Workers' Self-Management in Algeria

WORKERS' SELF-MANAGEMENT IN ALGERIA

Ian Clegg

NEW YORK AND LONDON

Copyright © 1971 by Ian Clegg
All Rights Reserved

Library of Congress Catalog Card Number: 73-178709

First Printing

Monthly Review Press
116 West 14th Street, New York, N.Y. 10011
33/37 Moreland Street, London, E.C. 1

Manufactured in the United States of America

CONTENTS

	Glossary	6
1	Workers' Councils: A Historical Perspective	7
2	A Colonial Prehistory	23
3	The Formation of the *Comités de Gestion*	39
4	The *Décrets de Mars*	57
5	The Economy: The Heritage of Colonialism	75
6	Class and Ideology in Algeria	95
7	The Political Stage, 1963–8	116
8	The Bureaucratic Emprise on the *Comités*	142
9	Workers and Managers	162
10	The Lessons of Algeria: Workers' Councils in Advanced Economies	177
	Appendix I: The Décrets de Mars	201
	Appendix II: La Charte d'Alger	210
	Appendix III: Economic Indices	221
	References	225
	Index	237

GLOSSARY

In order to help the reader, who may become confused by the proliferation of abbreviations, a short glossary is included. It is divided into two sections: the first dealing with political and military bodies, the second with post-independence economic bodies.

ALN	*Armée de Libération Nationale*
ANP	*Armée Nationale et Populaire* (ex ALN)
CCE	*Comité de Coordination et d'Exécution* (of the FLN)
CNRA	*Conseil National de la Révolution Algérienne*
CRUA	*Comité Révolutionnaire pour l'Unité et l'Action*
FFS	*Front des Forces Socialistes*
FLN	*Front de Libération Nationale*
GPRA	*Gouvernement Provisoire de la République Algérienne*
MTLD	*Mouvement pour le Triomphe des Libertés Démocratiques*
OAS	*Organisation de l'Armée Secréte*
OS	*Organisation Spéciale*
PCA	*Parti Communiste Algérien*
PPA	*Parti du Peuple Algérien*
PRS	*Parti de la Révolution Socialiste*
UDMA	*Union Démocratique du Manifeste Algérien*
UGTA	*Union Générale des Travailleurs Algériens*

*

BCA	*Banque Centrale d'Algérie*
BNA	*Banque Nationale d'Algérie*
BNASS	*Bureau National d'Animation du Secteur Socialiste*
CCAA	*Conseil Communal d'Animation d'Autogestion*
CCRA	*Centres Coopératifs de la Réforme Agraire*
CORA	*Coopératives de la Réforme Agraire*
CRC	*Caisses Régionales de Crédit*
ONACO	*Office National de Commercialisation*
ONP	*Office National de la Pêche*
ONRA	*Office National de la Réforme Agraire*
ONT	*Office National des Transports*
SAP	*Sociétés Agricoles de Prévoyance*

*

Translations in this book, unless otherwise indicated, are those of the author. In the transliteration of Arabic or Kabylie names, the French system has been used.

I

WORKERS' COUNCILS:
A HISTORICAL PERSPECTIVE

THE slow demise of classical colonialism in the 1950s and early 60s witnessed the largely peaceful surrender of the institutions of political power by metropolitan governments to indigenous political *élites*. In only two areas was there a protracted and violent struggle for liberation from the colonial *emprise*. For over ten years France was involved, first in Indochina and then in Algeria, in attempting to crush movements for national independence by the large-scale use of armed force. The passions inspired inside France by this struggle caused the end of the Fourth Republic and emphasized political divisions with a violence that is still clearly manifested. For many of the French, Vietnam and Algeria came to symbolize the extension and the actuality of the conflict between colonialism and national liberation, capitalism and socialism. Ho Chi Minh and Ben Bella joined Mao and Castro as the personifications of this revolt and became heroes of the left. The modes of economic and social organization of these revolutions became a source of identification between the socialist theory of the industrialized West and the chance of practice in the Third World.

This book is not a history of the Algerian revolution. It is concerned with a specific product of that revolution: the workers' committees set up to manage the agricultural estates and factories of the colonial bourgeoisie in the summer of independence, 1962. These committees were formalized as a system of economic management known as *autogestion* (self-management). *Autogestion*, with its emphasis on decentralization and democracy, its opposition to the rigid forms of bureaucratic socialism, came to be regarded as the real revolutionary achievement of independence. For many socialists *autogestion* came to symbolize not only an escape from the authoritarian Russian model but a clear example of the possibilities of developing a libertarian and revolutionary socialism in the Third

Workers' Self-Management in Algeria

World. Yet within five years the hero, Ben Bella, had been removed from power and *autogestion* in practice all but replaced by centralized state control.

The following description of *autogestion* in Algeria must not be regarded as the analysis of an isolated experience. Outside its own specific history Algerian self-management must be clearly situated within the wider history of attempts to create socialist modes of economic, social and political organization. It is part of the experience of the international revolutionary movement. In particular it is relevant to the whole problem of the forms of socialism in the Third World and the transplanting of a theory and practice developed mainly in the West. The development of a socialist ideology centred round self-management is mainly the work of the more libertarian sections of the Western left. These ideas have developed within the context of advanced industrial society. The question is whether, in terms of the present problems of the ex-colonial countries, the solutions implied by self-management are immediately relevant. Algerian *autogestion* thus assumes the proportions of an experiment in modes of revolutionary organization.

The *comités de gestion* (workers' management committees) set up in Algeria in 1962 were not, as will be made clear later, the practice of a conscious socialist theory. The elaboration of a theory to correspond with that practice emerged during 1963 and 1964, culminating in the *Charte d'Alger* – the official political programme of the Algerian revolution. The architects of this programme were clearly influenced by the experience of West and East European socialism, as well as China, Vietnam and Cuba. It is with this history that they sought identification.

Two distinct theoretical traditions, which often blend in practice, can be seen behind the formation of workers' councils in a revolutionary situation. Both are concerned not only with the destruction of capitalism and the disposition of power in the revolution but also with the question of work as a mediating factor in man's relation to his environment. These can be termed anarcho-syndicalism and the more orthodox Marxism-socialism.

The early nineteenth century saw the emergence of utopian socialist ideas that the worker should exert some form of control over the process of production. These ideas are clearly seen in *Le Nouveau Monde Industriel et Sociétaire* and *La Fausse Industrie* by

Workers' Councils: A Historical Perspective

Charles Fourier and the practical experiments of Robert Owen. Common to most of the utopian socialists was the feeling that work communities were an answer to the increasing degradation of man in the conditions of the industrial revolution. Their generalized ideal was a return to the small artisan communities existing before the industrial revolution; even though this golden age existed mostly in their own romantic vision of the past.[1] Beneath this rather effulgent romanticism lay the firm conviction that work could be made meaningful; that it was large-scale industry as well as capitalism that made it slavery. This basic hostility to industrialization and the emphasis on decentralized, small-scale economic and political units became the common factor for a whole current of utopian anarchist thought. It was expressed in America by Thoreau and Thorsten Veblen and in England by Ruskin and William Morris. Morris's *News from Nowhere* is probably the clearest expression of the form of such a utopian society. Kropotkin was perhaps the only one to place this utopianism within a strictly anarchist perspective in *Fields, Factories and Workshops* and *Mutual Aid: A Factor in Evolution*.

Utopian anarchism of this type is distinguished by its commitment to education rather than revolutionary violence as a means of destroying the twin evils of capitalism and the state. The more violent and opportunistic side of anarchist theory and practice stems from Bakunin, whose clashes with Marx split the First International. By the turn of the century this current had split into two clearly identifiable parts. The activities of the Bonnot gang in Paris, the Nihilists in Russia, the use of terrorism and assassination became the political outlet of the desperation of European romanticism which found its final cultural expression in Dada and Surrealism. The more orthodox current of revolutionary anarchism developed into anarcho-syndicalism.

Anarcho-syndicalism saw the workers' seizure of power in industry as an essential protection against the coercive power of the state. Achievement of their aims was most frequently seen as coming through a revolutionary general strike when the workers would occupy the factories. Their attitude to the state distinguished the anarcho-syndicalists from the orthodox socialist ideologues. Syndicalism and anarchism are marked by their clear hostility to the state: thus the revolution did not mean the seizure of the state but its replacement by freely associated communities of workers. The clearest examples of this anarchist-syndicalist tradition in practice can be seen in the Paris Commune, the Kronstadt commune during the Russian revolution, the Industrial Workers of the World in North America,[2] and the activities of the FAI and CNT in the Spanish Civil War. The ideological effect of syndicalism was much wider than this and affected the thinking and action of sections of the European trade-union movement until well after the First World War.*

These theories are, for the most part, situated in a revolutionary tradition that developed before Marx elaborated his theories and continued to develop parallel to them, though with a certain amount of cross-fertilization. They often lacked the total view of the mechanisms of capitalist society that marxism provided. Frequently, as Malatesta himself pointed out,[3] they did not appreciate the difficulties involved in the creation of a revolutionary praxis in the complexities of industrial society. What they did possess was a clear and definite hostility to all forms of authoritarian and bureaucratic organization. This led to the historical enmity between Bolshevism and libertarian socialism which found expression in Russia, the Spanish Civil War, Hungary and which preoccupies the left today.

For Marx and Engels, utopian communities, formed within capitalism, though important as experiments, were essentially mystifying. They did not tackle the problem of capitalism as a total system but merely ignored and were finally overwhelmed by it. For marxists, the liberation of the proletariat could only begin with the seizure of the means of production and the consequent overthrow not only of the capitalist economic system but its political, social and cultural superstructures. The proletarian revolution, as the negation of capitalism, was a historical and dialectical possibility that could only become actuality through the conscious action of the proletariat. For Marx the dictatorship of the proletariat was the first stage in the organization of revolutionary power. It is at this point that Marxism split from Bakuninist anarchism. Both Marx and Bakunin agreed on the concept of the dictatorship of the proletariat; but for Bakunin this implied an occult *élite* while Marx advocated the development of a highly conscious proletarian vanguard.[4]

* The General Strike of 1926 witnessed the final effort of syndicalism in England.

Workers' Councils: A Historical Perspective

Until the widespread series of revolutionary actions at the end of the First World War, the Paris Commune and the 1905 revolution in Russia were the first revolutionary attempts at the institution of a socialist society. There is no space here to go into the history of the Commune, but it had an important effect on prevailing socialist economic and political thought. The communards were basically inspired by the economic theories of Proudhon and the political theories of Blanqui, both of which were radically altered in face of the experience of the Commune. Proudhon had expressed profound opposition to the idea of 'association', stressing that it was as much in conflict with the freedom of the worker as with the 'economy of labour'. However, by 1870 even Paris had begun to experience an economy of scale and the individualist theories of Proudhon were jettisoned in face of the need to organize large-scale industry. This was done in the form of a grand union of all the separate factory councils. The Blanquists who favoured insurrectionism – the seizure of the state by a small disciplined body who would then swing the masses behind the revolution – ended up by creating a free communal federation to cover the whole of France.

In *The Civil War in France* Marx and Engels gave their approval to the conversion of the communards to the necessity of retaining some elements of state power until capitalism had been smashed finally. The experience of 1905 in Russia led Lenin and the Bolsheviks eventually to emphasize the necessity for a tight, disciplined party as the guiding force of the revolution.[5] The spontaneous forms of economic and political organization – the Workers' and Soldiers' Councils – which appeared in 1905 and again in 1917, owed little to the action of the Bolsheviks. They represented a loose federalized structure which was seen as a revolutionary alternative to the centralized and autocratic tsarist state. The internal pressures on the revolution soon came into conflict with the libertarian mode of organization represented by the councils. In November 1917 the councils were given complete managerial control of the factories but the following year they were turned into trade-union branches and became one part of the management *troika* of plant director, party cell secretary and secretary of the union branch. Impelled by the struggle to preserve the revolution, the Bolsheviks accepted the necessity of retaining some aspects of the bourgeois state.[6] Ensuing developments led to the crushing of the Kronstadt

Workers' Self-Management in Algeria

commune[7] and the workers' opposition.[8] This clash between centralizing and libertarian tendencies contains the classic dilemma of socialism. Before judgement is passed the situation must be subjected to vigorous analysis, for which there is no space here.

Workers' and soldiers' councils emerged in Hungary, Poland, Germany, Italy and Bulgaria during the revolutionary upsurge that shook Europe between 1917 and 1920.[9] In every case they were crushed by the success of the counter-revolution. Since then, every successive appearance of workers' councils has suffered the same fate. The councils set up in China during the 1924-7 rising[10] and those of the anarchists in Spain, 1936-9,[11] were ended by the military success of the right. The Hungarian councils in 1956 were smashed by Russian troops, attacked as 'imperialist' creations in almost the same terms as Trotsky's attacks on the Kronstadt commune.[12] Those that emerged in Poland in 1956 and Algeria in 1962 were rapidly institutionalized by the state and prevented from entering the political sphere.

The victory of the Allies and the Russian occupation of Eastern Europe in 1944-5 brought socialist or communist parties to power in Poland, Czechoslovakia, Hungary, Rumania, Albania, Bulgaria, Yugoslavia and East Germany by 1947. The governments of these countries copied in detail the Russian political and economic system.

The Russian model was developed in response to three main factors. The emphasis on the rapid development of heavy industry stemmed from a marxist assertion that this was an essential precondition of socialism. The internal logic of Bolshevism led to the creation of a centralized political authority, controlled by an increasingly undemocratic party organization. Extreme isolation in face of a hostile world after the revolution led Russia to create the industrial base by her own efforts under the strict discipline of the party. Already one of the most backward countries in Europe, ravaged by years of civil war, Russia had to undergo in a few decades the process of primitive capital accumulation that had taken centuries in the West. It had to accumulate the wealth, the technical knowledge, the labour force and the markets necessary for an advanced level of industrialization. By 1945 the forms of political and economic organization in Russia had been developed by Stalin from pragmatism to a full-scale ideology of the correct form of

Workers' Councils: A Historical Perspective

socialism. Until the middle and late 1950s this model was largely accepted, with a few exceptions, by most socialists to the left of the social democratic parties.

Under this system any form of direct workers' control of the means of production was sacrificed to the exigencies of building heavy industry and capital accumulation. Economists feared that, given any measure of freedom, the workers would pursue an egalitarian, ouvrierist* course to the detriment of both production and accumulation. On a political level it was feared that control within the factories might crystallize into a general political opposition. The fiction of ownership and control was preserved by regarding the party as the true representative of the proletariat, who thus owned and controlled the means of production by proxy. Within industry the factory council, usually consisting of party cell, party youth and union officials, preserved the fiction of workers' control at the point of production.

Recently the orthodox centralism of this system has shown signs of moving in a more liberal direction. The causes of this are economic rather than political. Lieberman and his followers in Russia have followed Oscar Lange[13] in pointing out the difficulty of exerting strict control over a sophisticated industrial economy. It is also felt that the profit motive instils a greater desire to increase productivity than calls to serve the cause of socialism. Generally this decentralization has not resulted in any change in the direction of increased participation in management but only in greater freedom for enterprise management and increased incentive payments to the workers.

There are, however, two East European countries where more than the purely ritual factory councils of the Russian model have been introduced. Despite the difference in the modalities of introduction and subsequent development, the councils in Poland and Yugoslavia highlight the political and economic dilemmas that their existence creates for orthodox socialism.

Poland had experience of revolutionary workers' and soldiers' councils between November 1918 and July 1919 and they appeared

* The term 'ouvrierist' here, and throughout the book, does not necessarily imply a value judgement. It is used to describe the ranking, by workers, of their own immediate material interests above wider national economic or political interests.

again for a short time at the end of the Second World War. In 1948 the nationalist wing of the Polish Communist Party (the Workers' Party) was defeated, the Polish Socialist Party was forcibly merged with the communists and a group closely aligned with Russia took over. From 1948 to 1956 the economy was closely patterned on the Russian model and any surviving councils disbanded as superfluous. This bureaucratic and centralized system proved unsatisfactory. Industry suffered from a shortage of raw materials and an anarchic system of prices and wages. Too much capital was invested in new factories built for political rather than economic motives. Over-emphasis on heavy industry led to a low level of agricultural and consumer goods production, causing inflation and widespread shortages. Real wages did not rise, and in some cases dropped between 1950 and 1956, housing was inadequate and consumer goods almost non-existent. The extreme dissatisfaction of the workers erupted in the strikes and riots at Poznan at the end of July 1956.

Two currents of opposition had already emerged by the end of 1955, both demanding decentralization. Technicians and economists accused political interference of causing the waste and inefficiency in industry. They advocated measurement of efficiency in money profits rather than plan fulfilment.* The workers' resistance to low living standards and state repression emerged as a general political opposition, proposing the establishment of workers' councils through which the workers could control the means of production themselves. After Poznan, workers' councils were set up in several factories.[14] Workers involved in this movement had wider political aims: besides ameliorating working conditions and wages, they hoped to create a national federation of councils that could form the basis of a democratic government. These aims were never achieved. But the government, under the newly returned Gomulka, was forced to accept the councils in the factories. Two decrees in November (10 and 15) extended the rights of nationalized enterprises and formalized the councils in law.

In this formal system the government retained the right to control most of the factors deciding the economic success of the enter-

* The main influence here is again Oscar Lange. Many of them were also impressed by Western methods of management and regarded Western economies as more successful.

Workers' Councils: A Historical Perspective

prise: the quantity and value of products, the total wages bill, the size of the profits, etc. Within this limiting framework the councils were authorized to establish the organizational structure of the enterprise and its work regulations, to fix wage rates and production norms and give advice on productivity – all within the framework of national agreements between the state and the (state-controlled) unions. The council elected a smaller body, known as the praesidium, to organize most of its work.

Despite the role played by the councils in the rise in productivity between 1957 and 1958, the government and party came to see them as a political threat. They represented a potential source of alternative power that could be used to channel and organize opposition. In 1958 a conference of self-management (CSG) was set up as the senior representative body in each factory. The CSG contained all the members of the council, the union shop-committee and the party cell; the council itself became a subordinate executive body. The praesidium was enlarged to include the director, shop-committee chairman and a party representative. Not content with seeing the party and state firmly in control of the councils, the government, at the end of 1958, changed the functions of the CSG from managerial to supervisory.[15]

The brief experience of workers' councils in Poland raises the important question of the basic antagonism between orthodox 'socialist' centralist ideology and the decentralizing, libertarian trend of the councils. The councils emerged as part of the historical response of the proletariat to conditions of economic hardship and political authoritarianism. Lenin returned to Russia in 1917 with the slogan 'All power to the workers' and soldiers' councils!' and the slogan has become part of the consciousness of the working class. Faced with the councils' challenge to Stalinism, Gomulka and the nationalist wing of the Polish Communist Party used them to their own advantage. The events of 1956 were used to free Poland from the overt domination of Russia and to establish Gomulka as a representative of Polish nationalism. The restriction of the councils to the economic field showed that the party had no intention of allowing its political hegemony to be challenged. The further limitation of the councils to a purely advisory capacity and their clear subordination to the party manifested that their political uses had ended. The logic of firm central control by the party inevitably leads it to oppose every manifestation of working-class organization that lies outside the ambit of the party. Within such a society the creation of workers' councils assumes the status of the development of a class struggle against the party bureaucracy in whose hands lies control of political and economic power.[16]

The Poznan riots and the appearance of workers' councils in Poland led to the return to power of the nationalist wing of the Communist Party which rapidly institutionalized and emasculated the councils. The same manifestation in Hungary was crushed by Russian troops. In Yugoslavia, however, it was the party itself which introduced workers' councils in an institutional form. Here the introduction of decentralization was accompanied by a reformulation of orthodox socialist theory and a consequent redirection of the theoretical role of the party. The Yugoslav system of self-management had the clearest effect on the formalization of *autogestion* in Algeria. The *décrets de mars*, giving the legal structure of Algerian *autogestion*, are based on the internal organization of self-management in Yugoslavia.

At the end of the Second World War, the Yugoslav communists under Marshal Tito, who had led the successful partisan resistance to the Axis powers, formed the government. The problems of reconstructing the shattered economy after four years of internal war, combined with the then generally Stalinist orthodoxy of the party, led to the creation of a highly centralized socialist state. In 1948 Yugoslavia was expelled from the Cominform and the period of close alignment with Russia ended. Basically the breach arose from the Yugoslav desire to run their own national programme of industrialization, rather than become part of the Russian economic empire. The partisan experience, with its emphasis on regional autonomy, had a marked pragmatizing influence on party theory. These factors combined with their refusal to work with the Russian MVD did not accord with Stalin's plan for Russian political and economic hegemony of East Europe. For a short period the shock of expulsion led the party to become more rigidly orthodox in the attempt to disprove Stalin's charges of nationalist deviation. Eventually the continued excommunication gave a stimulus to reconsider socialist theory.

An ideological basis for their new position was evolved, accusing

Workers' Councils: A Historical Perspective

Russia itself of deviating from marxism. The essence of the new position was that to counteract the tendency to autocratic centralism an immediate start must be made in the process of the 'withering away of the state', rather than waiting for a particular level of economic development or political maturity. The Yugoslav theoreticians drew their inspiration from Marx's comments on the state in *The Civil War in France*. They claimed that Marx advocated that an immediate start should be made in the destruction of the mechanisms of the bourgeois state. They accepted the necessity for state power to protect the revolution, but this state must be representative and not independent of the people.[17] This involved the institution of representative, democratic forms of administration in political and economic spheres. The Russian model of strict party control in every sphere was described as being the specific response to a specific situation and not a theoretical norm applicable to every situation.[18]

The Yugoslav party came to see itself as the enlightened guardian of Marxism-Leninism, acting as educators rather than rulers. The national working class in the early 1950s was too small and of too recent formation to formulate and press demands of its own. The party, therefore, was to develop forms of political and economic organization that had appeared elsewhere spontaneously in the course of revolutionary struggle. Since the early 1950s Yugoslavia has seen the gradual handing over of wide sectors of economic and political life to the people involved in them, accompanied by the reduction of state bureaucracy and the decreasingly authoritarian role of the League of Communists.

Almost all types of organization now have some form of self-management. This process has been gradual and until the mid-1960s there were still extensive state controls on the economic freedom of each enterprise. This was arranged through economic and political mechanisms: regulation of prices and markets, taxation, fixed wages, control of reinvestment and supervision by the party and unions of the organs of self-management. Since the New Economic Laws of 1965 there has been a rapid reduction in these controls. To create an economy capable of competing in the international market, subsidies to industry have been abolished and tariff protection removed. The law of supply and demand has been widely accepted as the best economic regulator. State control of production is minimal and enterprises are openly encouraged to compete with each other. For many, the theory accompanying the New Economic Laws represents a definite move in a capitalist direction.[19]

Self-management has been closely associated with economic motivation. In seeking to gain the workers' involvement in self-management the party has relied heavily on material incentives. The close connection between income and 'work done' has led to the development of a strictly economistic notion of self-management among the working class. They have accepted managerial and administrative responsibility because a significant proportion of their income is not fixed but depends on the economic success of the enterprise. This, accompanied by the removal of state controls from the market, has led to the appearance of a democratic but distinctly capitalist form of organization in Yugoslavia.

The dilemma facing those who genuinely believe in creating an alternative to Russian orthodoxy is that political decentralization and a high standard of living seem to tend towards the re-establishment of many of the values inherent in capitalist society. The reaction of a section of the party, under Rankovic, was to seek a return to this orthodoxy in order to re-establish socialism. The enlightened *avant-garde* of the Yugoslav party has attempted to introduce an advanced form of socialism by the use of law and economic incentives. In doing this it has been unable to raise the consciousness of the workers. In containing the class struggle it has come to resemble a liberal political *élite* rather than a Marxist party.

SOCIAL DEMOCRATIC AND CAPITALIST CONTAINMENT

Modern capitalism has seen the development of systems of participation that allow the worker greater control over management decisions than is possible under East European socialism. Indeed, workers' participation is rapidly becoming a part of the conventional ideology of capitalism. In many areas, both capitalist governments and management have outpaced the demands of the social democratic left. Some of the major facets of this ideology and its practice are worth including in this review as they form part of the philosophy of anticipation and recuperation that lies at the root of capitalism's containment of the workers' movement.

Western European social democratic parties have tended to

Workers' Councils: A Historical Perspective

orientate themselves round the ideology of nationalization. Traditionally they have strongly opposed the creation of workers' councils, preferring to vest control of the means of production in the state. Bernstein, in an early statement on the tenets of evolutionary socialism, produced the reasoning behind this orientation: 'All consume but all do not produce. Even the best productive association, as long as it is only an association for sale and exchange, will always stand in latent opposition to the community, will have separate interests opposed to it.'[20] The rationale behind social democratic opposition to workers' control of industry lies in an artificial division of society into workers and consumers. In this pluralist and entirely unsocialist definition the state assumes the role of custodian of the means of production to avoid one section of society exploiting another. Lacking any dialectical content, evolutionary socialism subsumes class conflict under the purely political capture of the bourgeois state. This emphasis on control of the bourgeois state rather than its destruction leads social democratic parties to become national rather than class parties. In this logic any overt manifestation of working-class militancy is taken as being hostile to the interests of the nation, and opposed.

It has been liberal capitalism rather than social democracy that has institutionalized workers' participation. The ideological foundations of capitalism's acceptance of workers' participation in management lie in a defined policy to contain and avoid social conflict by limited concessions. The legalization of organized forms of the workers' movement – parties, unions and workers' councils – has allowed capitalism to contain class conflict with its own economic and political system. The hegemonic ideology of the Western bourgeoisie has enabled it to develop a cultural consensus within which the idea of class conflict seems absurd. This ideology allows capitalism to recuperate the organized expressions of working-class hostility by institutionalizing them as part of the consensus. Two of the largest schemes of workers' participation on a national scale, in Germany and France, were promoted to preserve the national consensus in face of incipient class conflict.

In Germany, after the defeat of the Spartakist rising, the Weimar government attempted to placate labour by placing a works' council law in the constitution. These councils,[21] which were empowered to conduct plant bargaining and handle grievances, were dissolved under the Nazis, but reappeared in several industries at the end of the Second World War. The *Deutscher Gewerkschaftsbund*, the newly united union movement, took up the demand for workers' councils as the only means of ensuring democratic control of industry and preventing the re-emergence of Nazism. In this they received the grudging support of the Social Democrats who were more concerned with nationalization. The Christian Democrats put workers' participation in their 1947 Ahlener programme. In 1951 the CDU, now in power, passed a Codetermination Law instituting workers' participation in the coal and steel industries. The following year this principle was extended by the Fundamental Works' Constitution Law giving legal status to workers' participation in all private and public concerns.

Mitbestimmung, the ideology built round the works' councils, became a clear attempt to narrow political and economic differences between capital and labour, management and workers, thus opening the way to harmonious social and economic reconstruction. *Mitbestimmung* developed as the particular German form of the consensus created by capitalism to contain potential class conflict. As one liberal commentator put it: 'Codetermination became a vast educational scheme designed, over a period of years, to raise the workers' level of understanding and thereby to help bring about "social peace" and thus reduce the extent of the sphere of political conflict, or at least its violence.'[22]

At the end of the war in France the communists seized plants, sacked management for collaboration and set up workers' *comités de gestion* to manage the enterprises. Faced with the existence of these *comités*, de Gaulle legalized them in February 1945 but restricted their role in law to organs of communication between management and workers. In May 1946 their role was extended to include consultation and social welfare. De Gaulle's institutionalization of *comités d'entreprise* as an emasculated version of the *comités de gestion* was directed towards circumventing the potential threat to French capitalism represented by the communists in 1945-6. However, an ideology like *Mitbestimmung* never grew up round the French system. The hostility of the CGT towards collaboration with management and the historical militancy of the working class ensured that the *comités d'entreprise* gradually fell into disuse. The relative failure of the consensus in France appeared in the events of May 1968 when

Workers' Councils: A Historical Perspective

the factories were again occupied and demands for self-management on the Yugoslav pattern voiced.*

On a separate level management itself has become more and more influenced by ideas of cooperation with the workers. Until the 1930s most management accepted that industrial relations were inevitably governed by conflict.† Classical capitalist and Social Darwinist views of industrial relations were in fact further rationalized at the end of the First World War by F. W. Taylor's 'school of scientific management'.[23] Taylorism considered the worker purely as a machine with the aim of making optimum efficient use of his physical abilities. A gradual change in management attitudes became apparent as a result of Elton Mayo's experiments in the 1930s.[24] Mayo showed that output increased if workers felt that management was interested in them as people, rather than machines, and if it was prepared to grant them increased responsibility. Liberal theory, centred round this 'human-relations school', has also tended to place an ethico-philosophical emphasis on the moral dignity of human labour and on man's psychological need to understand and at least partially control his environment. Some form of participation in management is seen as fulfilling the worker's psychological needs; while failure to allow this reduces both his efficiency and willingness to work.[25] In the search for means to remove harmful conflict from industry, socialist theory on the causes of conflict has been used. The concept of alienation, removed from its Marxist perspective, has been used to describe the worker's feeling of dissatisfaction with his work and more responsibility urged as a solution.[26]

The growing acceptance by capitalism of some form of participation by the workers in the management of economic activity is influenced by the desire to avoid or contain conflict and so promote greater productivity. On one level it has sought to achieve this by promulgating the liberal ideology of the consensus, or national interest, by stressing the absence of any basis for class conflict. On another level, it is attempting to enlist the worker's cooperation by playing on his psychological and economic attitudes to work. In its

---

* In the context of Algeria, the organization of participation in French nationalized industries such as electricity, gas and mines is relevant. The Algerian government copied the French legislation in some detail when they set up nationalized undertakings to supersede autogestion.

† The experiments of Cadbury's at Bournville are a notable exception.

use of a combination of psychological and material bribes to promote cooperation, capitalism is not far removed from the Yugoslav party's use of similar mechanisms to encourage the workers to take responsibility for the administration of a socialist state. Both socialist and capitalist states are in fact seeking to contain class conflict through participation. Despite the formal differences in their ideologies, the ruling groups in both societies are using the same mechanisms to preserve their economic, social and political control.

This brief and over-simplified survey of the theory and practice surrounding workers' management of the means of production makes no pretence of being anything but a brief curtain-raiser to the Algerian experience of *autogestion*. *Autogestion* represents one more chapter in the search for appropriate forms for the revolutionary reorganization of the economy and society. The conflicts and dilemmas over the basis and forms of revolutionary authority in Algeria mirror those of most revolutionary situations. This book attempts to analyse the specific conditions surrounding and determining the outcome of these conflicts in Algeria alone. It is to be hoped that, on the basis of detailed studies like this, a realistic theory and strategy on the place of workers' councils can be developed.

2

A COLONIAL PREHISTORY

ALGERIA'S achievement of independence in July 1962 marked the culmination of nearly eight years of armed struggle for national liberation. This conflict broke the impasse between national aspirations and the colonial *status quo*. It did not solve any of the country's basic social or economic problems. At the moment of independence Algeria was left teetering on the verge of chaos, in conditions of a complete suspension of economic activity and near civil war. The establishment of workers' *comités de gestion* to manage the ex-colonial agricultural estates and industrial enterprises emerged as a response to this situation. The reasons for this specific response must be sought in the peculiarities of the French colonial enterprise in Algeria. This historical background has already been described by several commentators.* Here it is only necessary to draw out those factors which led to the development of the armed struggle and deeply affected the social, economic and political structures of independent Algeria.

The French conquest of Algeria involved the destruction of the pre-existing indigenous economic, social and political structures to an extent only surpassed in the colonization of America. It began as one of the last efforts of the Bourbon monarchy to restore its waning popularity among the French mercantile bourgeoisie and army, both of whom were severely restricted in their activities by the loss of colonies in the wars with England. The colonial project began as a politico-military adventure with little underlying economic rationale. The French army was soon faced with the necessity of consolidating the occupation they had achieved by force of arms. The answer to this problem was found in the deliberate project of mass settlement. The idea was expounded by Marshal Soult in the following terms: '... we cannot wait: it is absolutely imperative that we make *colons* and construct villages, summon all energies to

* See the references cited in the rest of this chapter

sanction, consolidate and simplify the occupation we achieve by arms'.[1] Settlement became the economic rationale for the military adventure.

The project of colonization by mass settlement, rather than the imposition of colonial authority on existing patterns of economic and social organization, could only be achieved by the destruction of these structures. The wrecking of the bases of the indigenous economy became a conscious plan whose effects were proudly described by the early conquerors.

> More than fifty fine villages, built of stone and roofed with tiles, were destroyed. Our soldiers made very considerable pickings there. We did not have time in the heat of combat to chop down the trees. The task in any case would have been beyond our strength. 20,000 men armed with axes could not in six months cut down the olives and fig trees covering the beautiful landscape that lay at our feet.[2]

This was written by Marshal Bugeaud, commander of the French forces in the early 1840s. Another army officer wrote: 'Since December we have made organized raids in all directions round Blida. These well-conceived raids have ruined or at least begun the ruin of the country.'[3]

The destruction was not confined to the countryside. Most of the urban centres were completely ruined, the inhabitants either massacred or fleeing forever. Oran, estimated to have 40,000 inhabitants in 1831, was reduced to 1,000 in 1838 and by 1881 still had a population of only 12,700.[4] The Muslim population that survived the brutalities of the army were driven back into the less fertile areas in the east and the *tell*, south of the coastal plain. Here, traditional methods of agriculture were unable to provide for the increased population and there was terrible famine. As for the colonizers, they measured the success of their policy in terms of the reduction of the indigenous population from near six million in 1830 to two and a half million in 1852.*

Resistance to the French conquest, though unsuccessful, was significant in the later awakening of some form of national consciousness. The Turkish administration had never controlled the

---

* Other more fanciful plans had envisaged shipping the whole indigenous population to the Canaries or Azores.

A Colonial Prehistory

country,* and even at the height of its power in the seventeenth century really only held the area round Algiers. In 1830 the administration, now decadent and enfeebled, rapidly collapsed in face of the French invasion of Algiers. The tribes of the interior, for long only nominally subordinate to the Ottoman *dey*, came together to form the basis of a new national state. This was the work of the emir Abdel Kader who succeeded in uniting the normally divided tribes – both Berber and Arab – and in bridging the traditional gap between town and rural areas. He created a centralized state running from Oranie in the west to the Constantinois in the east. He largely destroyed the old political structures of feudalism and created an efficient army; while on an economic level the state promoted development in mining and artisan activity and removed the feudal levies from the rural economy.

For a short period, between 1837 and 1841, Abdel Kader was recognized by the French as autonomous ruler of most of western Algeria. Driven on by the logic of their enterprise, the French broke the treaty as soon as they had consolidated their first gains and by 1847 Abdel Kader was forced to surrender. But it was not until 1857 that the Berber tribes in the Kabylie mountains were forced to submit.[5] Apart from the Sahara, which remained in a state of incipient revolt well into this century, the final large-scale rising against the French occurred in the Kabylie in 1870–1, but this was only a regional and tribal affair. The only opposition to colonialism after this was sporadic banditry and individual terrorism on behalf of the landless and desperate peasants. The wholesale physical desecration of the country, engineered by the colonizers, destroyed any economic or social basis for national consciousness for decades.

The rigid opposition of the *pieds-noirs*† to any compromise with the later reawakened aspirations of Algerian nationalism, and the extreme polarization of the two communities led inevitably to the armed conflict declared in 1954. The pathological extremism of

---

* Ottoman rule was established in Algeria in 1518 and by 1541 had been implicitly accepted by the Spanish.

† Technically, the term '*pied-noir*' is an epithet denoting a European Algerian born in Algeria. In post-independence Algeria it has become almost indistinguishable from the term '*colon*', which technically denotes the European Algerian born outside Algeria. The two terms are used indiscriminately in this book.

the *pied-noir* ideology has its origins in the history of the *colons* and the process of colonization.

The early French conquerors of Algeria idealized their actions as a continuation of the Crusades and the reimposition of Western civilization on North Africa, discontinued since the fall of the Roman Empire. At the height of the campaigns against Abdel Kader, a French traveller wrote in 1844:

> The goal of our African campaigns is more vital and more sacred than the goal of our European wars... it is the sacred cause of civilization which is at stake; the immortal cause of Christianity, which according to God's promise will dominate the world, and the French nation is bound by providence to fulfil this destiny.[6]

In the same tone General de Bourmont, conqueror of Algiers, told his troops: 'You are continuing the Crusades.' This belief in the innate superiority of things European, and especially French, this sense of mission became the dominant ideology of the settlers. It led them to construct a Manichaean vision of their world within which they advanced, inexorably, to their own destruction.

The extreme diversity of the origins of the settlers (as well as their basic similarity) was essential in forming the structures of their consciousness. The first large settlement came in 1848 when the defeated republican workers were transported to Algeria, followed in 1851 by more political deportees and the unemployed of Paris. The German annexation of Alsace-Lorraine in 1871 produced a wave of refugees who settled in Algeria. After 1880 a large number of French peasants, ruined by phylloxera in the vineyards, emigrated to Algeria. This French element, the product of years of social upheaval, political defeat and poverty, was reinforced by refugees form Italo-Slav unifications, the Balkan wars, political defeat in Spain and the upheavals of two world wars. In 1876, 153,000 of the 344,000 Europeans were of non-French origin and by 1954 over half the million *colons* fell into this category.

The diverse origins of the *colons*, their lack of any real racial or cultural unity and their desperate need for identity led them to discover their basic unity in defence of the privileges accorded them by the French administration and their hostility to the Muslim masses. This appeared in an assertion of their basic Frenchness, in a fervour for things French that far surpassed its equivalent in the

A Colonial Prehistory

metropolis. In this vision they, the outcasts of Europe, became the true guardians of French civilization. In this dream world they felt threatened on one side by the Muslims whom they had dispossessed and on the other by a treacherous metropolis made effete by liberalism. This Manichaeism, which carries its own nightmares, led the Algerian *colons*, like the settlers of Rhodesia and South Africa, into a pathological resistance to change. The small minority of large agricultural, industrial and commercial entrepreneurs had a more rational foundation to their hostility to reform: they feared it would undermine their economic and political hegemony. Yet, despite the objective existence of divisions between the settler bourgeoisie and the working class, any class conflict was subsumed under the necessity of preserving *Algérie Française*.

The power of the *pieds-noirs* lay precisely in the economic, social and political privileges accorded them by the metropolis. Although by 1848 Algeria had become legally part of France most of the administration was in the hands of the army. It was not until the settlers had revolted against Napoleon III in 1870 that the power of the army was reduced* and civilian political institutions were created. These were largely similar to those already existing in France. The three departments of Algiers, Constantine and Oran were represented in the French parliament. On a local level the communes were divided into two categories: *communes de plein exercice*, where the Europeans were in a majority and the mayor was elected, and *communes mixtes*, where there was a Muslim majority and a European administrator was in control. In 1889 a law, automatically naturalizing the children born in Algeria of alien parents, was passed thus giving the new generations the same civil rights as Frenchmen. These moves gave a clear substance to the *colons*' dreams of integration with French culture and polity. How little this affected the metropolitan French they were to discover in 1962.

Over and above the normal political rights of France, the *colons* wrested special local privileges from the metropolitan government. They gained administrative and financial autonomy as well as a numerically disproportionate parliamentary representation in France. The key organs of their autonomy were the *Conseil*

---

* The army continued to control the Sahara until independence.

Supérieur* and the *Délégations Financières*.† Both of these were originally merely advisory bodies to the colonial administration. By the 1930s they had achieved considerable autonomy and had become invested with the symbolism of *colon* independence from an increasingly liberal metropolis.

Only those Muslims who conformed with the provisions of the *senatus consulte* of 1865 had similar political and juridical rights to the *colons*. This granted French citizenship to Muslims who were prepared to abandon their exemption to French law on matters like marriage and property. As an attempt to assimilate the Muslim population, the *senatus consulte* was a complete failure: between 1836 and 1934 only 2,500 of them took advantage of its provisions. Those who did not take out French citizenship were not only denied the right to vote but were also subject until 1946 to a separate legal code – *le code de l'indigénat* – which made them liable to summary justice. The political and juridical separation of the Muslims was further emphasized by their lack of opportunities in education. The Muslims – some ninety per cent illiterate in 1950 – were as late as 1954 only receiving school places for nineteen per cent of their school-age population.[7] Underlying this separation between *colons* and Muslims was an economic gulf which for the mass of Muslims served as a total barrier to any hopes of progress or personal advancement within the colonial situation.

The colonization of Algeria cannot be described in economic terms as the impact of an advanced industrial economy on a backward agricultural economy. After the conquest the metropolitan project of large-scale settlement meant that land had to be provided for the immigrants. This could only be achieved at the expense of the existing Muslim population. Every rising was followed by the widespread confiscation of Muslim lands – private, tribal and communal – which were then distributed to the settlers, along with improvement grants, by the administration.‡ The early economy of

---

* Created in 1876 to offer administrative advice to the Governor General.

† Created in 1878 to consider the administration's budgets. Both these organs contained a few Berber and Arab notables nominated for their trustworthiness, i.e. the *Délégations Financières* had forty-eight Europeans, seventeen Arabs and six Berbers.

‡ Thus, for instance, after the 1870–71 Kabylie revolt, 524,000 hectares of land was confiscated.

A Colonial Prehistory

French Algeria was thus based on the small plots of the settlers. But it did not long remain so: the years up till the declaration of armed struggle witnessed the growing concentration of land-ownership in the hands of a small and powerful body of *colon* magnates. By 1954 there were only 20–30,000 land-owners (four per cent of the European population). The average holding was 108 hectares and in total the European sector produced some sixty per cent of the gross agricultural revenue. Over eighty per cent of the European population lived in towns, some fifty per cent alone being in the urban areas of Algiers and Oran.[8]

The *colons* were never entrepreneurs in the true sense of the word: the state had provided land and finance at the start and in 1954 sixty per cent of total new investment was still being provided by the state, while forty per cent of all private capital savings was exported to France. Algerian capitalism, based on agriculture and mineral extraction, was content to export agricultural products and raw materials in return for industrial and luxury goods from France. The sectoral imbalance of the economy is marked by the following table:[9]

Sector	Gross domestic product 1954 (per cent)
agriculture, livestock, fishing	33·4
industry, mines, construction	27·4
transport, commerce, services	39·2

The tertiary sector of the economy was vastly over-inflated, particularly in relation to the secondary sector. The real situation of both these sectors can be seen from the fact that in 1954 out of some 38,000 enterprises only 668 had over fifty employees. The average number of employees per enterprise was 10·45.[10] The Algerian industrial and service sectors were dominated by artisan activity. The inability of the economy to become in any way self-supporting was marked by a growing and chronic trade deficit that had to be made up by the metropolitan government.

The specific structure of the Algerian economy formed the basis for the political dominance of a small group of magnates. The concentration of ownership, in particular in viticulture, created the foundation for the economic and political dominance of this group. Before the advent of oil and gas, wine formed some fifty per cent of the annual trade receipts of the economy.[11] The small producers were unable to challenge the monopoly of the magnates because of the high capital costs of viticulture. The owners of the large estates, usually rentiers, became closely associated with the Bank of Algiers and the government, through the *Délégations Financières*. Here they formed a political bloc that vigorously defended Algerian agrarian capitalism against metropolitan interference. Owing to its small size the secondary sector never produced a class of bourgeois entrepreneurs sufficiently strong in economic terms to wrest political predominance from the agricultural interest. The absence of a strong industrial bourgeoisie meant that there was no strong political force for whom a policy of liberalization might have proved politically and economically necessary.

In contrast with the mainly urbanized *pied-noir* population, the majority of the Muslims were involved in agriculture. There was a small group of relatively prosperous proprietors. With only 25,000 Muslims owning fifty or more hectares of land, this group was very small in comparison with the mass of peasants who survived on subsistence agriculture.* Those working in the European sector of agriculture provided a cheap and inexhaustible labour supply. Some 108,000 workers formed a permanent labour force; while some 434,000 were seasonal or day labourers working for less than 100 days a year. In industry and commerce, ninety per cent of all activity was controlled by Europeans. Out of a total labour force of 569,000, roughly 330,000 were Muslims. Here the polarization between the communities is clearly visible in terms of income. Of the total workforce, 3·9 per cent (ninety-three per cent of whom were European) earned over one million AF a year; while 35·5 per cent (ninety-five per cent of whom were Muslims) earned less than 200,000 AF a year.[12] Thus even those Muslims fortunate enough to find employment represented a destitute and impoverished proletariat in comparison with their European fellow-workers.

The Algerian economy and class structure are dealt with in detail further on. Here only a few factors need stressing. The growing Muslim demographic pressure caused the progressive collapse of the traditional agricultural sector as the main means of support for the indigenous population. The European economy, stagnant from

* The table on p. 97 gives a clearer breakdown of the composition of the Muslim agrarian population.

A Colonial Prehistory

the 1930s, orientated to agriculture and lacking any large-scale industry, was totally incapable of absorbing this potential labour force. The landless agricultural workers either searched desperately for seasonal work on the colonial estates or migrated to the urban areas. Here they formed a classic sub-proletariat – unemployed or at best irregularly employed. At independence, the heritage of colonialism was an economy directed towards the maintenance of a small sector of the population and incapable of even employing fifty per cent of the rest: an economy which was progressively draining the country of its natural capital and was totally dependent on the metropolis for its survival.

The growing numbers and desperation of the Muslim population only served to increase the fears of the *pieds-noirs* that any concessions would bring down the whole structure of European dominance. Unable to accept even the most innocuous reforms forced on them by the French government, the *pieds-noirs* remained totally hostile to any Muslim demands. In response, the Muslims progressively abandoned the moderate aims of their middle-class leaders for the violent course of national liberation by armed struggle.

NATIONALIST POLITICS AND REVOLUTION

The total disintegration of the superstructures of Muslim society in face of the colonial project made it impossible for any unifying force, based on traditional authority or ideology, to emerge as a successful opposition to colonialism. Apart from isolated military actions in the Sahara, the crushing of the last Kabylie revolt in 1871 inaugurated a period of almost complete Muslim quiescence which lasted until the 1920s. At this point two separate trends of political opposition to colonialism emerged. The theory and action of these two currents dominated Algerian nationalism right up until the declaration of armed struggle in 1954 and then, with modifications, until after independence. Two conflicting solutions to the national problem characterized the political currents before 1954. These were complete national independence from France or assimilation – the granting of civil rights to the Muslims which would render them completely equal to French citizens. The ideological developments stemming from these opposed solutions have had a direct and material effect on the political positions taken up over the orientation of independent Algeria. The deep political divisions that have shaken Algeria since independence have their roots in the early nationalist politics of forty years ago.[13]

In 1924 the emir Khaled, grandson of Abdel Kader, with the support of the French Communist Party (PCF), set up an organization – the *Étoile Nord Africaine* – among emigrant Algerian workers in Paris.[14] By 1926 the *Étoile* had come under the leadership of Messali Hadj whose personality was to dominate the left wing of Algerian nationalism for the next twenty-five years. The links with the PCF were finally broken in 1934 after five years of argument during which Messali accused the communists of trying to subordinate the *Étoile* to their own political aims. The political programme of the *Étoile* demanded complete independence for Algeria with full political and trade-union liberties and a comprehensive programme of agrarian reform. The *Étoile* and the organizations that grew out of it drew most of their support from the emerging Muslim working class in the larger urban centres and in France. The leadership were mainly petit-bourgeois intellectuals influenced to a certain extent by left-wing ideology.

The foundation of the *Fédération des Élus* in Constantine in 1927 represented the political emergence of the more liberal, Westernized Muslim middle class.* Rather than independence, they confined their demands to comparable rights with the *pieds-noirs*. One of the most prominent of the *Élus* was Ferhat Abbas, who, with Messali Hadj, was to dominate Muslim politics until 1954. Another important grouping, the Association of the 'Ulemas, was formed in 1932. Originally created to purify Islam from decadent modern trends, the 'Ulemas came to lead a large educational, religious and political movement emphasizing Algeria's Islamic specificity and separation from Western culture. Their motto was: 'Islam is my religion; Arabic is my language; Algeria is my fatherland.' While Messali Hadj and Ferhat Abbas represented different currents of Western-influenced political thinking, the 'Ulemas represented the traditions of pre-colonial Algeria. The organizational strength of the 'Ulemas was never very well developed, but in ideological terms they had a great effect on the peasants.

The years between 1936 and 1954 saw several occasions when the

* The *Élus* grouped Muslims who had been elected as *délégués financiers, conseillers généraux, conseillers municipaux,* etc.

A Colonial Prehistory

possibility of introducing liberal reforms of the type demanded by the assimilationists were thwarted by the *colon* lobby. During the Popular Front period the French government elaborated the Blum–Violette project[15] which aimed at enfranchising some 30,000 of the better educated middle-class Muslims. The hopes of the *Élus* were dashed when the *colon* lobby in the French parliament prevented the examination of this project until after the fall of Blum's government. After this setback the *Élus* split and the more militant, under Ferhat Abbas, launched the *Union Populaire Algérienne*. In 1937 Messali Hadj founded the *Parti du Peuple Algérien* (PPA) as a specific political party to replace the *Étoile*. The PPA was banned two years later, at the outbreak of war in 1939, but remained in clandestine existence.

After the defeat of the French at the beginning of the Second World War, the *colons* in Algeria supported the Vichy government. Their hatred of the 'decadent' and liberal politicians who they felt had betrayed France led them to throw their lot in with Marshal Pétain and his collaborationist policy. The Vichy French suppressed all Muslim political parties and this, combined with the disillusion suffered by the moderates in 1936–7, made the elaboration of a common front possible. The Allied landings in 1942 effectively defeated the supporters of the Vichy government in Algeria and, for de Gaulle and the Free French, represented the start of the liberation of French soil. In February 1943 Ferhat Abbas, now driven from his moderate position, issued the *Manifeste des Élus Algériens*, openly espousing the right of Algerian self-determination. The next month de Gaulle, seeking to create a political balance against the mainly pro-Vichy *colons*, brought in by decree the Blum–Violette proposals. This gave 60,000 Muslims access to French citizenship. But for most nationalists such measures were by now too little and too late. The same week Abbas launched the *Amis du Manifeste de la Liberté* (AML) as a common front for all the tendencies of Algerian nationalism.* At this point Abbas appeared to be dominating nationalist politics while Messali Hadj's PPA remained banned after the defeat of the Vichy forces.

A period of intense nationalist activity followed, culminating in a series of spontaneous demonstrations and riots in May 1945. The centre of much of this activity was Setif and the resulting reprisals in this area are estimated to have ended in the deaths of 40,000

* The *Manifeste* is the *Manifeste des Élus Algériens* issued by Abbas.

Muslims. Most observers would see this as the point at which many nationalists realized that force was the only means by which they could achieve their objectives. But it was not until nine years later that this final step was taken. The interim was taken up with increasingly futile attempts to gain even the limited political representation allowed them in law.

Although de Gaulle refused to consider any of the demands for self-determination,* he did institute a limited form of political representation for the Muslims. The Statute of 1947 created two colleges in the Algerian assembly and municipal councils – the upper for French citizens, the lower for local citizens (Muslims). The strength of the nationalists was revealed in the municipal elections in October 1947 and the assembly elections in April 1948. Two new nationalist parties, both created in 1946, contested the elections: Messali Hadj's *Mouvement pour le Triomphe des Libertés Démocratiques* (MTLD), a front for the banned PPA, and Ferhat Abbas's *Union Démocratique du Manifeste Algérien* (UDMA). Between them they took a high percentage of the second college seats in the municipal elections and were only prevented from doing the same in the assembly by widespread electoral falsification. For the next six years the nationalists were systematically prevented from achieving even a restricted representation by administrative manipulation. A French MRP deputy, M. Fonulpt-Esperaber, said of the March 1949 elections: 'It is beyond argument that, in the district I visited, the election was neither free nor sincere. It is not the voters who chose the successful candidate. The administration chose him by using the tested methods which, in Algeria, are the fruit of disgraceful experience.'[16]

Apart from the Muslim nationalist organizations themselves, the only other organizations which played any role favourable to nationalist aspirations between 1936 and 1954 were the Algerian Communist Party (PCA) and the *Confédération Générale du Travail* (CGT). The PCA was created out of the Algerian region of the PCF in 1936. Its membership was mainly European and it

* At the time of the statute's promulgation, de Gaulle said on 18 August 1947: 'Algeria has been wrenched from a thousand years of anarchy by French conquest ... French sovereignty! That means that we must never put into question, for any reason, external or internal, the fact that Algeria is our *domaine*.'

A Colonial Prehistory

remained largely controlled by its parent body, the PCF. In 1936, while supporting the Blum–Violette proposals, the PCA permitted the dissolution of the *Étoile Nord Africaine* and Messali Hadj's imprisonment. Later, in 1945, the PCA denounced Messali Hadj's use of violent political rhetoric as being a direct cause of the Setif riots.

Despite its subordination to the metropolitan party's strategy and politics, the PCA has a certain importance in the development of nationalism in Algeria. It was the only European group in Algeria to carry on a dialogue with the Muslim nationalists that was based on mutual respect. It provided an important theoretical and tactical training ground for a number of militants. Most of them, in fact, received this training in the CGT rather than the PCA. From its formation in 1921 the CGT accepted Muslims as members both in France and Algeria and demanded Algerian independence. During the period of agitation leading up to the Popular Front, Muslims and Europeans went on strike together in Algeria. However, in the years following 1945 the nationalist movement gradually split away from the CGT. In 1952 the MTLD set up a special section for establishing cells in factories. Finally, in 1956, the *Union Générale des Travailleurs Algériens* (UGTA) was set up as a separate legal trade-union organization with both socialist and nationalist aims.*

Undoubtedly the failure of the PCA and CGT to take full cognizance of nationalist demands must be attributed to the attitude of the Russian party. During this whole period the Third International adhered rigidly to the Stalinist doctrine of socialism in one country. The claims of anti-colonialism were subordinated to the preservation of socialism in Russia or at most its extension to the West. This policy helped to emphasize the already deep separation between the *pieds-noirs* and the indigenous working class. It also ensured that the nationalist movement, despite its eventual socialist orientation, would always remain suspicious of, and indeed hostile to, the Communist Party.

By 1950 nationalist politics had been reduced to a state of stagnation and ineffectiveness in face of exclusive *colon* control of the political, administrative and economic machinery of Algeria. The

* The CGT, in Algeria, became the *Union Générale des Syndicats Algériens* (UGSA).

UDMA and MTLD were caught in a dilemma: legal means to secure their ends had proved futile, yet the memory of the fate of the Setif riots made them afraid to espouse open recourse to violence. Their impotence was only increased by their mutual electoral competition for the support of the Algerian masses. While the official leaders of the nationalist movement were engaged in a meaningless ballet, aping the activities of Western political parties, the foundations for an armed rising were being laid outside the ambit of conventional politics.

In 1947 a group of the more extreme members of the MTLD set up a clandestine operational body – the *Organisation Spéciale* (OS). In 1950, following activities such as bank and arms raids, the OS was denounced by the MTLD and its members removed from all responsibility in the party. At its national congress in 1953 the MTLD voted to pursue an open and legal course towards independence and, after an attack on Messali's followers, Ben Khedda was elected the new general secretary. The leaders of the OS continued to work clandestinely, forming the *Comité Révolutionnaire pour l'Unité et l'Action* (CRUA) with the explicit task of preparing for an armed rising.[17]

The CRUA issued its declaration of war in November 1954 and simultaneously announced the formation of the FLN. Up until mid-1955 the activity of the nationalist military groups amounted to little more than sporadic terrorism and banditry.[18] During late 1955 and 1956, support for the FLN increased rapidly. In April 1956 Ferhat Abbas and Ahmed Francis of UDMA were driven by the failure of their moderate politics to announce their support for the FLN. At the same time Tewfik Al-Madani of the 'Ulemas and Ben Khedda of the MTLD also rallied to the FLN. The FLN had now become a true national front, but their action had sown the seeds for future political splits. During 1956 the French government finally recognized the seriousness of the revolt and raised the number of troops in Algeria to 400,000.

Following the rallying of the more moderate nationalist elements a meeting of the FLN was held in the Soummam valley in the Kabylie. Here a vague ideological programme was drawn up and the revolution given a definite ruling body in the *Conseil National de la Révolution Algérienne* (CNRA) with an executive, the *Comité de Coordination et d'Exécution*. The meeting decided that politically and

A Colonial Prehistory

militarily the guerrillas of the interior were to have precedence over the political and military leaders outside the country in Egypt, Tunisia and Morocco. The CNRA never implemented this decision and from Soummam dates the split between the maquisards and the external leaders which was to bedevil Algerian politics and envenom personal relations in the years after independence. In October of the same year (1956) five of the major leaders of the FLN were captured while overflying Algeria. These men – Ben Bella, Ait Ahmed, Rabah Bitat, Mohammed Khider and Boudiaf – who had all been members of the CRUA, were imprisoned for the duration of the war. In this way the *chefs historiques*, as they came to be known, were kept separate from the intense rivalries within the FLN and were able to play an influential political role on their release at independence.

From 1957 onwards the FLN lost ground militarily. The French army, under General Challe, was able to contain and then eradicate all but a few pockets of guerrilla resistance. The use of air power and napalm to clear cover made movement inside the country almost impossible. The construction of mined and electrified barriers along the borders with Tunisia and Morocco kept the better trained and armed elements of the *Armée de Libération Nationale* (ALN) from coming to support the guerrillas or moving in supplies. One of the most successful moves in countering guerrilla activity was the policy of *regroupement*, initiated by General Challe. This strategy, learnt from the British in Malaya, involved moving the rural population out of areas favourable to the guerrillas and resettling them in camps under military guard. An estimated two million peasants were treated in this way, creating vast social and economic problems for the future.

Though losing militarily, the FLN managed, after the formation of a provisional government (the GPRA) in 1958, to gather considerable international support and recognition.* The same year, de Gaulle was returned to power in France and the Fourth Republic was declared to be at an end. His return was engineered from Algeria by the professional army officers working in close alliance with the *pieds-noirs*. Both felt that the metropolitan politicians were not taking

* In 1958, the Political Commission of the UN recognized Algeria's right to independence. On 19 December 1960, the UN Assembly voted in favour of this.

a sufficiently hard line with the guerrillas. They were determined that Algeria should not be betrayed as Indochina had been. Ironically, it was de Gaulle himself who soon came to see that the Algerian war could only be ended by self-determination.

In the context of the present analysis it is not necessary to go into the long and tortuous negotiations leading up to independence.[19] Weighing heavily with de Gaulle was the impossibility of retaining up to a million soldiers and their administrative support in a country where the majority of the population supported the demand for national liberation.* Despite the military success of the French army in containing the guerrilla activity, the cost of the continued organization of repression added to the already heavy burden of supporting the Algerian economy. Economically the government felt that Algeria's close links with the French economy and the *colon* domination of all sectors of the Algerian economy would act to reduce the effects of independence. This represented the by now classic, neo-colonialist argument that economic exploitation is more profitable without the expense of political control. Politically, the presence of an armed right-wing bloc just across the Mediterranean from France meant that the stability of France could be threatened at any time by another military *coup*.

Prolonged negotiations with the GPRA led to the signing of the Évian Agreements on 15 March 1962 with an immediate ceasefire and a provision for a referendum on independence on 31 June. Under the Évian Agreements it was assumed that Algeria would choose independence but remain closely tied to France with no radical changes in social or economic organization. The reality was very different.

* De Gaulle witnessed this for himself during his visit to Algeria, 9–13 December 1960, when he was met by Muslim crowds chanting '*Vive l'Algérie Musulmane!*' (see Albert-Paul Lentin, *Le Dernier Quart d'Heure* [Paris, 1962]).

3

THE FORMATION OF THE *COMITÉS DE GESTION*

THE political, economic and social history of the Muslim and European communities in pre-independent Algeria had far-reaching consequences for the development of Algeria as an independent state. The total polarization between the two groups and the concomitant exclusion of the Muslims from political and economic power led inexorably to an impasse where violence became the only solution. Just as inevitably this violence only increased the separation between the two communities, to a point where reconciliation became an impossibility. The mass exodus of the *colons*, fleeing their shattered dream world, meant not only the end of *Algérie Française*; more importantly for Algeria it meant the disappearance of a whole bourgeoisie, of capitalists, administrators and technicians. At this precise point, the always precarious unity of the FLN split into dissenting factions. Algeria was left in a state of almost total economic and political paralysis. It was in this situation that the *comités de gestion* made their appearance.

De Gaulle's evident intention to end the war and grant some form of independence to Algeria provoked an increasingly hostile reaction among the *colons* and many professional army officers. Their desperation in face of this 'betrayal' emerged in the formation of the *Organisation de l'Armée Secrète* (OAS) in February 1961 and the abortive military *coup* of 22–5 April 1961. The OAS was a blend of right-wing officers still bitter over their betrayal by politicians in Indochina[1] and the more fanatical *colons*. The tactics of the OAS reflected the pathological universe of the *pied-noir* in its totality. Their only ideology was *Algérie Française*, the preservation of the colonial structures in all their forms. To this end they employed terrorism and assassination in the attempt first of all to intimidate the French government* and then to provoke the FLN into retaliation.

---

* Among these efforts were the assassination of two French *commissaires*, Goldenberg and Gavoury, the attempted assassination of de Gaulle and the bombing of the HQ of an anti-OAS brigade.

When this failed they ordered a general offensive, aimed indiscriminately at both French and Muslims.* In June a policy of *'terre brûlée'* was declared, inaugurating an orgy of destruction. With his dream crumbling the *pied-noir*'s response was to destroy this world. If *Algérie Française* could not be preserved then Algeria must be reduced to what it had been in 1830. The Muslims should not have the benefit of anything created by the *colons*.[2]

The widespread destruction of buildings, machinery, communications and administrative records was accompanied by the exodus of some ninety per cent of the European settlers. In the light of *colon* dominance of Algeria's economic and political organization it should be clear how great a void this departure would create. It represents an event unparalleled in the history of liberation from colonialism. The *colons* formed almost all Algeria's agrarian and industrial capitalists, administrators, managers, doctors, teachers, engineers and skilled manpower. There were not only few Muslim entrepreneurs able to take over in production or commerce; there were no indigenous technical or managerial strata. The economy ground to an almost total halt, creating unprecedented unemployment. Even the firms controlled from France ceased production as their managerial staff were largely *colons*.

This catastrophic situation was made infinitely worse by the breakdown of the political and administrative machinery at the moment of independence. Algeria fell apart into a whole series of political conflicts, with at least three potential governments and other less well defined groups attempting to establish their claim to revolutionary authority. None of these, during the summer of 1962, was capable of establishing sufficient authority to end the chaos that followed the departure of the *colons*. The political and ideological conflicts of this period left their stamp indelibly on the whole history of independent Algeria: they had their roots in the conflicts of the years before independence.

I have already mentioned the basic splits in the nationalist move-

---

* The OAS finally lost the support of most of the army when on 23 March in the rue d'Isly they killed seventeen French soldiers and wounded seventy. As an example of the terrorism against Muslims, at the beginning of May, the OAS perpetrated the following events: 3 May, sixty-two Muslims killed in Algiers; 7 May, 100 Muslims killed in Algiers; 10 May, thirty Muslim women killed in Algiers and Oran.

The Formation of the Comités de Gestion

ment. The FLN was an alliance of necessity between the moderates of the UDMA, the Islamic purists of the 'Ulemas, and the various left-wing factions descended from the MTLD. Compounding this basic heterogeneity were the differences between those who had remained in the maquis and the political leaders in Tunis, Rabat and Cairo. The existence of the well-armed units of the ALN under Colonel Boumédienne and the return of the five *chefs historiques* added further complications to an already divided FLN.

The traditional differences in the FLN had been between the 'easterners' who based their nationalism on the Arab and Islamic nature of Algeria and the 'westerners' who favoured retaining close ties with France. The first overt indication of more profound ideological differences came at the CNRA meeting in Tripoli in May. This was called to discuss the future of independent Algeria following the conclusion of the Évian Agreements. The meeting soon developed into a sustained attack on the GPRA, not so much on its prime minister Ben Khedda, who had replaced Ferhat Abbas in September 1961, as on the triumvirate of Boussouf, Ben Tobbal and Krim Belkacem who really controlled the GPRA and CCE.[3] The attack was mounted by a heteroclite alliance of the *chefs historiques*, the leadership of the ALN and some moderates under Ferhat Abbas. The immediate cause of the clash was over the ceasefire arranged between the OAS and the GPRA but it had its roots in a whole series of disagreements over the direction of the war and the shape of independent Algeria. The unstable nature of this alliance is clear from the hesitant participation of Boudiaf and Ait Ahmed who had old grievances against Ben Bella and his authoritarian tendencies, and, as socialists, had deep suspicions of Boumédienne and the ALN.*

* See Hervé Bourges, *L'Algérie à l'Épreuve du Pouvoir* (Paris, 1967), p. 27. The enmity to Ben Bella dated from early in the war: cf. a document Abane Ramdane planned to send Ait Ahmed and which was captured by the French: 'Whether you like it or not, and this is my conviction and that of all the "brothers" of the Interior, Ahmed [Ben Bella] is doing everything in his power to appear as the supreme leader of the revolution.' Quoted by Serge Bromberger, *Les Rebelles Algériens* (Paris, 1958), p. 135. These enmities were deepened by the assassination of Abane Ramdane, a left-winger, and one of the leading figures of the FLN after the arrest of the *chefs historiques*, by a right-wing faction of the CCE led by Boussouf: see Mohammed Lebajoui, *Verités sur la Révolution Algérienne* (Paris, 1970), pp. 158–62. For Ben Bella's own feelings about the FLN at Tripoli,

Workers' Self-Management in Algeria

Despite the obvious, and at times extreme, differences between the various factions when the project on the future of independent Algeria, elaborated by Ben Bella,* was voted on there was no open opposition. The *Projet de Programme pour la Réalisation de la Révolution Démocratique et Populaire*, known as the Tripoli Programme, represented, in ideological terms, a victory for the left-wing elements of the FLN. In accepting a 'socialist option' for Algeria it destroyed the whole basis of the Évian Agreements.

The first part of the document analyses the conduct of the war. The previous leadership (especially the GPRA) are criticized for a lack of ideological precision, for having an authoritarian and paternalistic attitude to the masses, and having 'petit-bourgeois' tendencies towards bureaucracy.

> The ideological idleness of the FLN, its feudal mentality and the petit-bourgeois attitudes which these produce indirectly, risk turning the future Algerian state into a mediocre and non-democratic bureaucracy in reality if not in its ideology.[4]

The old leadership is indicted for taking the control of the revolution out of the hands of the 'internals' and so creating a gulf between leadership and masses and the resulting depoliticization of the masses.

Having criticized the FLN for its past deviations and failings, the Programme goes on to elaborate the bases for a 'socialist option'.

> The analysis of the social context of the liberation struggle shows that, in general, it is the peasants and workers who are the active base of the movement and have given it its essentially popular character.[5]

> Ideological combat must follow the armed struggle; the democratic and popular revolution will follow the struggle for independence. The democratic and popular revolution is the conscious construction of the country according to socialist principles and with power in the hands of the people.[6]

---

see Robert Merle, *Ben Bella* (Paris, 1965), based on a taped interview. A good overall account appears in Edmond Bergheaud, *Le Premier Quart d'Heure ou l'Algérie des Algériens: de 1962 à aujourd'hui* (Paris, 1964).

* Ben Bella claimed that he drew up the programme while in prison at Aulnoy, stating: 'The sovereignty of Algeria had been recognized, but only as a formality and the reality could take many shapes. Here lay the weakness of the FLN: it had neither policy nor doctrine.' Quoted by Merle, op. cit., p. 123.

The Formation of the Comités de Gestion

In its discussion of the economy, the Programme opts for freedom from the dominance of neo-colonialism, state planning with workers' participation, agrarian reform with land redistribution and creation of state farms. It elaborates a programme of industrialization with the long-term view of nationalizing transport, banks, insurance, external trade and mines. On all of these points the Tripoli Programme was making statements of intention rather than actual practical plans.

The surprising and temporary unity achieved over the programme was lost when the CNRA approached the task of choosing the future government and reorganizing the party. Ben Bella proposed to create a *Bureau Politique* at the head of the FLN containing a more representative selection of militants than the GPRA; this would form the core of the new government.[7] This move was seen by the members of the GPRA as an attempt to reduce the power of the government in favour of the party and the army, and they refused to accept it. The crisis became open on the eve of independence when the GPRA dismissed Colonel Boumédienne and two other commanders (Mendjli and Slimane) of the ALN from their posts. Ben Bella refused to sanction the decision. The ALN rejected it as illegal, and Khider, one of the *chefs historiques*, resigned from the GPRA.

On 3 July, after a massive vote for independence, Ben Khedda and the now depleted GPRA arrived in Algiers to set up their government. On the 11th Ben Bella arrived in Tlemcen with the ALN from Morocco and on the 22nd announced the formation of the *Bureau Politique* as the supreme government.* On the 25th Boudiaf (who had refused a seat in the *Bureau*) and Krim Belkacem declared their opposition to Ben Bella and the *Bureau* from Tizi-Ouzou in the Kabylie. Two days later, Ait Ahmed left Algeria in protest against Ben Bella. During this period the leaders of the *willayas*, the *maquisard* regions,† set up their own local fiefs, sometimes allied to the GPRA, sometimes to the *Bureau Politique*,

* Its members were to be Ben Bella, Mohammed Khider, Hocine Ait Ahmed, Rabah Bitat (all imprisoned in France), Said Mohammedi and Hadj Benallah.

† The *willayas* were set up to control military and political aspects of the guerrilla struggle. There were six *willayas* and Algiers was recognized as a seventh autonomous region. They were W. I Aurès, W. II Constantinois, W. III Kabylie, W. IV Algérois, W. V Oranie, W. VI Aumale-Sud.

or the Tizi-Ouzou group, or as in the case of Willaya IV in the Algiers region, owing allegiance to no one. Meanwhile, outside Algiers, in the old French administrative centre of Rocher Noir, the *Exécutif Provisoire* set up, according to Évian, as the only legal government till elections were held, vainly attempted to keep some administration going.

By September the *Bureau Politique*, backed by the only competent armed force – Boumédienne's army of the frontiers – had gained control of most of Algeria and held elections on its own single list. The detailed history of the political manoeuvres and armed clashes that preceded Ben Bella's victory does not belong here.[8] Despite clashes in which thousands were killed outright, civil war was avoided by the general reluctance of leaders and people to prolong the agony of nearly eight years' struggle with France. For a few months the political divisions that have riddled Algeria ever since independence were papered over.

Thus, at the moment of independence, Algeria was plunged into an almost unparalleled economic, social and political dissolution. The war had resulted in some one million deaths leaving at least 400,000 orphans. Half a million refugees were returning from Tunisia and Morocco. Two million peasants were in *regroupement* camps, their villages, crops and livestock abandoned or destroyed.*
Over a million hectares of the best land had been abandoned by the *colons* and the time of harvesting and ploughing was approaching. Much of the machinery in agriculture and industry had been sabotaged by the owners before they left. Over two million agricultural, industrial and commercial workers were unemployed. The schools were closed and there were few teachers to staff them. The number of doctors had dropped from nearly 3,000 at the beginning of the year to 600. Above all, there was no political authority capable of dealing with the immediate social and economic problems.

It was in this situation that *autogestion* made its appearance. During the summer and autumn *comités de gestion*, composed of workers, were set up in a large number of industrial and agricultural concerns. Their immediate role was to recommence production, provide employment and safeguard these national assets. Their long-term effect was to institute a practice of social and economic organiza-

---

* For instance, the number of sheep in the country is estimated to have dropped from six million in 1954 to under three million in 1961.

The Formation of the Comités de Gestion

tion, which, with its concomitant theory, was to dominate Algerian national political ideology in the following years.

Nearly all commentators on the *comités de gestion* describe their emergence as spontaneous.[9] Only a few right-wing opponents of independence see the *comités* as a carefully conceived plot designed to prevent the return of the *colons*:[10] a conspiracy theory that does not fit the facts. But while agreeing on the spontaneity of the creation of many of the *comités*, the observers are not agreed on the motivation of the workers who took over the farms and factories. Most of the descriptions of independent Algeria are by Frenchmen and reflect the strong, romantic identification of the French left with the Algerian revolution and with Ben Bella as its personification. This has led them to bend the events of the summer of 1962 to fit their own political orientations. The lack of precise details about the period has aided this process.

The basic implication of 'spontaneity' is that, in the absence of any legitimate authority, the industrial and agricultural workers, with little or no political direction from above, acted to secure the economic resources of the country. Alain Marill talks of: '. . . the spontaneous actions of the workers and peasants who did not want to lose the wealth abandoned by its former owners. It was in a situation where the absence of power was total, where economic enterprises were abandoned, that the workers once more became conscious of the reality of their national problems.'[11] The point in question is whether the industrial and agricultural workers occupied and managed the farms and factories from a basic ideological commitment to socialism and a rational estimation of the nation's economic problems or whether they were motivated by their own immediate economic self-interest. Most commentators have taken the line that the workers were consciously identifying with a revolutionary socialist tradition. For these purists the idea of material self-interest on the part of the workers is never as revolutionary as the sacrifice of individual interests to those of the nation or class.

The official position of FLN militants has always been to affirm the basic communitarian ideas of the workers and peasants, heightened by the national liberation struggle, as the foundation for *autogestion*. In this it differs little from Yugoslav claims that the origins of self-management can be seen in the collective organization of the historical peasant *zadruga*. As *autogestion* became the fundamental basis of the theory and practice of the Algerian revolution it is not surprising that it should be surrounded by a mythical opacity. A recent FLN pamphlet described the origins of the *comités* in the following terms:

> In an upsurge of revolutionary enthusiasm, workers and peasants alike were quick to react and they demonstrated a firm determination to re-establish the rights which they acquired as a result of their fierce struggle. They occupied closed factories and businesses and many of the rich agricultural estates which had been abandoned and they began to reopen them at once. Fully conscious of their new responsibilities, they organized themselves with admirable control and elected their '*directions collégiales*' [management committees].* In this way the system of autogestion emerged quite naturally as the logical conclusion of a continuing development of thought and action and the revolutionary accomplishment of the working class.[12]

This is one of the clearest statements on *autogestion* as the conscious and enlightened identification of the Algerian working class with a classic revolutionary tradition.

For those like Mohammed Harbi, one-time editor of *Révolution Africaine*† and close associate of Ben Bella, who believed in the necessity of an *avant-garde* party to lead the masses, the enthusiasm of the above passage was not so attractive. While appreciating the revolutionary verve of the workers, Harbi places much more stress on the eventual codification of *autogestion* and the leadership given by the FLN.[13] At the other extreme, right-wing commentators see the establishment of the *comités* not as the spontaneous action of the workers, but as stage-managed by the army which was seeking to impose by force the ideas of Mao and Castro. Between these extremes lie those who doubt the revolutionary content of the seizure of the factories and farms, whether it was spontaneous or stage-managed.[14] Grigori Lazarev remarks, quite accurately, that the FLN were basically orientated towards redistribution of land to the *fellahs* (peasants) rather than the establishment of

---

* *Direction collégiale* is an important concept in the Algerian revolution – the idea of collegiality as a mode of democratic leadership is similar to that of democratic centralism. Opposition to Ben Bella and Boumédienne has been partially based on their infringement of this.

† *Révolution Africaine* is the weekly organ of the FLN published in Algiers.

The Formation of the Comités de Gestion

state farms in their war-time propaganda. He stresses that the workers were basically conservative and motivated by self-interest. 'In the climate of economic anarchy following independence the agricultural workers [*salariés agricoles*] wished to conserve their own positions and so appeared as a stabilizing element, and their initial conservatism paradoxically ensured a certain continuity of management.'[15]

Amidst the fiercely partisan evaluation of the revolutionary content of the *comités de gestion*, the background events are at least clear; although, as might be expected, they are in isolation capable of misinterpretation. With the massive departure of the *pieds-noirs*, the small national Algerian bourgeoisie and petit-bourgeoisie moved in to purchase their property. Furniture, cars, then apartments, land and businesses were offered at ridiculously low prices by panic-stricken *colons* desperate to realize at least some of their capital assets before leaving. The ability of the Algerian Muslim middle class to buy up this property was, in fact, severely limited by its small size and extreme lack of liquid capital. However, in face of such sales the *Exécutif Provisoire* published a decree on 24 August allowing prefects to requisition abandoned industrial and agricultural enterprises and nominate managers to administrate them until the return of the owners.[16] These properties came to be known as the *biens-vacants*. The *Exécutif Provisoire* still fondly believed that the majority of the settlers would return once a government had been elected. In reality this interim measure had already been outpaced by other elements in Algerian society. On the one hand, there were the 'spontaneous' and 'anarchic' activities of the workers and peasants and on the other the more organized methods of the ANP, FLN and foremost of the *Union Générale des Travailleurs Algériens* (UGTA).

In Algiers the workers, earlier confined to their own areas of the city by OAS activity, had started moving down into the European areas by 20 June. Here they occupied empty apartments and, at times, their factories which had been closed, in many cases, since the OAS crisis had begun in April.[17] This pattern was repeated in the other large urban centres. In the countryside the permanent workers on the large colonial estates were, in many cases, carrying on with the normal work of harvesting, fruit-picking, etc., even though they were severely handicapped by the lack of machinery. All through the summer and early autumn these occupations continued, often taking violent and conflicting turns. At Céligny crops and buildings on farms bought by Muslims from the colonial owners were burnt by irate peasants who felt that they had not benefited by this transaction.[18] In Meloug the sub-prefect, supported by local army units, put a private Muslim owner into a large estate only to be driven off by the local agricultural workers who had already occupied it.[19] Elsewhere the permanent workers banded together to prevent ex-combatants or seasonal labourers from moving into estates which they themselves now controlled.[20]

The evidence on the large majority of the occupations of colonial property is scanty because of the anarchic conditions of the time. But from what evidence exists, it seems clear that many of the 'spontaneous' initiatives taken by the workers amounted to an attempt to preserve their jobs, and therefore income, at the expense of any outsider, whether capitalist, ex-combatant, peasant or seasonal worker. In many cases the ex-combatant and the army were not welcomed as liberators. Both during the war and in the aftermath of independence the ALN/ANP* had directed their terrorism against workers on the European estates because they regarded them as compromised with colonialism. In fact, many of the permanent agricultural workers on the large estates in the coastal plains had been geographically distant from a war that had mainly taken place in the mountains and the large towns. They regarded the ex-combatants, who were mostly peasants, not as heroes of the liberation struggle but as outsiders and competitors. In the political anarchy and economic breakdown of the summer the main objective of the workers was to secure their own economic livelihood; a revolutionary initiative to seize the means of production for the nation was only a secondary consideration.

The conscious seizure of factories and farms as an explicit part of the struggle against colonialism lay very much more with national organizations like the UGTA, the FLN and the army, even though their ideological motives were different. The role played by the UGTA in the creation of the *comités de gestion* was, without doubt, the most important. The UGTA, formed in 1956, had remained a national organization separate from the FLN during the war. Although prevented from taking an active role in the military

* The Army of National Liberation (ALN) changed its name to the *Armée Nationale et Populaire* (ANP) after independence.

The Formation of the Comités de Gestion

resistance by the French control of the towns, its basic structures remained in existence. After the ceasefire it rapidly gained in membership* and importance as the only sizeable organization already securely based inside the country. Many of its officials had Marxist leanings after training in the French CGT or East European countries during the war. However, the theoretical separation of the UGTA from orthodox Communist theory and practice had already become apparent by 1958-9 when articles appeared in its paper, *L'Ouvrier Algérien*, describing Russia as 'state-capitalist'. This early ideological stance foreshadowed the UGTA's firm commitment to autogestion and its opposition to the authoritarian nature of Ben Bella's régime. From the beginning of the factional struggle for political power it determined to stay uncommitted and retain the autonomous role of the UGTA as the only real representative of the working class.[21]

As early as February 1962 the UGTA was pressing for a definite socialist orientation to post-independence Algeria.

Independence is inseparable from the Revolution, but the Revolution is more important than independence. . . . To bring about the Revolution is to see to it that one political, economic and social order disappears and is replaced by another in which all national resources and important means of production are socialized, and the country is economically and socially managed by the labouring masses.[22]

To a certain extent these demands were taken up by the Tripoli Programme. By early July the internal UGTA leadership, especially Lassel and Bourouiba, had decided on the forced occupation of factories and commercial enterprises in Grand Alger and Oran.[23] Their stated reasons were twofold: firstly to prevent the nascent Algerian bourgeoisie from getting a firm foothold in the economy and secondly to provide work for the starving workers. To emphasize their complete condemnation of the fratricidal activities of the leaders of the FLN they organized a giant demonstration in Algiers in August with the slogans ' *'sba' a snine, Barakat*' ('Seven years, that is enough') and 'Give us bread'. They also covered Algiers with the slogan '*Un seul héros – le peuple*' as a protest against the growing personality cult in the FLN.

From the start, the UGTA had decided on *comités de gestion* composed of workers as the appropriate form of revolutionary

* In July 1962 it claimed a membership of 300,000.

organization of the means of production. To this end they set up a *commission d'autogestion* to advise workers on the formation of *comités de gestion*. During September the UGTA extended its activities to the countryside. In the Kabylie and Constantinois the peasants had already taken over most of the European land; these were generally quite small holdings and not susceptible to the formation of *comités de gestion* unless they were rationalized and unified. The UGTA concentrated on the Mitidja and the Cheliff where the European holdings had generally taken the form of large estates. They set up the first *comités* in Boufarik, Blida and Orléansville, where the *comité* members were all permanent workers from the estates.[24]

By now the creation of *comités de gestion* had a definite political content: the creation of basic democracy to act as a force against the growing autocratic tendencies of the FLN leadership. The UGTA attacked the *chefs historiques* who had not shared the experience of the people during the war and now wanted to impose their rule by force of arms.[25] In August they were joined, tacitly, by Boudiaf who had formed the *Parti de la Révolution Socialiste* (PRS). The PRS accused the FLN leadership, specifically the *Bureau Politique*, of preparing a police state of personal dictatorship. Of the FLN as a party the PRS announced that it '... after having been the catalyst of all popular energies during the liberation struggle can no longer pretend to be a revolutionary movement'.[26] In this they were joined by the *Amicale Générale des Travailleurs Algériens*, the UGTA's sister organization representing Algerian workers in France. The PCA eventually came out in support of the *Bureau Politique*, ironically, as one of Ben Bella's first measures was to make it illegal.

Although the UGTA had been the first to set up *comités de gestion* in the larger towns and in the Mitidja and the Cheliff, the other national organizations were also acting to secure the abandoned European means of production. The army, as it moved in from Morocco and helped set up the *Bureau Politique* in Tlemcen, placed large parts of western Algeria under its direct control. European land was either redistributed to ex-combatants or, if large estates were concerned, placed under the direct control of army units. In many cases spontaneously formed management committees were forcibly dissolved and the original permanent workers expelled. This process has continued sporadically to the present day and the army

The Formation of the Comités de Gestion

still controls an unspecified number of estates.* The army was impelled by several motives. It wished to secure a political base by distributing land to ex-combatants, whose loyalty was to the army rather than any other organization or group. Like the UGTA, it was also intent on preventing the bourgeoisie from gaining a foothold in the economy and making the return of the *colons* difficult, if not impossible. Its political ideology, inspired by Mao and Castro, not only led it to believe that revolutionary authenticity lay in the countryside but that control of the means of production should lie with the state. Thus the army believed in peasant cooperatives and state farms rather than autogestion. At the same time, many of the *willaya* leaders were attempting to place their own supporters on European farms in their areas with a view to establishing a basis for future political and, if necessary, military support. Despite the later disbandment of the *willayas* by Ben Bella the ex-guerrilla leaders could always count on a certain amount of support from their local fiefs in any conflict with the central government. As for the FLN itself, it was not until late October that it officially began to set up *comités de gestion* in both agriculture and industry; though certain of its militants had worked alongside the UGTA from the beginning.

By September Ben Bella was firmly in power as the prime minister of the newly elected Assembly. One of the first acts of the new government was to issue a decree on 22 October instituting *comités de gestion* in vacant agricultural estates.[27] At this point the right of the owner to return was still retained; if he did so, *autogestion* was to become *cogestion*. The following month, on 23 November, this principle was extended to industry and mining.[28] At the same time as the October decree, another was published forbidding any transactions in abandoned European property – the *biens-vacants* – and allowing prefects to annul any such transactions since independence.[29] The *comités de gestion* set up after this date were generally appointed by the local administration rather than being elected by the workers. Even before the 22 October decree had been issued a telegram was sent to all prefects asking them to give priority to ex-combatants in any elections or appointments to *comités*. This once

* This process is not generally known in Algeria. My evidence comes from a document in the possession of Soliman Lotfallah, a one-time *conseiller* to Ben Bella, seen in 1965.

again represented the basic orientation of the party and army towards the peasantry rather than the industrial or agricultural proletariat. The full institution of *autogestion* as a specific system of economic management and the official basis of Algerian socialism did not come until the following March, with the *décrets de mars*.

The modalities surrounding the emergence of the *comités de gestion* can be traced to the combination of circumstances in the summer of 1962. The history of extreme separation between the Muslim and *colon* communities made it likely that independence would be followed by a profound social, economic and political caesura. This likelihood was deepened into certainty by the experiences of the war and ensured by the flight of the mass of the *colons*. The composition of the FLN as a tacit alliance between traditional Muslim political groups agreed only on national liberation, the wartime division between the interior and the exterior, the lack of any clear plan on the future of independent Algeria, all combined to make the eruption of factionalism almost inevitable. Finally, the dislocation of the already moribund traditional social and political structures caused by the war made the emergence and adoption of unconventional solutions likely.

The account of the various modes in which European property was taken over makes it clear that there was no one coherent ideology or motivation acting as a mediation. The official explanation has been put in terms of a national aptitude for cooperation. 'Thus this collective management is the culmination of a natural collective mentality that 130 years of exploitation only reinforced and which ripened radically during the seven and a half years of revolutionary opposition to colonialism.'[30] Most of this statement is based on a romantic and entirely erroneous appreciation of the social structures and ideology of the peasants. (I shall go into social structure and ideology in greater detail in a later chapter.) The traditional structures of Algerian society, based on the tribe or clan, were irremediably shattered by the impact of the conquest. The political authority of the tribal chiefs was annexed by the colonial administration and the extended family became the basic unit of social and economic cooperation. The FLN certainly recruited the majority of its guerrilla cadres from the peasants and shepherds in the interior, but their motivation for joining the liberation struggle differed from that of their leaders. The peasants were fighting for a return to the

The Formation of the Comités de Gestion

past, for a return of their lands stolen by the Europeans, for Islam, for the memory of Abdel Kader. They were not fighting for communitarian socialism or the establishment of cooperative economic enterprises. Their rigid opposition to any form of cooperatives has forced the government to delay its programmes of agrarian reform several times since independence.

The FLN claimed to draw its revolutionary authenticity from the peasants but at no time during the war did it seek officially to put socialist ideas across to them. A study of André Mandouze's *La Révolution Algérienne par les Textes* shows no mention in any of the FLN–ANP's declarations of socialist thinking about agriculture or industry. The word socialism is, in fact, not mentioned at all. For agriculture there are promises of agrarian reform, while industry is talked about in terms of removing the colonial exploitative structure by building a national manufacturing industry. The revolution and the ideology offered the Algerian people were national and democratic rather than socialist, peasant-based rather than urban. In this context, the Tripoli Programme represented a belated attempt to impart a coherent ideological and practical direction to the revolution. Despite its acceptance of socialism as a guiding ideology, the actual recommendations of the Programme amount to little more than promises of land redistribution, creation of state farms and the eventual nationalization of some fields of industry and commerce. In any case, it is doubtful whether the recommendations of the Programme reached more than a small minority of the workers or peasants in the confusion of the summer and autumn.

In the light of this discussion on the motivation for the occupation of the *colon* farms, it is interesting to look at the types of action taken in geographical and class terms. The areas where there were large numbers of peasants in close proximity to European holdings were the Kabylie and the Constantinois.* The peasants in these areas had been in contact with units of the ANP for much of the war and had been closely affected by the promises of agrarian reform. Their conception of this was individualistic rather than cooperative; for them the European farms, which were mainly small units, were to be redistributed to individuals or families and farmed in a traditional

---

* To a certain extent, the same is true for parts of the Oranais, but the effect of peasant occupations was masked by the army take-over of the *biens-vacants*.

manner. Their conservatism has appeared in their continuing hostility to any reform that posits the amalgamation of individual units. They attacked the *traffiquants* who had bought some of the land, not so much because they were bourgeois but because they were outsiders. Similarly they opposed even ex-combatants if they were not from that area. For them it was a matter of reclaiming land that had been expropriated or bought from them within historical memory. Much of this land was later reappropriated by the government and *comités de gestion* set up to manage them.

It was on the richer coastal belts, where the *pied-noir* holdings were large estates, that agrarian *autogestion* really took hold. Here it was not peasants with their 'traditions of cooperation' who were involved but permanent agricultural workers, workers who in many cases had long ceased to have any connection with the traditional society of the peasants.[31] These workers had a privileged position among Muslim agriculturalists; they had a permanent paid job. They had become proletarianized through their relation to the means of production, which was that of wage labourers within a cash nexus as opposed to the peasant's relation to his own land. On many of the estates the permanent workers attempted to preserve them as an integral whole and continued to manage production as it had been under the *pieds-noirs*. They tried to keep out, not only the *traffiquants*, but often also the army, ex-combatants and seasonal workers – the landless agricultural sub-proletariat. Their motives were a confused mixture of economic self-interest and revolutionary consciousness. Their immediate reaction to the absence of the *pieds-noirs* was to continue production in order to realize some income from sales. Indeed, they were so desperate for wages that in the early months they often sold machinery and vehicles and mortgaged the harvest to local or foreign speculators to raise money for their immediate needs. This represented a sizeable loss of capital goods.

The industrial workers were in a position similar to the permanent agricultural workers: in relation to the mass of urban workless and occasionally employed they were an *élite*. Again they had been thoroughly proletarianized through their employment in industry or commerce and were even further removed from the traditions of peasant society than the workers on the large estates. Having been without wages for three months, in many cases their

The Formation of the Comités de Gestion

first concern was to recommence production in order to pay for their immediate material survival.

It is too simplistic, however, to attribute economic self-interest as the only motivation of the industrial and agricultural workers for occupying the means of production, or indeed to denigrate them for having such a motivation. During the course of the war little had been said about the future modes of ownership or control of the means of production. The only organization with a mass base to have an explicit socialist ideology was the UGTA and it had only acquired this mass base since the ceasefire, while until the middle of the summer its activities had been mainly confined to the large towns. There was thus an almost total lack of overt socialist education or organization until the late summer of 1962, though a number of workers had been affected by the vaguely socialist content of the PPA and MTLD. However, their relation to the means of production and their consequent objective proletarianization had created a certain consciousness of their position. They were able to translate the national hostility to the *colon* as exploiter into a class hostility to the *colon* as capitalist. This class consciousness was rudimentary in that it did not have a well-defined political orientation. The occupation of the factories and farms was a collective activity and represented the collective expression of their immediate and overriding interests both individually and as a class – escape from starvation. For them this came before any consideration of the wider political meaning of their action. Later the accumulated effect of the liberation struggle, the efforts of the UGTA to realize the implications of the occupations, and their own success did create a greater degree of consciousness. But to condemn economic self-interest as unrevolutionary because it does not contain a specific ideology is to misconceive the basis of class consciousness.

The appearance of *comités de gestion* on the *colon* properties faced the new government with a *fait accompli*. The FLN had not, officially, considered a socialist policy until Tripoli and even then it was contained in the vaguest of terms. The actions of the workers and the UGTA drove Ben Bella and his associates to make a definite step in the direction of social control of the means of production. The objective effect of the workers' actions was to make the return of the *pieds-noirs* almost impossible and to withdraw large sectors of the economy from immediate and direct control by capitalism. It provided an opportunity for Ben Bella and the FLN to produce a theory and practice of Algerian socialism. The workers' seizure of the means of production turned independence into revolution. In so doing they secured for Ben Bella the reputation of a revolutionary leader, placed for a time on a level with Castro. But from October 1962, when the party and state assumed the mantle of this new revolutionary authenticity, the history of the *comités de gestion* was one of containment by party and state. Lacking any revolutionary theory on the respective roles of party, state and workers' councils, Algerian socialism fell in pawn to the new social forces created by independence. The nascent national bourgeoisie of administrators, party officials and technicians turned to attack the *comités* as an explicit threat to their own developing class interests.

4

THE *DÉCRETS DE MARS*

WITH the formation of *comités de gestion* during the summer and early autumn of 1962, a mode of economic and social organization arose even before the new state itself came into being. Before any firm decision on the role of the state, its structure or its ideology had been taken, the *comités* had created a practice with profound theoretical implications for the future of the state. Ben Bella and most of the party leaders were caught completely unawares by this *fait accompli*. As we have seen, the first reaction of the new government was to temporize. In the 22 October and 23 November decrees the *comités* were accepted as useful expedients. It was not until March 1963 that Ben Bella's government formally accepted the *comités de gestion* as an integral part of the nation's economic organization and defined their practice as the keystone of Algerian socialism. The so-called *décrets de mars* appeared to set the seal of government approval on the events of the summer. For a short time it looked as if party and state were firmly committed to the idea of *autogestion* as the specific Algerian version of socialism.

This chapter will delineate the formal, legalistic structure of *autogestion*, running from the decrees of March 1963 which established the structures and responsibilities of the organs of self-management in the enterprise through to the attempts to create a coherent economic and administrative superstructure for the separate enterprises. It should be borne in mind that, although the various decrees and government directives had the force of law, their actual application was highly incoherent. On one level the attempted imposition of a uniform structure on a mode of organization whose origins were not uniform created the likelihood of deviations. More importantly, the more or less well defined hostility to *autogestion* among many members of the state and party machinery meant that no real mechanism existed for enforcing the decrees. Within the political and economic conflict over *autogestion* the exact organization of each enterprise came to reflect its own specific juncture within that conflict.

Thus what is outlined here as the organization of *autogestion* is to a large extent an ideal type rather than actuality. Later chapters will look at the way the apparent intentions of the decrees were thwarted. A distinction between the institutions created or legalized in early 1963 and those (mainly administrative superstructures) created later should be borne in mind. For most militants the decrees of March remained an ideal, vested with a certain amount of revolutionary authenticity; conversely, the superstructure represented the ever-encroaching power of the new *élite* seated in the state and party machinery.

THE 'DECRETS DE MARS'

The exodus of the *colons* left some one million hectares of land, a thousand industrial enterprises[1] and thousands of small shops abandoned. The number of housing units left empty is hard to estimate, but Humbaraci[2] gives a figure of 200,000 for Algiers alone. These then were the *biens-vacants*. The decrees of 22 October and 23 November instituted *comités de gestion* in the *biens-vacants* in agriculture, mining and industry, where the enterprise had over ten employees. The *comité* members, numbering three, were appointed by the local prefect or party officials. For administrative purposes they were placed under the supervision of the *Bureau National pour la Protection et Gestion des Biens-Vacants*, which acted through the office of the local prefect.

These measures were solely the recognition by the government that a *de facto* situation existed. The political leaders had been caught completely unprepared by the flight of the *pieds-noirs* and the abandonment of their property. The Tripoli Programme had based its assumptions on the premise of a gradual and orderly expropriation. The necessity of creating well-defined and permanent organs of management that were under the control of the government was obviously of paramount importance. From the government's point of view this important sector of the economy could not be allowed to remain in confusion and uncertainty. It had to regain control of a sector which had already acted in a spontaneous and extra-governmental fashion. It was essential not only to impose some

The Décrets de Mars

measure of control but, just as important, to elaborate an ideology that would contain it.

The first signs of the creation of an official theory and practice round the *comités*, as opposed to a stop-gap legalization, came in December 1962. On the 4th, in a speech to the National Assembly, Ben Bella remarked:

> These management committees, democratically elected, will allow a real economic and social improvement for the workers who will, under this system, be closely associated with responsibility for their concerns. This measure constitutes a first step towards agrarian reform and foreshadows the socialization of production and distribution circuits in the industrial and commercial sectors.

The wording of this speech shows that Ben Bella had still not fully accepted the idea of complete self-management. At this stage it was still not clear what was to happen to the European lands: in a speech on 10 November Ben Bella referred to redistribution but on 12 December he referred to state farms. *Autogestion* is not mentioned at this point.

The *décrets de mars* represented a radical acceleration in Ben Bella's attempt to create a socialist praxis. But, as so often, Ben Bella was the figurehead rather than the architect in this process. The *décrets* were formulated by a group whose main figures were: Mohammed Harbi, editor of *Révolution Africaine*, Soliman Lotfallah, an Egyptian, and Michaelis Raptis, alias Pablo, a leading figure in the Fourth International.

The first decree – 18 March 1963[3] – dealt with the question of the *biens-vacants*. It defined the criteria of *vacance* in industry, commerce, agriculture and housing. They were those 'certified as abandoned or which stand idle or fail to function normally without a good cause'.[4] This meant that a declaration of *vacance* could be issued for cessation of activity or non-occupation for two months, an abnormal level of production or the non-exercise of the rights and obligations of proprietorship for two months. The second decree – 22 March[5] – declares that, in general, all industrial, mining and agricultural enterprises certified as *biens-vacants* shall be managed by their workers.

In his speech on 29 March, Ben Bella explained the reasons for the government's action. He emphasized that the revolution had no wish to chase out the *colons* and that, although they were saboteurs, the *Exécutif Provisoire* had asked them to return to help rebuild the country. Even his own government had left them the possibility of returning if they were prepared to collaborate with the *comités de gestion*. He went on:

How many of them came back and agreed to cooperate with the *comités de gestion*? What national government, worthy of the name, could have allowed itself to let this situation deteriorate? One day Algeria had to go back to work. One day the government born of the Algerian revolution was bound to organize the management of the enterprises and concerns abandoned and betrayed by their former owners. The Algerian workers have proved their ability to rise to this challenge. They had to be given the opportunity to carry on with their undertaking. [He goes on to say that those certified as vacant are] once and for all, definitively, *biens-vacants* and as such their management is once and for all, definitively, in the hands of Algerian workers. From now on we will speak no more of *biens-vacants* but of enterprises under *autogestion*.[6]

Some 1,200,000 hectares of land and 1,000 industrial and commercial firms were affected by this decree. Not all of them were placed under *comités de gestion*: the second decree (22 March) allowed those considered to be of 'national importance' to be placed in the public sector and managed by the state. This was later used by the government as a legal means for restricting the development of *autogestion*. The *décrets de mars* did not nationalize all European property in Algeria, only the *biens-vacants*. A series of later decrees extended the conditions governing appropriations.[7] A decree issued on 9 May 1963[8] allows property and enterprises to be put under state protection for causing public disturbance in its methods of management or production. This decree was an enabling device to allow the government, through the local prefect, to take over any enterprise they wished. In fact it was mainly used by the UGTA who, by calling strikes in particular enterprises, forced their nationalization.

Outright nationalization has usually been brought in by decrees dealing with particular sectors. The only decrees dealing with all sectors are one issued on 26 July 1963, but retroactive to 1830, declaring to be the property of the state any property seized by or given to collaborators with colonialism. The other, issued on 27 August 1964, allowed the confiscation of the property of those

The Décrets de Mars

attacking the security of the state, independence or the socialist objectives contained in the *Charte d'Alger*. Apart from the land affected by the legislation on the *biens-vacants*, another million hectares of European land was nationalized on 30 April 1963, and finally all European lands were nationalized, without indemnity, on 1 October 1963.[9] Since then, all transport, mining, banking and insurance have been nationalized and decrees dealing with industry, oil, gas and commerce are still being issued.

THE STRUCTURES OF 'AUTOGESTION'

In his speech introducing the *décrets de mars* to the people of Algeria, Ben Bella discussed the question of how the *biens-vacants* ought to be managed:

> Two solutions presented themselves: Should they be managed by the state? Should they be managed by the workers? In fact it was impossible to hesitate. The principle of self-management of the enterprises by their workers was already written into the realities of the Algerian revolution by the spontaneous and conscious actions of the working masses. The powerful movement of *comités de gestion* which had spread throughout the country only awaited legislation in all its revolutionary entirety. . . . With the *assemblées générales*, the *conseils des travailleurs* and the *comités de gestion* the workers of Algeria take their own destiny in hand.[10]

The basic decree regulating the organs of *autogestion* within the enterprise is that of 22 March.[11] In form and operation these organs are very similar to those in the basic Yugoslav system of self-management, from which the Algerian scheme was largely copied. In outline the scheme consists of a pyramidal elective structure representing the workers and a director who represents the interests of the state.

The organ from which, in theory, all power is delegated is the *assemblée générale des travailleurs*, composed of all the regular, full-time workers of the enterprise. Seasonal workers are expressly excluded from membership (Article 4). This exclusion created much antagonism in the agricultural sector where a large number of temporary, or seasonal, workers are taken on in the summer and autumn. It had the effect of preserving the privileged position of the permanent workers and excluding the landless peasants who had often participated in the independence struggle more directly than the permanent workers.* In effect, two classes were created among the workers of each agricultural enterprise. The most commonly expressed reason for this exclusion was that the seasonal workers would not have the long-term interests of the enterprise at heart and would, consequently, act in an openly instrumental fashion. The ultimate decision on the membership of the *assemblée* lies with the director (Article 5). In view of the tensions that developed between the director's identification with the administration and the workers' opposition to the administration, this factor soon led to the exclusion of workers on political grounds.

The *assemblée* must be called at least once every three months by the *conseil des travailleurs* or the *comité de gestion*. It can also be convened on the initiative of one-third of its members. All voting is by secret ballot and a quorum of two-thirds is needed to validate decisions. The *assemblée* elects the *conseil* or, when the enterprise has fewer than thirty employees and there is no *conseil*, the *comité de gestion*.

The *conseil* is elected from members of the *assemblée*. It should have a basic membership of ten, plus one extra member for every fifteen permanent workers above the basic thirty.† The *conseil* may not exceed a maximum of 100 members. At least two-thirds of its members must be directly engaged in production work so as to ensure a proper representation of shop-floor workers. Members are elected for a term of three years, one-third of the membership being re-elected every year. The *conseil* should meet at least once a month, called by the *comité* or on the initiative of one-third of its members.

The *comité de gestion* is elected either by the *conseil* or, in its absence, by the *assemblée*. It has a membership of from three to eleven (there is no numerical relation to the number of employees) of whom two-thirds must be engaged in production work. Members are elected for three years on the same basis of partial yearly elections as the *conseil*. It must meet at least once a month and 'as often as the interests of the enterprise require'; it is usually called by its president.

---

* The term 'landless peasants' is not an intentional obscurantism. It refers to the large percentage of rural inhabitants who had lost all or most of their land by expropriation, *régroupement*, etc.

† Thus, if the enterprise has forty-five workers the number on the *conseil* will be eleven, if it has sixty, twelve – and so on.

The Dècrets de Mars

Two-thirds of its members, including the director who is a *de jure* member, must be present to validate decisions. Decisions are made by a simple majority with the president holding the casting vote. It can admit members of the *conseil* or *assemblée* to its meetings on a consultative basis. The president, who holds office for one year, is elected by the *comité* from among its own members.

The *décrets de mars* state that the director represents the state in the enterprise. However, just before his fall, Ben Bella, bowing to the workers' growing opposition to administrative interference, changed the director's legal position. The *arrête* of 29 May 1965 states: 'The director does not have the status of an agent of the state. On the contrary he has all the rights and advantages stemming from the position of a permanent worker, apart from the right of being a member of any other organ besides the *comité de gestion*' (Article 2). The director is automatically a voting member of the *comité* but may not be the president. He is appointed by the appropriate administrative body (see later explanation) with the agreement of the local *Conseil Communal d'Animation d'Autogestion* (CCAA). He can only be dismissed for a 'serious offence' or 'obvious incompetence' or if the CCAA withdraws its recognition. The 29 May 1965 *arrête* set up a *Commission Nationale de Recrutement et Discipline* for directors in the industrial sector, which has to be consulted before a director may be dismissed.* The director should be appointed by competition unless lack of cadres makes nomination necessary. The *arrête* also institutionalized the existing arrangement where smaller enterprises with no director had *comités de gestion* appointed from among their workers.

This then is the basic legal structure of the organs of autogestion within the enterprise. But, as I shall show later, even the simple requirements on elections were almost never fulfilled in practice. The actual functions of these self-management bodies, as delineated by the *décrets de mars*, are much more diffuse and here the legal requirements have remained in almost complete abeyance. The *assemblée* is the body which must approve and sanction the plans and actions of the other bodies. Thus it 'adopts' the development

* The Commission is composed of an FLN representative as president, representatives from the Ministry of Industry and Energy, the Ministry of Labour, and the UGTA and three representatives of the *comités de gestion* nominated by the Ministry of Industry.

plan, the annual equipment, production and marketing programmes, and 'approves' arrangements on work organization and the final accounts. The peculiar terminology of the decree shows that its authors seem to have regarded the *assemblée* as a rubber-stamp rather than a democratic organ with full powers to delegate or revoke authority. This attitude stems from the avant-gardist conception of socialism among those responsible for elaborating the decrees. Their constant fear was that the majority of the workers would ignore their responsibilities and act in their own self-interest.

The *conseil*, where it exists, makes decisions on the purchase and sale of machinery, and on long- and medium-term loans. It 'approves' the internal organization of the enterprise and examines the accounts before they go to the *assemblée*. An official statement on the role of the *conseil* stresses that it was inserted between the *assemblée* and the *comité* 'in order that the latter does not become a body cut off from any practical contact with its base and that bureaucracy and apathy do not develop'.[12] In the decrees the *comité* has a much more positive managerial role than the other organs. It draws up the development plan, the annual programmes for equipment, production and marketing, and decides on the way these should be implemented. It regulates the organization of production, fixes short-term loans, buys raw materials and draws up the accounts. Where no *conseil* exists the *comité* undertakes its functions.

The president of the *comité* 'convenes', 'presides over' and 'directs' meetings of all the organs of self-management and countersigns the minutes. He countersigns all documents involving financial transactions and represents the enterprise in law. The director, as the 'representative of the state', checks on the legality of all economic and financial transactions undertaken by the enterprise and may veto any decision that does not conform to the law. He keeps the accounts of the enterprise, holds the day-to-day funds and signs all documents involving financial transactions. He is secretary of all three self-management bodies and keeps their minutes. In the prevailing conditions of widespread illiteracy, especially among agricultural workers, the director is often the only literate member of the concern. This allows him considerable scope for manipulation. The director also assumes, 'under the president's authority', responsibility for the day-to-day running of the enterprise in conformity with the decisions of the *assemblée*, *conseil* and *comité*.

The Décrets de Mars

The extreme vagueness of the *décrets de mars* on the relative powers of president and director contained the seeds of an almost inevitable jurisdictional conflict. Even assuming a large degree of harmony between the interests of the state and the workers, the uncertain definition of the roles of president and director would have led to conflict. In a situation where the workers were increasingly hostile to any form of administrative control, the director as a representative of the administration was immediately regarded with suspicion. Ben Bella attempted to justify the position of the director in his 29 March speech:

In your self-managed enterprises it is necessary that there is someone to represent and safeguard the interests of the national collectivity to which you belong. In your self-managed enterprises there must be someone professionally qualified who can give you the benefit of his technical experience. Your enterprises must achieve a high level of productivity and you must be able to help the economic development of our country. In your self-managed enterprises there must be someone who can serve as a communicating link between your enterprises and the state which is responsible for the national development plan.

This director, whose nomination depends on your agreement, this director is a worker like you who will share your griefs and joys and participate, with you, in the socialist construction of our country. Make his job easy. Help him. Guard him like the apple of your eye.[13]

Ben Bella's rather euphoric vision of the director was very rapidly made a hollow mockery by the real state of affairs, as indeed was everything else about the *décrets de mars*.

THE SUPERSTRUCTURES OF 'AUTOGESTION'

Having accepted the *comités de gestion* and given them legal standing in the decrees of March, the main problem facing the state was how to incorporate them into some form of national planned economic system. Apart from the *biens-vacants*, the remainder of the nationalized European lands and state undertakings like railways, gas and electricity, the rest of the economy remained in private hands and the market prevailed as the sole medium of exchange and distribution. If Algeria was to be socialist and achieve economic independence, it was clear that there must be some form of central control over economic activities. A choice had been made to allow the nascent socialist sector to be run by its workers, yet some form of central control had to be instituted.

During the campaign for elections to the self-management bodies, in May 1963, Ben Bella expressed his feelings:

Certainly self-management does not mean for us a completely decentralized control of the economy, taking no account of the economic imperatives on national, regional and communal levels. The enterprises under self-management act within the general framework of the country's economic plan and strictly fulfil their financial obligations towards the national and communal effort.[14]

This statement did not do full justice to the dilemma the government found itself in. On the one hand there was a vague hostility to the full centralism of the Russian model which was compounded by the obvious inadequacy of the state machinery to achieve this; on the other hand there was the fear that the workers, if left to themselves, would pursue sectional rather than national interests. The same month, Bachir Boumaza, Minister of the Economy, outlined this problem. 'The great difficulty in *autogestion*, an essentially evolutionary formula, is to find the right mean between the anarchic, ouvrierist tendency of the base and the centralizing, bureaucratic, *étatiste* current at the top.' In face of the need to construct some form of machinery that would supervise and correlate the activities of the *comités* and give them financial and technical aid, the government began to create an administrative superstructure.

In the absence of any real theory on what the relations between the enterprise and the centre should be, the superstructure was pieced together in an *ad hoc* fashion. Each successive stage in this process placed the *comités* more firmly under central control until the administration came to control every essential aspect of the economic activity of the *comités*, rendering the concept of *autogestion* derisory. Finally, apart from agriculture, where such a process did not seem feasible, the *comités* themselves were dissolved and the enterprises integrated into *sociétés nationales* run on state capitalist lines. It was not the superstructure itself which crushed *autogestion*: some form of integration and cooperation were essential if the *comités* were to survive and expand. But from the beginning, as we will see later, the state machinery was largely staffed by the personnel of the ex-colonial administration and were on the whole hostile to *autogestion*. At first the machinery was merely incom-

The Dècrets de Mars

petent, but as time went on it became the means by which this new *élite* entrenched itself politically and economically. The contradiction between base and superstructure lay less in the inevitable tensions any such organization contains than in the class antagonisms between administration and workers.

In general terms the government resorted to the Yugoslav formulation defining the ownership and control of the means of production under self-management. Legally, it was held that the workers had a right to the usufruct while the enterprise itself belongs to the nation, national sovereignty being vested in the people. In managerial terms, the workers had control over the principal economic and financial means of the enterprise: capital utilization, choice of investment, production methods, etc. – always within the limits of the national plan. In his 15 May 1963 speech, Ben Bella referred to the workers' duty to the state in managing the enterprises entrusted to them in the way most beneficial to the community.* In return, he promised that 'the state, as representative of the national community, engages to provide all possible aid in capital, machines, administrative personnel and social services of various sorts. . . .' Under this contractual acknowledgement of mutual obligations various *organismes de tutelle* were to be set up to guide and aid the *comités*, rather than impose direct managerial control. The reality was very different from the intention.

With the decision to turn the *biens-vacants* over to the management of the workers, the *Bureau National des Biens-Vacants*, set up in October 1962, was dissolved. On the same day as the first of the *décrets de mars* the *Office National de la Réforme Agraire* (ONRA) was created as the supervisory agency for the *comités* in agriculture. It joined the *Office National de Tourisme* (ONAT) which had already been set up to supervise hotels, restaurants and cafés under *autogestion*. In many ways these were not new organizations. They were both developed directly out of pre-existing colonial bodies and used what remained of their administrative and financial infrastructure and personnel.[15] A few days later, on 4 April, the *Bureau National d'Animation du Secteur Socialiste* (BNASS) was set up with the functions of 'education, stimulation, coordination and supervision of the socialist sector'.[16] This represented an attempt by the Harbi group

---

* This statement, of course, ignores the cardinal fact that the workers seized the enterprises and not the state.

to create a single unitary organization which would deal with the whole of the socialist sector. But with agriculture already under ONRA its scope was restricted mainly to industry. Later in the year it was still further restricted by the transfer of *comités* in road transport to an *Office National des Transports* (ONT), cooperative fisheries to an *Office National de la Pêche* (ONP) and *comités* in the building industry to the Ministry of Public Works. Then, on 11 January 1964, *comités* in industrial, artisan and mining enterprises were placed under the supervision of the Ministry of the Economy.*

Thus in less than a year the self-managed sector had been split up into its respective economic divisions. BNASS was left without any real function and eventually dissolved. For many militants in Algeria the subordination of the *comités* to specific bureaucracies in 1963-4 meant the end of the honeymoon with the government. BNASS had been seen as a means by which workers in *autogestion* could participate in the solution of their common problems. On the pretext of rationalization the government forced the *comités* into a form of organization that was explicitly economic rather than political and economic. This process was carried to its near ultimate conclusion in 1967 when ONRA was dissolved and the *comités* in agriculture placed under the direct control of the Ministry of Agriculture, the ONT was wound up and *comités* in road transport formed into one state company, and many *comités* in industry were dissolved.

From the first temporary legislation on the *biens-vacants* in October and November 1962, the *comités* were subordinated to an increasingly bureaucratic external administrative structure. Only once was there an attempt to create an integrated structure above the level of the enterprise which the workers could participate in. In June 1964 a decree reorganizing the socialist sector of industry, was issued. In view of the diversity and small size of many of the *comités* and their difficulty in competing with the private sector, it was felt necessary to create the conditions for consolidation and greater self-reliance in production, marketing, technology and finance. The decree envisaged the creation of *unions*, on a regional

---

* Decree 64.8. Later, on 8 June, a further decree (64.175), which was part of the reorganization of the socialist sector of industry, divided the enterprises into two parts: enterprises of 'national importance' came under the direct supervision of the ministry; those of 'local importance' under regional or departmental subdivisions of the ministry.

The Décrets de Mars

and national scale, which would consolidate horizontally *comités* with similar activities and vertically those with complementary activities. Apart from its obvious economic value this measure stemmed from the demand by the workers and the UGTA for a more democratic form of integration between the various *comités*.

Not many of these integrated organizations were set up: those that were rapidly formed differing modes of organization. The closest to the original intentions were bodies like the *Union Régionale du Bois de l'Algérois* and the *Union Nationale des Industries Métallurgiques et Électriques Socialistes*. These comprised most of the *comités* in a particular branch of industry on a regional or national level and were managed by a *conseil d'administration* composed of all the presidents of the constituent *comités*, plus a state-nominated director. Their function was to provide raw materials and spare parts and market the products of the constituent *comités*. A central office (*Bureau d'Études*) also provided technical and financial information. Each *comité de gestion* remained free to decide its own internal policies.

The same process of economic rationalization was achieved by other integrative organizations; but here consolidation meant either a reduction in the powers of the *comités* or even their dissolution. In the *Complexe Métallurgique d'Algérie* (COMETAL) and other similar complexes* the individual units lost their *comités* and were run instead by a foreman (*chef d'atelier*) nominated by the complex director. The workers were represented by an elected council with consultative powers only. The dissolution of these *comités* proved to be a forerunner of the more widespread attack on them in the name of economic rationalization.

The *décrets de mars* also tried to link the *comités* at the level of the commune. The second decree envisaged the creation of a *Conseil Communal d'Animation d'Autogestion* in each commune.[17] The intention was to devolve down to the commune as much of the administration as was consonant with the limiting framework of the national plan. The CCAA was to be composed of all the presidents of *comités* in that commune, plus a representative from the army, the party and the UGTA and one from the communal administration.

---

* Other complexes similar to COMETAL are the *Complexe Industriel du Bois* (CIB), *Complexe d'Ameublement et de Menuiserie de l'Algérois* (CAMA) and *Complexe Laitier de l'Algérois* (COLAITAL).

Like much of the early legislation, the CCAA was based on the Yugoslav model – in this case the communal producers' council. An official version of the role of the CCAA ran as follows:

> It is absolutely essential that the various enterprises in the commune are linked as they face a certain number of common problems.... The essential tasks of the CCAA are to help the *comités de gestion* to co-ordinate the activities of the enterprises, study all the problems and arbitrate in the conflicts which may arise within enterprises.... The CCAA can and must become a centre for propaganda and education. Together, the presidents of the *comités* must confront their experiences and study their difficulties.... The experiences of each will profit all.[18]

Besides these functions, the CCAA were to give or refuse consent to directors appointed by the supervisory authority and mediate in conflicts between directors and presidents. Basically it was seen as a cushion between state and enterprise which would allow the development of local democracy under the watchful eye of the party and army. In fact, very few CCAA were ever set up. Their non-existence was paralleled by the absence of any communal elections until 1966. In any case, central machinery was implacably hostile to all such manifestations of local independence.

FINANCE AND MARKETING IN 'AUTOGESTION'

The efforts to provide finance for the *comités de gestion* and organize the sales of their products reflects the same process of initial vagueness followed by increasing centralization as did their more general administration and supervision. As with the other superstructures, the reasons for creating some form of integrated financial and marketing organizations lay, initially, with a quite rational desire to integrate the socialist sector in agriculture and industry. But the mechanisms created on this basis soon came to determine the total operation of the *comités*, making a farce of their formal autonomy.

Within the self-managed enterprise, the allocation of income, either as wages or profits, was laid down by the decree of 28 March 1963 (the third of the *décrets de mars*).[19] The income of the enterprise was basically divided into three parts – state, enterprise and workers – with a further division of the workers' part into regular wages, social security benefits, production bonuses and shared profits. The decree is extremely vague on the exact method of allocating either the gross or net income of the enterprise. In an official clarification it was stated that the net income of the enterprise should not be less than fifty per cent of the gross income. The allocation of net income is in the hands of the *assemblée* which should divide it approximately into eighty-five per cent for income of the employees and fifteen per cent for enterprise funds. For the workers, one of the most important provisions of the scheme was the institution of productivity bonuses and profit-sharing (Article 4 of the decree). They had occupied the factories and farms to continue production and therefore to get an income; one of the main, immediate attractions of *autogestion* was its promise to increase income through a more equitable distribution of profits. In fact, as I show later, they only once received any distribution of profits in excess of their normal wages. In any case, the whole of the decree was rendered academic by the fact that, within a short time, no self-managed enterprise actually controlled its own funds. These came to be held and administered by state agencies.

The financing of the self-managed sector is very vague and has never been formally defined. At their formation the *comités* were in an extremely difficult financial position. The *pieds-noirs* had taken with them the cash assets of the *biens-vacants* and, where possible, removed, sold or sabotaged the capital goods such as machinery. Often they were forced to sell still more capital assets in order to provide survival wages. To a certain extent agriculture was better provided for than industry. The *Sociétés Agricoles de Prévoyance* (SAP), which had provided credit, raw materials and technical assistance to small European farmers before independence, continued to function. Partially subsidized by the French government, they provided cash, tractors and seed to the *comités* on an *ad hoc* basis during the autumn of 1962. After the creation of ONRA in March 1963, the SAP came under its supervision and continued to provide raw materials and technical assistance. Later in that year they were dissolved and their functions taken over by the *Centres Coopratifés de la Réforme Agraire* (CCRA), a subsidiary of ONRA.

ONRA became not only the supervisory organ for the *comités* in agriculture and a source of raw materials and technical aid but also the main source of financial assistance in terms of short-term loans, usually repaid after the harvest. This exercise was largely academic as the *comités* funds were held by ONRA anyway, through its subsidiary CCRA. After the dissolution of ONRA in 1967, the funds were transferred to the *Caisses Régionales de Crédit*. In short, this meant that the *comités* never had control over their funds: all taxes, etc. were removed at source by the state agencies, while wages were, or were not, doled out by the same bodies. We shall see, later on, the effects of this removal of financial autonomy.

The initial plight of *comités* in industry was very similar to those in agriculture. Up until the so-called reorganization of the socialist sector in June 1964 the *comités* were in fact worse off than agriculture. Although two government agencies were legally empowered to loan money – the *Caisse Algérienne de Développement* for long-term loans and the *Bureau d'Études de Réalisation et d'Intervention Industrielles et Minières* for intermediate loans – in practice very little assistance came from this source. The *comités* were driven to rely on private sources, or in a few cases direct loans from the state via the local prefect. With no capital resources, most enterprises remained hopelessly in debt, unable to reach full production. In face of this financial strangulation the *Banque Centrale d'Algérie* (BCA) was made the bank for *comités* in industry as part of the June 1964 reorganization.[20] Like the CCRA in agriculture, the BCA held all enterprise funds and carried out all but the smallest financial transactions for them. The growing desire for rationalization and centralization under Boumédienne was reflected in the eventual creation of the *Banque Nationale d'Algérie* on 28 April 1966 as a specific bank for all *comités de gestion*. In practice the *Caisses Régionales de Crédit* continued to manage the funds of agricultural *comités*.

The flight of the *colons* affected not only production but the whole mechanism for marketing products. The expropriation of the *biens-vacants* had allowed the state to control a certain sector of production, but the advantages to be gained from this would be lost if products were to be distributed by private commerce and profits channelled away from the state. To deal with this problem the government set up two agencies to deal with marketing – the *Office National de Commercialisation* (ONACO) and the *Coopératives Régionales Agricoles* (CORA). ONACO was created in December 1962 to deal with foreign trade in agricultural produce, equalize consumption and production, convert products ill-adapted to their markets and cut the cost of living by importing and stocking food. The bulk of agricultural produce was sold to the traditional metropolitan

The Décrets de Mars

dealers and the remainder went to nationalized processing plants. In July 1963 ONACO was given a monopoly in the sales of fruit, vegetables and sugar; cereals and wine were dealt with by special government agencies. The same year ONACO organized a chain of retail outlets – the *Magasins Pilotes Socialistes* – which were to provide the public with food at low prices in competition with the largely private retail food market. The CORA were established as a sales and marketing organization for internal sales only. Despite the good intentions of this scheme it was not very successful in achieving its objects, as I will show in more detail later. For several years the *comités* still sold to private buyers where possible as they paid in hard cash unlike ONACO and CORA; but ONACO was unable to affect prices very greatly since the international market determined the level of wholesale prices while, internally, the private sector often undercut the *Magasins Pilotes Socialistes*. In industry, despite the attempt to rationalize the *comités* in 1964, the provision of raw materials and the marketing of finished products remained in private hands. With no official 'socialist' marketing organization the *comités* suffered at the hands of a private sector only too anxious to prove *autogestion* a failure.

The *décrets de mars* only established the organization of self-management on the level of the enterprise and expressed vague ideas on the possible role of the *comités de gestion* in national economic and political life. They were an ideological *prise de position* rather than a coherent plan for the management of the means of production. They did little more than legalize the *de facto* occupation of these means of production by the workers. By themselves the *décrets de mars* cannot be regarded as the sole content of Algerian autogestion, but as a particular moment in an ongoing process. I have outlined the organization of *autogestion* above the level of the enterprise which followed the *décrets* because these superstructures must be regarded as an integral part of the Algerian experience. Whatever the form taken by these superstructures, the attempt to consolidate the individual *comités* into a coherent economic and political force was for a short time accepted by workers, union, party and state as a necessary development for *autogestion*. That they became bureaucratic malformations does not affect their position as part of the formal system of *autogestion*. The structures I have portrayed were developed over a period of five years, from 1962 to 1967. The process is purposely temporarily removed from its proper background to clarify the formal operation of *autogestion*, because there is no exact moment at which *autogestion* can be frozen and described in its entirety.

The historical process from which I have abstracted this description is one of increasing bureaucratic control by the state. The original intentions of the *décrets de mars* and the gains of 1962 were soon lost in this labyrinthine administrative superstructure. As one commentator was forced to acknowledge:

In practice and in effect every activity of the self-managed enterprise is controlled and even directed by the state agencies [ONRA and BCA]: contracts with suppliers, sales contracts, the annual plans for production, sales, raw materials, machinery, etc. are all decided by the supervisory agencies.[21]

In order to understand why *autogestion* first became a hollow and meaningless façade and was then actively sabotaged it must be reintegrated into its historical context. The rapid imposition of bureaucratic structures on the *comités* is directly related to the economic, social and political circumstances of Algeria. In the years after independence Algeria witnessed a continuous struggle for power between its emergent national bourgeoisie and the working class, with the mass of the peasantry and unemployed as disillusioned and impoverished onlookers. *Autogestion* stood at the centre of this conflict. For its supporters it represented not only the real gains of independence but a revolutionary mode of dealing with Algeria's very real economic problems. For them the solution lay in involving the mass of the workers directly in the country's future, in giving them complete economic and political power. Originally the party and state accepted most of this premise while stressing the need for leadership; but in time *autogestion* became a threat to their developing hegemony. As they moved, more and more firmly, towards a centralist conception of political control, the *comités* came to be seen as an anarchic hindrance. The following chapters describe this struggle and the economic and social factors that form its background.

5

THE ECONOMY: THE HERITAGE OF COLONIALISM

THE conflict that has most overtly determined the content of Algerian socialism has been over modes of economic organization and development. In this respect Algeria is similar to most newly independent countries seeking to free themselves from dependence on the colonial metropolis and from neo-colonialism as a whole. Class conflicts tend to gell round competing and opposed theories of economic development, rather than finding precise expression in the political sphere. However, these conflicting theories of economic organization are clearly related to social structure in terms of conflicting class interests. In Algeria this class conflict emerged in the shape of two solutions to the country's economic problems – *autogestion* and state capitalism, independence from international capitalism and reliance on it.

The origins of independent Algeria's economic problems lie in the structures of the *pied-noir* economy. The principal characteristics of this economy were a sectorial imbalance towards raw material production and services with an overall tendency to stagnation. This stagnation and the circumstances of the war made the Algerian economy heavily dependent on France, and in particular the French state, for new capital investment and aid to offset trade and budgetary deficits. Algeria was typical of colonial territories in being dependent on the metropolis for most of its transformed products. Raw materials produced by agriculture and mineral and hydrocarbon extraction were exported in return for industrial and luxury goods. There was no classic entrepreneurial bourgeoisie and thus no class capable of creating a true industrial infrastructure. The closeness of the metropolis meant that any such industry would have been in competition with established French capitalism, while the poverty of the Muslim population severely restricted the size of the potential market. The lack of local capital was another important factor in restricting the growth of industry. Profits made by *rentier* capitalism out of agriculture were either invested in local property and services, exported to the metropolis and invested there, or consumed in the hedonistic life-style of the *colon*. The metropolitan or foreign companies exploiting minerals and hydrocarbons also exported their profits.

The flight of the *pieds-noirs* and the occupation of their property by *comités de gestion* made it possible for the Algerian government to annex large sections of primary production (excluding hydrocarbons) and parts of the secondary and tertiary sectors. But this did not solve any of the underlying economic problems; the question of dependence within independence remained. Algeria was still heavily dependent on France as a trading partner, was still incapable of transforming most of its primary products and still suffered from a chronic lack of investment capital. There was a severe shortage of trained manpower and a mass of underemployed or totally unemployed in both urban and rural areas. The physical effects of the war itself made the situation even worse. The question of how to resolve these problems without abandoning some of the expressed ideals of the revolution has been at the base of most of the political conflicts that have shaken Algeria since independence.

The scarcity of figures makes it difficult to look at the details of this economic predicament. The pre-independence statistics are reliable for the European sectors but tend to become indeterminate for the Muslim. The destruction of records by the OAS, the scarcity of statisticians and the inability of untrained book-keepers to provide raw material for those that do exist have made the compilation of records since independence extremely difficult. The political implications and tendency to bias in the statistics that are produced make an accurate assessment of the economic situation after 1961 almost impossible.

I have characterized one major economic legacy of colonialism as stagnation. A brief survey of output in several areas will serve to establish this. In agriculture, cereal production between 1850 and 1910 achieved a growth rate of 1·7 per cent a year, but was completely stagnant between then and 1955. The average yearly production of cereals in the period 1911–15 was twenty-one million quintals; it was exactly the same between 1951 and 1955. Wine, one of Algeria's staple exports, had a long-term growth rate of three per

The Economy: The Heritage of Colonialism

cent up till 1940 but after 1945 this declined to almost nothing. The total growth rate of tobacco was 1·6 per cent a year; while olive oil actually declined from the 1930s. Only the relatively new fruit and vegetable sector achieved a satisfactory growth rate of three per cent a year between 1925 and 1940 and rose to nine per cent a year between 1945 and 1955. The global agricultural growth rate between 1880 and 1955 was only 1·3 per cent per year. This was in a sector that, before the advent of hydrocarbon extraction, accounted for thirty-three per cent of the gross domestic product and some seventy per cent of exports. In mining and industry the average growth rate between 1910 and 1930 was 6·8 per cent a year but it fell to 1·3 per cent a year between then and 1955.

The increasing stagnation of the economy from the 1930s was clearly reflected in the alarming rise in the import–export deficit. The table below gives these figures to 1955 in milliards of AF.[1]

	1880	1910	1930	1955
exports	31	68	127	165
imports	31	68	127	240

By 1960 this deficit of 75 milliard AF had become one of 4,351 million current NF. Between 1955 and 1960 imports tripled.

Samir Amin, the Maghrebine economist, sums up the Algerian colonial economy in the following simple table.[2]

Total annual growth rates, 1880–1955 (per cent)

agriculture	1·5
industry	3·1
services	2·0
total production	1·9
population	1·6
production per head	0·3

The incapacity of the colonial economy to achieve a high growth rate is underlined by the figures for the last twenty years when the growth in production remained almost static and the population growth rose to three per cent a year, and is likely to increase to four per cent.[3] Amin sums up his analysis of the colonial economies of the Maghreb as follows:

Workers' Self-Management in Algeria

It was undoubtedly the structure of colonialism itself which, despite vigorous efforts, made these results so disappointing. Under colonialism the economic growth of the Maghreb could in no way be called stable and integrated. This instability, which is typical of this kind of colonial administration, acted as the most powerful brake on the acceleration of economic development and finally left a tragic heritage of economic and social problems to the independent states of French North Africa.[4]

The inability of the colonial economy to provide for the needs of Algeria as a whole was recognized by the Gaullist administration in France soon after it came to power. The Constantine Plan, published in 1959, represented the first serious attempt by the metropolitan government to get to grips with Algeria's economic problems. The increasing financial burdens of both the war and underwriting the Algerian budget forced it to consider the basic failings of the Algerian economy. Writing at the same time as the Constantine Plan, René Gendarme emphasized that the low growth rate was due to a lack of capital: 'Development demands the accumulation of local capital and above all the aid of imported capital.'[5] The Plan agreed with this identification and envisaged large injections of metropolitan capital, both state and private, to readjust the sectorial imbalance in favour of industry: The small size of the entrepreneurial bourgeoisie, the *colon* opposition to metropolitan interference and war-time conditions combined to doom this initiative to failure. There was no *colon* group capable of using such capital for either the expansion of existing industries or the creation of new ones. The structure of the economy and the culture of *colon* society were inimical to this mode of development. Vigorous development of industry by the state would have been the only possible way out of this impasse. Yet the traditional hostility of the *colons* to metropolitan interference ruled this out. In the event, only thirty-five per cent of the capital allotted was ever invested: much of it was returned to France by the *colon* bourgeoisie as their private investments. This fulfilled René Gendarme's statement: 'One of the fundamental problems of the Algerian economy [is] the injection of public capital in Algeria and its return to the metropolis in private form.'[6] Despite its radical innovations, the Constantine Plan would not have solved many problems: it only envisaged the creation of 2,500 jobs a year.

The situation of the economy became catastrophic when the flight

The Economy: The Heritage of Colonialism

of the *colons* followed the disruptions of the war. The paucity of statistics makes it impossible to gain an accurate picture of this situation. Industry and the tertiary sector were the most immediately affected, though the effects on the budget and investment capital were more serious in the long run.

It has been estimated that, if oil and natural gas are excluded, there was a drop in overall production of twenty-eight per cent in the period 1959–63; while in the tertiary sector there was a drop in net production of thirty-six per cent in that period.[7] In construction and public works, which at the time formed the largest single employer in the non-agricultural sector, production dropped fifty-five per cent in 1963 in relation to 1962, and the number employed plummeted from 200,000 to 30,000. Cement production dropped from 1·3 million tons in 1962 to 0·6 million in 1963. In mining there was a drop in production of twenty per cent in 1963. In metallurgy production dropped fifty per cent in 1963. There was a reduction in the production–consumption of electricity of seventeen per cent in 1962 and a further five per cent in 1963.[8] Another source lists the following levels of utilization of productive capacity in the months after the ceasefire.[9]

	per cent
textiles	50
olive oil	71
fish-canning	14
fruit-canning	40
sugar-refining	0
chemicals	40
metallurgy	25

The effects on agricultural production were felt less immediately as crops had already been planted before independence and the actions of the *comités de gestion* meant that most were saved and harvested. In agriculture, the main problem was not production but the disruption of the normal commercial mechanisms for marketing the produce. Only thirteen per cent of the produce of the *colon* farms was usually transformed in Algeria; while foreign sales represented some forty-two per cent of the value of the country's exports. Much of the commercial export machinery had been owned or operated by the *colons* and their flight effectively destroyed most of the existing arrangements. The effects of this were catastrophic. Fruit exports dropped by twenty-two per cent in 1962-3 and by a further twenty-seven per cent in 1963-4. Vegetable exports dropped by thirty-nine per cent in 1962-3 and by a further forty-three per cent in 1963-4.[10] Only forty per cent of the 1962-3 wine production was ever marketed. Most of the wine, fruit and vegetables that could not find a market were left to rot. The disruption of internal markets and the lack of processing plant made it impossible to consume the surplus internally. Cereals, grown on the large colonial estates, continued to be transformed for internal consumption. But the collapse of large sectors of traditional agriculture resulting from the *regroupement* policy, the use of napalm and the general socio-economic breakdown meant that whole areas of the country faced starvation. Only large gifts of American grain kept famine at bay.

The only sector which remained largely unaffected by both the war and the events of independence was hydrocarbons production. The geographical position of the wells, mainly in the desert, removed them from the scene of conflict; while the FLN had no great desire to sabotage such a national asset. As both oil and natural gas production were largely controlled by the French state and large international companies, the flight of the *pieds-noirs* had little effect on production and manning.

The only immediate benefit of the recession was the effect it had on the level of imports. We have already seen that by the mid-1950s the Algerian economy was marked by a growing excess of imports over exports. The collapse of the *colon* economy and the flight of the *pieds-noirs* drastically reduced the market for imported goods. Thus, despite the recession in those industries oriented towards processing and handling such goods, it had the effect of markedly reducing the value of imports. In 1960 the value of imports was 6,298 million NF; in the chaotic year of 1962 this fell to 2,424 million NF and in 1963 it rose to 3,900 million NF. At the same time, the value of exports was rising due to the steady increase in oil and natural gas production. Thus by 1963, 1960's apparent trade deficit of 4,351 million NF had been reduced to one of 435 million NF. (See Appendix III, Table 4 for full trade figures, 1960-68.) The benefits of this dramatic change on the economy as a whole were less apparent. The reduction of the deficit was only obtained at the expense of a severe reduction in employment in both industry and the services. It can be estimated

The Economy: The Heritage of Colonialism

that the number of jobs in these two sectors shrank by roughly two-thirds. What Algeria was experiencing was the complete collapse of the significant part of its internal economy which had been geared to the needs of around one million *colons*.

The break with France meant that the chronic trade and budgetary deficits could no longer be covered by the metropolitan budget. The events of 1962 further worsened the budgetary situation. In that year tax revenue dropped by forty per cent, leaving the government heavily deficitory and reliant on external aids merely to cover its administrative costs.* More seriously the crisis left a deep imprint on the availability of capital. In 1962 bank deposits dropped by forty per cent as a result of the transfer of private European funds to France. In 1963, out of total investment receipts of 2,245 million dinars (DA),† Algeria only provided 154 million itself. In fact in that year foreign sources provided forty-eight per cent of the total government revenue. (See Appendix III, Table 1 for details of government revenue and expenditure, 1962–8.)

The chronic stagnation of the colonial economy, its under-capitalization, its heavy reliance on the metropolis for financial aid, its inability to provide employment for more than a tiny fraction of the Muslim population and its near total disintegration in 1962 are the background to the problems of independent Algeria. The question facing Algeria was how to achieve economic development without totally compromising the ideals of the revolution. If the country had to remain dependent on neo-colonialism for aid then these ideals would remain illusory; Algeria would be open to pressure in both her internal and external politics. The Tripoli Programme had aimed to achieve this independence through nationalization, agrarian reform and industrial development. The flight of the *pieds-noirs* and the formation of *comités de gestion* enabled the government to nationalize some sectors of production. They did not solve any of the basic problems. The basic orientation of the economy towards export of raw materials, the chronic lack of investment capital for industrial or agricultural development, and the massive unemployment still remained unchanged.

* It has been estimated that the French government were paying around £700,000 a month in the second half of 1962 merely to keep the Algerian administration functioning.

† The Algerian dinar (DA) has official parity with the NF.

Workers' Self-Management in Algeria

In the first flush of enthusiasm following the *décrets de mars* Ben Bella treated autogestion as an economic panacea for all the problems outlined above. *Autogestion* was not just an advanced form of socialist economic organization, it was to provide the capital necessary to create development. 'The resources furnished by the *comités de gestion* will in the years to come be an essential source of finance for industrialization.'[11] The government did not feel capable of nationalizing the whole of the industrial and service sectors immediately. A period of cooperation with internal capitalism and existing representatives of metropolitan or foreign capital was felt to be necessary. But it was felt to be essential that, apart from this, Algeria should generate the capital and energy necessary for future development. The influence of China and Cuba weighed heavily on many of the militants in the party and the UGTA. They felt that these countries had faced similar problems to those they were now facing. The half-formed ideas of the Tripoli Programme found expression in the *comités de gestion* and Algeria was committed to the '*option socialiste irréversible*'. If Algeria was to follow the Chinese example and attempt to develop by her own efforts then capital must be generated internally.

By the end of 1963 a choice had been made to rely as far as possible on Algeria's own resources. As quoted above, Ben Bella announced in October that the nationalized sectors under the *comités de gestion* were to be an important source of capital for development. It also became clear that a rejection of foreign capital would mean that Algeria would have to rely on labour power rather than machinery. China had chosen to create an industrial base by using labour-intensive rather than capital-intensive production. Algeria's natural capital lay in the vast numbers of un- or underemployed. If this large reserve of manpower could be put to work on creating an industrial infrastructure then foreign investment could largely be dispensed with. In a speech to the National Assembly in December 1963, Boumaza, Minister of the Economy, outlined the government's position, saying that 470 million working days had to be provided for every year.

> Even if we do not achieve this immediately we must provide 100 million, that is, we must create work for 500,000 people. Thus each year permanent jobs for a 100,000 people will be created. This is only possible if costs are kept low; otherwise we will be unable to industrialize and

The Economy: The Heritage of Colonialism

construct the schools and hospitals that we need. Our efforts will not be profitable unless we use very little capital equipment and unless we confine ourselves to feeding workers rather than paying them a real salary.[12]

Boumaza was not by any means the most outspoken proponent of the Chinese model; but this speech shows how far the government were orientated towards the use of labour-intensive methods. In fact, Boumaza was much more favourable to the more classic socialist model of central control rather than the decentralization implied by *autogestion*.

In the light of the government's policy enunciated in 1963, *autogestion* (and intensive use of labour power) became the official basis of the road to economic success. The fate of *autogestion* was tied directly to the success of the government's wider economic policies. Thus as the bureaucracy in the party and state began to develop clear class characteristics it became clear that the concept of *autogestion* presented a political threat. Because the accepted Algerian socialist orthodoxy was *autogestion* they could not attack it in direct ideological terms. But they were able to condemn it for being a cause of the country's continuing economic difficulties. The interest that they, as a class, had in promoting central control and state capitalism could be masked by the claim that they were acting in the national economic interest. It was on this basis that by 1967 the policies of 1963 had been almost totally reversed and that those responsible could still claim to be the legitimate inheritors of the ideology of the revolution.

It is undeniable that the years after 1962 saw no real economic improvement. The vital question is whether the *comités de gestion* can be held responsible for the economic failures of this period; whether the reversal of policy was based on any real assessment of the validity of *autogestion* as an economic model for an underdeveloped country. To decide this it is necessary to look at the operation of various sectors of the economy in this period.

AGRICULTURE

The legacy of colonialism for agriculture in Algeria was the sharp division between the modern European sector and the traditional Muslim sector. In effect this was a division between production for profit and production for subsistence. Before independence there were 22,037 European land-holdings amounting to 2,726,000 hectares and an estimated 630,732 Muslim holdings on 10,075,000 hectares. In 1960 the modern sector produced a value of 175 milliard AF and the traditional sector produced 145 milliard;[13] but the first sector produced this with 100,000 workers, the second with some eight million (including families). Not only was the average size of the European holdings far larger than the Muslim holdings but their productivity was much higher.* The Muslim holdings were in the least fertile areas of the country where the colonial policy of land settlement had driven them.

The division of land-holdings has not changed in essence since independence. Out of an area of some 2,381,700 square kilometres only 42·5 million hectares are utilizable for agricultural purposes and only about 14·5 million are actually under cultivation. Of this area some 2·5 million hectares, representing the majority of the *colon* holdings, are in the socialist sector, another 11·27 million are owned privately and the rest is owned communally. The division of holdings in the private sector has been assessed as follows by the government:[14]

over 100,000 holdings	under 1 hectare
over 300,000 holdings	1–10 hectares
160,000–180,000 holdings	10–50 hectares
16,000–17,000 holdings	50–100 hectares
8,000–9,000 holdings	over 100 hectares

In the socialist sector the European holdings have been rationalized and consolidated. This process has produced some 2,300 units with an average area of just over 1,000 hectares each.[15] Each unit is managed by a *comité de gestion*.

It is in this division between the modern and traditional sectors that some of the most basic of Algeria's economic problems lie. Out of a total population of twelve million some nine million are supported by agricultural production – eight million in the traditional sector and one million in the socialist sector. The small-holdings in the traditional sector are incapable of feeding those dependent on them, let alone adequately employing the estimated million-plus active rural male population. Increasing demographic pressure and the

* As the actual labour force on the traditional holdings is not known, no comparison in terms of productivity per head is possible.

The Economy: The Heritage of Colonialism

destruction caused by the war have forced large numbers of the rural population to migrate to the towns in search of both food and work. Here they barely survive on charity and intermittent employment and form a vast economic burden.*

The modern sector employs a total of 150,000 permanent workers (about ten per cent of the active rural male population). Production in this sector has remained largely equal to what it was before independence if climatic factors are taken into account. (See Appendix III, Table 5 for figures on agricultural production.) The maintenance of production levels in the first years of independence is a very real achievement when it is considered that the amount of machinery available to *comités de gestion* dropped by sixty per cent in 1962–3.

The apparently inequitable distribution of land between the two sectors was sanctioned on the grounds that the ex-*colon* properties were to provide the surplus capital required to transform the traditional sector and invigorate industry. But far from providing capital for investment in other sectors, the self-managed sector of agriculture was found to be forty-five per cent deficitory in 1966. One commentator noted:

The budget has called for a contribution from the agricultural and industrial sectors under *autogestion* which have till now been a dead weight, and even an unimaginable burden on a country which decided that its future lay in the principles of *autogestion*.[16]

However, in the light of the overall maintenance of production levels (and productivity per head) the *comités de gestion* can hardly be accused of incompetence. As I have already pointed out, the financing and arrangements for marketing in this sector were in the hands of government agencies and not under the control of the *comités*; any failure to produce profits must be laid at their door. The level of government investment expenditure on agriculture dropped from 803 million DA in 1963 to 118 million DA in 1966. (See Appendix III, Table 3 on investment expenditure.) Thus many *comités* were unable to make good the losses in capital equipment incurred at independence. But what was really at fault was the system of marketing, controlled by the state through ONACO and the CORA. These agencies were incapable of replacing the old private marketing circuits and either exported agricultural produce at uneconomic prices or at times did not manage to sell them at all. The resulting

* The fate of this group is discussed more fully in the next chapter.

loss of income forced the *comités* to borrow from the state to finance both capital investment, turnover costs and even wages.* The immediate result of this situation was the dissolution of ONRA as the controlling agency for agricultural *comités* and the imposition of direct supervision by the Ministry of Agriculture.

INDUSTRY

Before independence the manufacturing and service industries numbered about 155,000 small artisan concerns and some 9,600 companies.[17] Manufacturing never formed more than twenty per cent of the gross domestic product in this period. Most of the volume of production and the majority of the labour force were concentrated in only 1,600 companies. Barbé estimated that less than a thousand of these concerns accounted for over fifty per cent of the labour force in manufacturing and services. This distinction can be elaborated in terms of those concerns with paid workers (about 37,750 with 350,000 workers) and the rest which were of a family or individual nature and paid no actual wages. There are no exact figures for the number of employees in manufacturing and services; but Barbé estimates that in 1954 regular and irregular employees totalled 239,000 Europeans and 330,000 Muslims.

It is impossible to compare figures for overall production, employment or capital value for the period before and after independence. Owing to the complete dislocation of activity the sample cannot be the same. However, if the service sector and artisan activity are left aside and only the larger enterprises involved in manufacturing are considered, limited comparisons are possible.

The last survey of industry made by the colonial authorities before the contraction of business at the end of the war was in 1957.[18] This covered 1,586 enterprises employing a total of 96,405 employees – 60,450 Muslims and 35,955 Europeans. According to this survey the two divisions employing most workers were metallurgy–mechanical–electrical with just over 22,000 employees and the food-processing industry with just over 28,000 employees. Together these represented more than half the labour force in manufacturing outside the artisan sphere. The European labour force was con-

---

* Later chapters contain more details on the financial suffocation of the *comités*.

The Economy: The Heritage of Colonialism

centrated in engineering, food-processing, textiles and paper. In engineering the loss of the skilled European labour force, which outnumbered the Muslims four to three, was particularly damaging.

The situation of industry after independence is impossible to verify with any real accuracy. The national census of 1966 determined that there were 164,000 employed in the secondary sector (including mining). However, this figure includes those working in tiny individual or family concerns of an artisan nature. A survey on employment in industry in the spring of 1966 is more comprehensive and gives some opportunity for comparison with levels of employment before independence.[19] This survey concentrated on the same area as the 1957 survey and determined that the number of concerns was 425, employing some 31,400 workers. In relation to 1957, this represents a drop of nearly sixty per cent in the number of firms and employees. This calculation can only be a rough one as there is no real basis for relating the findings of the two years. What seems clear is that the jobs vacated by the Europeans were not, to any great extent, taken up by Algerians. In manufacturing, if artisan production is excluded, the total drop in employment was sixty per cent while the number of Algerians employed dropped by fifty per cent.

The drop in employment was paralleled by a reduction in the level of output. There are no figures available for the service sector which suffered a catastrophic shrinkage on the departure of the *colons*. In manufacturing, the only verifiable publicized indices appear to show that the reduction in output was not as severe as the drop in numbers employed. However, these indices only cover a small number of activities – cement, superphosphates, steel, tobacco, cotton and shoes – and thus do not give a complete picture; especially as both cotton and shoes are new industries. From the evidence available, every sector shows signs of continuous expansion since 1963; though it was not until 1968 that 1958 levels of output were achieved. (See Appendix III, Table 6 for indices of industrial output, 1958–68.) Relating output to employment, it would appear that production per head is higher than it was before independence. But, in the absence of any real figures, this can only be an informed guess.*

---

* It is unlikely that increase in output per head can be accounted for by increased mechanization as there was almost no investment in capital equipment during this period.

Workers' Self-Management in Algeria

Algerian industry can be divided into three main groups according to the mode of ownership and management – self-managed, state controlled and privately owned; a further small group is composed of firms that are part private and part state-owned (*entreprises mixtes*). The 1966 survey of industry gives the following division for manufacturing, mining and services.[20]

type of ownership	number of concerns	number of employees
self-managed	218	14,934
state	411	44,113
private	599	40,570
mixtes	22	1,758
total	1,250	101,375

Since that time, the balance of ownership has shifted in favour of the state sector. Mines, insurance, banks, oil and petrol distribution have been completely nationalized; in May and June 1968 over forty companies in food, chemical, mechanical and construction industries were nationalized. The self-managed sector has shrunk as a large number of concerns in both the service and manufacturing sectors have been incorporated into state controlled companies. In 1966 the socialist sector (self-managed and state controlled) employed about the same number of workers as the private sector. If firms of an artisan nature are ignored the private sector now probably employs about twenty-five per cent of the industrial labour force.

In spite of the fact that enterprises under *autogestion* employed some fifteen per cent of the labour force in manufacturing and services their participation in actual output is much lower.* About forty-five per cent were of a semi-artisan character (i.e. severely under-capitalized); of the total thirty per cent were in building and public works, thirty-five per cent in food and drink, and only about six per cent in basic industrial production; the rest were in the service sector. Most of the relatively capital-intensive firms run by *comités de gestion*, like the steel works ACILOR and the *Verreries de l'Afrique du Nord* (VAN), had been placed under direct state management by 1965. Thus the enterprises under *autogestion* were basically labour-intensive. The reasons for this lie in the structure of the

* There were no figures available on the relative levels of output of the various sectors.

The Economy: The Heritage of Colonialism

colonial economy. As I have already pointed out, the *pieds-noirs* showed little desire to invest capital in industry, being content to invest it in property, services or export it to the metropolis. The small number of modern, capital-intensive firms were owned by metropolitan or foreign companies. Apart from a few cases like ACILOR, VAN and ALUMAF, these were not abandoned at independence. Thus the concerns occupied by the *comités de gestion* at or just after independence were the relatively small and unimportant enterprises owned by the *colons*. The metal, chemical and textile industries remained dominated by private ownership. It is important to stress that this is foreign ownership: there is an almost complete absence of Algerian national private capitalism in industry. The nationalization of this sector had to depend on government action. The state sector, usually managed through *Sociétés Nationales*, consists of enterprises nationalized by the government since independence, enterprises originally under *autogestion* but later placed under state control, and new enterprises created with the aid of foreign loans such as the Annaba steel complex and the Draa ben Khedda textile works.

In the first years of independence, apart from the overall difficulties of the Algerian economy, the *comités* in industry were faced with two immediate problems. They were in competition with a modern private sector capitalized from abroad. More immediately they were desperately short of capital with which to buy raw materials and give credit to customers, let alone invest in new capital equipment. As noted in the last chapter, government aid to this sector in the first years after independence was almost non-existent and it was not until the middle of 1964 that any attempt was made to organize it on a rational basis.

In this situation the potential development of *autogestion* in industry rested entirely on political and ideological decisions at government level. In agriculture the government had had no choice but to legalize the occupation of the *colon* estates by the *comités de gestion*. The fact that agricultural products formed some forty per cent of the value of exports made it necessary to create financial, technical and marketing organizations to consolidate the initiatives of the individual *comités*; though even here, as we have seen, these very agencies were responsible for many of the failings in agriculture. In industry the government, in view of the accepted socialist option,

Workers' Self-Management in Algeria

had two choices: it could either extend *autogestion* as the main form of management or it could institute a form of state management. It had also to decide whether it was going to develop a labour-intensive or capital-intensive industry. In the event Ben Bella made none of these decisions. There was no extension of the nationalized sector and *autogestion* was left to fend for itself in a limbo. Under Boumédienne there was a rapid extension of the nationalized sector accompanied by a sustained attack on *autogestion* and the decision to use foreign capital to develop capital-intensive industry.

HYDROCARBONS AND MINING

Oil and natural gas represent the largest single section of Algeria's exports. Non-agricultural exports form about sixty per cent of the country's total exports and of these hydrocarbons form about eighty per cent. Before independence all production of hydrocarbons was in the hands of foreign companies, mostly French. Production of crude oil on a commercial scale began in the Sahara in 1958.* From 1·2 million tons in 1959 production rose to a ceiling of twenty-six million tons in 1964 and 1965, when it was limited by the capacity of the two pipelines to take oil to the coast. The opening of a third pipeline in 1966, together with fresh discoveries, allowed production to be boosted to thirty-three million tons in 1966. Natural gas production from Hassi R'Mel began in 1961 at 231 million cubic metres and had risen by 1967 to over 2,000 million cubic metres. Reserves are estimated at three million million cubic metres. France is Algeria's largest customer for oil and natural gas. A contract signed in June 1967 covers the sale of 3,500 million cubic metres of gas to France, beginning in 1971.

Under Boumédienne the government set up a state-owned company, the *Société Nationale pour la Recherche, la Production, le Transport, la Transformation et la Commercialisation des Hydrocarbures* (SONATRACH), through which it has gained a stake in this rapidly expanding industry. SONATRACH owns the third oil pipeline to the Arzew refinery and has a fifty per cent stake in S.N. Repal (a French state company) which, with the *Cie Française des Pétroles*, owns the Hassie Messaoud oil field and the Hassi R'Mel

---

* The principal oil fields are at Hassie Messaoud in Central Algeria and the Polignac Basin near the Libyan border.

The Economy: The Heritage of Colonialism

gas field. In 1966 SONATRACH bought BP's distribution network in Algeria and its share in the Arzew refinery. A year later the Esso and Mobil marketing organizations were nationalized and in May 1968 the remaining networks were taken over and SONATRACH became the sole domestic distributor. The present gas liquefaction plant at Arzew is owned by the French firm *Cie Algérienne du Méthane Liquide* (CAMEL). A new liquefaction plant is being built at Skikda and will be jointly owned by SONATRACH, the French state oil company and the *Cie Française des Pétroles*.

The relative ease with which the Algerian state has gained a stake in oil and natural gas production is unusual for third world countries. The reason for this lies in the large share that the French government had in oil exploration and production before independence. The original Sahara oil code of 1958 provided for a fifty–fifty profit-sharing between the operating company and the government. This arrangement was transferred to the Algerian government in the Évian Agreements. In 1965 the government's share was raised to fifty-three per cent and then to fifty-five per cent in 1969. The French and Algerian states cooperate in research and production through their respective state-owned companies – SOPEFAL and SONATRACH. The tradition of state involvement in the production of hydrocarbons allowed the Algerian government to acquire a stake without any great difficulty. French state involvement has also helped Algeria avoid blatant exploitation by the big international oil companies. The private firms that are in operation cannot transfer more than fifty per cent of the gross turnover abroad. Despite all this, Algeria's profits from hydrocarbons are restricted by the price levels fixed and maintained by the international companies.

Apart from hydrocarbons, Algeria exports other minerals, the main ones being iron ore, lime phosphates and zinc. All mines in the country have been nationalized. The small concerns, mainly owned by *pieds-noirs*, were put under *comités de gestion* in 1962–3. The larger mines, mainly owned by metropolitan companies, were nationalized by decree in May 1966. As Appendix III, Table 7 shows, production, with the exception of that of iron ore, dropped significantly in the years following independence. One of the main reasons for this was the reluctance of foreign companies to continue investing capital in face of government hostility to private ownership. Since nationalization in 1966, production in the two main areas – iron ore and lime phosphates – has increased considerably.

From this brief survey it is clear that the war and the events of independence had a disastrous effect on the immediate situation of the Algerian economy. Industrial production was set back almost a decade; internal markets were severely disrupted, losing almost a million of the most wealthy consumers; exports of agricultural products were completely disorganized; only oil and natural gas production remained unaffected. Although the enormous deficit in foreign trade was reduced, the country continued to suffer from a severe lack of capital for development. In 1963, as we have seen, out of a total investment receipt of 2,245 million DA, Algeria herself only provided 154 million. By 1965 the amount of foreign aid had dropped drastically and, despite an increase in the Algerian contribution, total investment receipts stood at only 967 million DA.

It was at this point that oil and natural gas proved to be the main factor that could allow Algeria to achieve a trading surplus and maintain investment levels. In 1966 a new pipeline to the coast was opened. In that year Algeria's own contribution to her investment receipts rose from the previous year's level of 337 million DA to 900 million, of which oil accounted for 750 million. In 1968, although foreign aid dropped to 250 million DA, Algeria's contribution had risen to 1,340 million (oil – 1,000 million). At the same time, in 1967, the foreign trade account ceased to be deficitory, returning a surplus of 374 million. Undoubtedly, by the end of the 1960s, Algeria's position was better than that of most other underdeveloped countries. Oil and gas receipts, combined with severe restrictions on imports and the export of capital, had brought her to a position of being able to generate at least some of the capital needed for internal development.

But long before this became apparent, the fate of *autogestion*, as a mode of economic organization, was already being sealed. In a speech in January 1964, less than a year after the *décrets de mars*, Boumaza, then Minister of the Economy, presaged the move towards centralization.

In face of those who are impatient to see everything nationalized we must reply that first of all the means of management must be created. Before allowing the masses total control of the economy we must organize them, create economists, men fit for their new responsibilities.

The Economy: The Heritage of Colonialism

... The obstacles in the way of immediate and complete socialization make a phase of organization necessary.[21]

Boumaza still favoured the intensive use of labour in order to avoid relying on external aid, but economic development was to be strictly centralized. After 1965 this tendency was even more emphasized, but the economic theory and political ideology had also changed. Under Boumédienne capital-intensive development has been favoured, while the classic socialism of Boumaza has been replaced by state capitalism. Nationalized enterprises have been formed into publicly owned companies encouraged to function in a normal capitalist way, based on the model of nationalized industry in France. The historical political process of this policy reversal is detailed in a later chapter. The implications for *autogestion* are clear: the new middle class of administrators and technocrats condemned *autogestion* for the continued economic malaise and assumed firm control of the economy themselves.

Whatever the theoretical merits of the development of capital-intensive industry, its immediate applications show little return. In 1963 342 million DA was invested in the creation of new industries designed to create jobs for 7,000; but full production was not reached until 1969. This represents a creation of only 1,160 jobs a year.[22] This is a drop in the ocean compared with the figure of two million unemployed. If the population increase is taken into account Algeria needs to create new jobs at the rate of 100,000 a year if near full employment is to be achieved in twenty years' time.[23]* In fact the Algerian government has come to rely on emigration as a means of solving many of its economic problems. There are 800,000 Algerians living abroad and those working represent twenty per cent of all Algerians in full employment. In 1967 the FLN stated that:

The essential advantage of emigration is expressed both in terms of employment and as an appreciable contribution to economic development in alleviating the social burden of real and hidden unemployment which weighs heavily on the productive sector of the population. Also, emigration, by the currency it sends back [1,000 million NF annually], has the remarkable advantage of allowing two million peasants if not

* It is estimated that, at the present rate of growth, the Algerian population will have quadrupled from twelve million in 1966 to forty-eight million in thirty-five years' time.

to progress, at least to survive, and slows the exodus to the towns. Moreover this considerable amount of currency has the effect of rendering our balance of payments positive.[24]

Economically Algeria is in the same position as most other ex-colonial countries. The colonial economy was based on the production and export of raw materials and the provision of services for the *colon* population. Industry, when it exists, is geared to the transformation or assembly of materials from the colonial metropolis. Not only is such an economy geared to the needs of the colonizing country, it is also to a large extent owned and controlled by that country. Political independence does not bring economic independence. Even if nationalization is used as a means to free production from foreign control the economy is still dependent on neo-colonialism for markets and for capital. Thus, despite political independence and even nationalization, in 1968 over fifty per cent of all Algeria's trade was with France which also supplies capital and technical assistance.

Algeria's economic problems are rooted not only in the general conditions of the aftermath of colonialism but in its own specific and tragic circumstances. The mode of economic organization opened up by the FLN's socialist orientation and the formation of *comités de gestion* in 1962 was immediately called into question by Algeria's economic dependence on a capitalist metropolis. Algeria's economic situation has been instrumental in determining the whole content and direction of her 'socialist option'.

6

CLASS AND IDEOLOGY IN ALGERIA

THE outline of Algeria's economic structure, its basic problems and possible modes of development dealt with in the last chapter give one side of the situation within which *autogestion* developed. The social structure and class ideologies which will be discussed in this chapter have also been instrumental in shaping the history of *autogestion*. Unless these are understood, the encroachment of the state on *autogestion* will appear either as fortuitous or as the result of purely economic considerations and not as one single but vital aspect of a protracted and indistinct class struggle. This is not to take the social structure or the economic situation as the sole determinants of the course followed by *autogestion* in Algeria. The effervescent and chaotic political life of the country has a certain independent existence of its own. However, the underlying factors affecting the relationship between the *comités de gestion* and the state are firmly rooted in the consciousness and attitudes of the workers and the bureaucracy.

The national struggle for independence and the following economic and social revolution were intimately connected with the ideologies and attitudes of the various classes in Algeria. If we are to look for reasons why the independence struggle and the official option for a socialist mode of development through *autogestion* petered out in a form of state-controlled managerial capitalism we must look both at the economic situation and at class attitudes to independence and its aftermath. Similarly, to understand the workers' attitudes to *autogestion* there must be some understanding of their consciousness and value system as a class.

In this formulation of the Algerian class structure the main identifying criteria will be relationship to the means of production and the existence of distinct forms of consciousness. The main divisions are as follows: peasantry, rural and urban sub-proletariat, agricultural and industrial working class, the traditional middle class and the new administrative middle class.

PEASANTRY

The application of the term peasantry to a society whose pre-colonial structure was tribal loses some of the clarity of its original European context. However, in Algeria the original tribal structures were destroyed by the French as social, political and economic units. They continued to exist in the realms of sentiment only. The extended family is now the only viable indigenous social, political or economic structure in the traditional rural areas. Despite the division of economic activity into arboriculturalist, pastoralist and simple agriculture, the social structure is invariably uniform. The relationship to the means of production is also similar in that the natural environment is not acted on with a view to transformation. It is existed with in simple biological terms. Work itself is seen in the pre-capitalist spirit of subsistence rather than profit. Almost no money is used and where it is, it is expended in immediate consumption rather than accumulated as capital.

The vast mass of the Algerian rural population is not involved in *autogestion*. But, because of its size and the recent rural background of a large percentage of the urban population, its attitudes to modern economic and social organization are highly significant. In the light of recent theories[1] on the peasants as the revolutionary class of the third world it is important to determine the reaction of this class, and of those workers whose immediate background lies within it, to *autogestion* or any other form of socialism.

The paucity of statistics makes it difficult to determine the make-up of the rural population with any exactitude. In 1964 roughly seventy-five per cent of the population, i.e. eight million, lived outside the urban communes. The official figures give the active male population in rural areas as 1,250,000 and estimate employment at 750,000.[2] But the criteria of active population, employment and unemployment are difficult to apply to a traditional rural economy. The assessment made by Chaliand (see Table, p. 97) is more revealing.[3] Despite the wide discrepancy between this and the official figure it can be taken as a fair representation as it corresponds to the 1956 figure of 2,772,000.[4] The table shows that those who can be placed in the category of peasant by their relation to the means of production form only a third of the active rural population. The majority do not work their own land. They fall into two categories: those with

Class and Ideology in Algeria

number	characteristics
100,000	full-time workers in agricultural *autogestion*
450,000	seasonal or day labourers
1,000,000	unemployed, i.e. no land or work
450,000	existing on 1–10 hectares
170,000	existing on 10–50 hectares
25,000	existing on 50 or more hectares

permanent employment in the modern sector and the vast majority of nearly one and a half million who with their dependants form a drifting, landless sub-proletariat.

Purely traditional economic, social and political structures and consciousness are found, therefore, among only a small percentage of the Algerian population. But in terms of consciousness, the traditional value system still has a large though possibly immeasurable effect on both the sub-proletariat and the working class. One of the most important aspects of this value system, and the one that is the most vital in determining attitudes to post-independence forms of political and economic organization, is the concept of time.

Modern economic and social organization, whether capitalist or socialist, demands an ability to predict and calculate the future as the basis of economic rationality: it demands a determinate attitude to time and to the future. Traditionally, in rural society, foresight or prediction is confined to the tangible: it involves no rational speculation on an abstract future. Time is intimately connected with the immediate: with the cycle of the seasons. The total dependence of primitive agriculture on nature means that there can be no planning outside that of the immediate seasonal cycle. All that can be determined is that autumn will follow summer and spring, winter. Time becomes circular. But even here there can be no ultimate certainty: the caprices of nature – too much rain or too little – can interrupt this pattern catastrophically. Even the life of the individual is socially regulated in the cyclical pattern of birth, puberty, marriage, old age and death. This pattern too can be interrupted at any time by outside forces. The traditional concept of the future is of something that might or might not happen according to the unknowable will of the external: nature deified as god. In these circumstances, the member of a traditional rural society can have no grasp of time as modern society sees it. For modern society time is a linear projection of past and present into the future: a future which, despite all the inevitable uncertainties, is predicated on its past.

Submissiveness to time underlies the traditional attitudes to economic organization: to cooperation, money, credit, profit and trade. Money is characterized by an indeterminacy of use and time for use; whereas in an economy characterized by barter everything has an immediate and tangible use. There exists a vast conceptual gulf between traditional and modern economies. With the injection of a traditional into a modern economy the problem of money becomes immediately apparent. Because of his inability to conceptualize money as having any tangible reality, the peasant will be tempted to change the indeterminate into the determinate by the conversion of money into goods. In any case, the idea of saving is alien. One of the characteristics of a backward rural economy is its inability to save an agricultural surplus. Therefore, traditionally, this surplus is consumed.

All through such societies there is an attempt to deprive economic transactions of their strict economic meaning by accentuating their social significance or function. The consumption of the surplus is used to promote social status or emphasize social solidarity. The market is used to create or re-define social rather than economic relationships.[5] In such circumstances the concept of credit or profit, the whole basis of modern economic organization, is alien. Not only do they make time an object of calculation, but they also posit the creation of a relationship of inequality not based on social or religious considerations.

Competition, then, in its capitalist economic sense, is foreign to traditional societies – not only foreign but dangerous in that it threatens to unbalance the pre-existing social and political status system. Conversely, in many ways the concept of cooperation is just as alien. Economic or social cooperation within the family or 'clan' exists because the social group pre-exists the accomplishment of the task. But any attempt to persuade members of such a society to cooperate on an economic or social level outside the existing structures immediately postulates the problem of imposing a group structure that exists only in reference to future ends. In this sense cooperation demands a determinate attitude to time: the idea that time can be controlled. It is this difficulty in visualizing the future

Class and Ideology in Algeria

rather than the famed 'peasant individualism' that balked the colonial administration and still balks the Algerian government in its attempts to promote economic cooperation in rural areas.

It must be emphasized that this subjection to the external, which has been characterized as a fatalism or resignation specifically due to the Islamic religion, is not in fact due to the religion itself. Islam is strong in Algerian rural areas because it is in harmony with the peasant 'spirit' and the traditional value system. In fact the Koran, like the Bible, can be adduced to approve the effort to change the environment by personal endeavour just as often as an injunction to remain in harmony with it. 'It is not Islam which has imposed a fatalistic conception of the world, but the rural character of the society that has led to a fatalistic interpretation of the religion.'[6] Pierre Bourdieu, an acute analyst of the social structures of pre-independence Algeria, clarified this position when he stated: 'The link between Algerian society and the Muslim religion is not that of cause and effect but rather that of the implicit to the explicit or, as we could equally say, of the experienced to the formulated.'[7] In the context of the Weberian analysis of the relationship between religion and economic development[8] it must be stressed that it is not Islam itself which has presented the development of a 'capitalist spirit'. Some heterodox sects, particularly the Mozabites, bear a close resemblance to Calvinism in their doctrine and have developed forms of capitalism.* The intrinsic block in the development of advanced forms of economic organization, whether capitalist or socialist, lies with the character of traditional society and its externalized religious formulations rather than with religion itself.[9]

In the light of these considerations of traditional society it is difficult to countenance the thesis that the peasantry is the revolutionary class of the third world. In particular, they contradict the ideas of Frantz Fanon, who based his own analysis, in part, on the experience of the Algerian struggle for independence. This is not to disparage the activities of the peasants during that struggle but to question the motivations and forms of consciousness ascribed to them by revolutionary theorists. Here, we must note that the traditional Marxist attitude to the peasants is also inadequate, especially in its application to the third world. In his *Eighteenth Brumaire of*

* The Mozabites, numbering some 58,000, owned about 4,000 commercial establishments in pre-independence Algeria.

Louis Bonaparte Marx discusses the French peasants, stating that: 'their mode of production isolates them one from another instead of bringing them into mutual intercourse'; that there is no 'wealth of social relationships'; that the peasant economic unit 'acquires its means of life more through exchange with nature than in intercourse with society'.[10] As we have seen, the destruction of the economic and political bases of clan or tribal solidarity by colonialism ended in a similar isolation of the family unit in Algerian rural society. Marx feels that the peasantry can be described as a class in that their mode of life, interests and culture separate them from other classes. But he goes on to say: 'In so far as there is merely a local interconnection between these small-holding peasants, and the identity of their interests begets no community, no natural bond and no political organization among them, they do not form a class.'

The inadequacy of Marx's definition when applied outside its specific context of France in the 1840s lies in its assumption that there can be no identity of interests that may bridge the separation engendered by the mode of production. Bourdieu isolated this common identity among the Algerian peasants involved in the struggle for liberation:

Thus it is that even the future is conceived of in the light of the past and the criticism or refusal of the present arises not so much from the condemnation of the present and the past, but from the striving memory of the ancient order, the basis of pride and the supreme defence against self-doubt.[11]

The traditional rural population rose against colonialism because they had been savagely oppressed and exploited for over a century. But they fought for the memory of Abdel Kader's Algeria. They did have a common identity; but what bound them was a desire to recreate the past. Thus it is not true to say, as some strict Marxists have, that the peasants cannot participate in revolutionary struggle. Objectively, the role of the Algerian peasant in the liberation struggle was a revolutionary one. Equally, in terms of the Fanonist thesis, it is untrue to say that, because they are actively involved in the struggle against colonialism, they form a revolutionary class. Subjectively, in terms of their consciousness, their role is not a revolutionary one. The experience of struggle does not necessarily destroy the traditional value system or social structure because it is not internalized as a revolutionary struggle. In Algeria, after the struggle, the peasants of the traditional rural sector returned to their classic isolation.

This thesis holds good for almost every revolution of this century: the peasant involvement in the struggle stems from the desire to recreate a seemingly mythical past rather than from a conscious commitment to a revolutionary ideology. As long as their relationship to the external world remains one of submissiveness to the perceived natural order, the peasantry will continue to lack the consciousness necessary to enable it to enter the struggle as a subjectively revolutionary force. In Europe the Algerian experience was paralleled in Russia and Yugoslavia, where the attempt to expand socialist modes of economic organization to rural areas, whether in terms of state farms or cooperatives, was met with marked hostility or even open opposition. In Algeria it was the permanent workers on the European estates, proletarianized by their relation to the means of production, who consciously or unconsciously created socialist forms of economic organization in the *comités de gestion*. The peasants merely attempted to redistribute these land-holdings with the aim of reincorporating them within the traditional system. Since then the *fellaghine* have remained almost totally separated from the political and economic conflicts that have determined the country's development. But the content and structure of the traditional value system have had an immeasurable effect in determining the attitude of other groups and classes towards forms of political and economic organization.

THE SUB-PROLETARIAT

The second broad class division in Algerian society is the rural and urban sub-proletariat: that is the mass of unemployed or irregularly employed. Despite the differences in geographical environment, these two groups can be regarded as basically homogeneous in terms of their relation to the means of production, and they have an almost identical socio-cultural system of beliefs and values. They are the human flotsam created by the inability of traditional agriculture to cope with a vastly increased population and by the social and economic destruction created by French military policy during the war.

Migration to the urban areas is the most important single factor in determining the rapidly changing numerical proportions within

Workers' Self-Management in Algeria

Algeria's overall social structure. It is also the factor which creates the greatest economic and social problems. The rapid growth of the urban population in the recent history of Algeria can be seen from the following figures for the Muslim population of urban communes.[12]

1959	1962	1963	1964
2,347,000	3,680,000	3,900,000	4,095,000

This high level of population growth in urban areas is concentrated in towns with a population of over 100,000. These account for fifty per cent of the total urban population and received sixty per cent of urban immigration from 1954 to 1960. The growth of the Muslim population of Algiers is perhaps the most astounding:

1959	1960	1966
293,000	588,000	943,000

The extremely rapid growth between 1959 and 1960 can, of course, largely be accounted for by Muslims fleeing from the war zones.

The difference between this rapid urbanization of the population, typical of the third world, and that of Europe in the nineteenth century, is the discrepancy that exists between the urban 'civilization' and the traditional peasant culture of the rural areas. Moreover, whereas in Europe industrialization largely preceded urbanization, in Algeria the situation is in reverse. Another difference is that, in general, this does not represent a numerical loss to the countryside: in Algeria, the rural population has continued to increase even though declining relatively *vis-à-vis* the urban areas. In Algeria the effect of the war and the *regroupement* policy helped speed up the exodus to the towns. The most important fact about the large majority of urban immigrants is that they do not become integrated into urban life through industrial or commercial employment. They remain separated, living in *bidonvilles* or shanty towns, with infrequent casual employment, and form a vast urban sub-proletariat.[13]

The recent rural background of a large proportion of the urban population becomes clearer if we look at the figures in more detail. Of the Muslim population of the three largest towns – Algiers, Oran and Constantine – just before independence, twenty-eight per cent of family heads were born there, 19·7 per cent came from smaller

Class and Ideology in Algeria

towns and 44·3 per cent came from rural areas.[14] In both these last cases two-thirds of the family heads moved directly to these three main urban areas with no intermediate stage. Particularly important in this movement is the fact that all those without employment at the time of the survey arrived this way. Those with employment had generally spent some time in a smaller town before moving to the cities. In the smaller towns 53·4 per cent of family heads were born there and 44·3 per cent came from rural areas. Only a minute fraction (1·5 per cent) had migrated from the big towns and these were professional or skilled workers. In these smaller towns it was found that fifty per cent of family heads under the age of forty had migrated from rural areas.

No reliable figures for migration have been published since independence but these migrations are symptomatic of what has become a normal demographic process in much of the third world. The reduction or eradication of certain diseases like malaria, and food subsidies, especially for children, by colonial authorities sharply reduced the death rate and increased life expectancy. The result in every case is that the rural areas are no longer able to support the increased population. In Algeria the process of migration was, as we have seen, greatly aggravated by the effects of the struggle for independence.

The French army, in order to cut the guerrillas off from local support, inaugurated a policy of moving the rural population out of the more inaccessible hill country into easily policed resettlement camps. It has been estimated that this policy affected some two million people, seventeen per cent of the population. Not only did *regroupement* mean the shattering of traditional socio-economic structures, it also meant the end of that particular relationship of the peasant to his environment which defines him in his role of peasant-to-himself. More significant for the future of Algeria, it helped to raise unemployment to a level of sixty per cent. In addition, by destroying the villages, crops and animals, it meant that many would never return to their previous economic activity.

Several studies have been made of the effect of *regroupement*[15] but they can be best summed up by the following quotation.

By depriving them of the assurance and security provided by the social and economic order of former days, by abandoning them to idleness or to makeshift forms of employment, by stripping them completely of any responsibility for their own destiny, by giving them the status of persons on relief, the authorities transformed these demoralized country dwellers into a sub-proletariat who had lost all measure of their former ideals of honour and dignity and who wavered between attitudes of resignation and ineffectual revolt.[16]

Regroupement and urbanization also meant the introduction of the concept of time-lost, as opposed to the traditional mode of time-passing: in other words, a modern economic notion of time. Without the security of traditional work the unemployed country dweller becomes conscious of time-lost or -spent: he becomes conscious of being unemployed.

If we add to those affected by *regroupement* the urban sub-proletariat forced to move to towns by demographic or war-time pressures, we are dealing with one-third of the Algerian population. In fact the situation of the urban sub-proletariat was, and is, very little different from that of those in resettlement camps. The *bidonvilles* virtually constituted enclaves of rural society within the urban environment. Often they contain members of the same clan segment. The older members make desperate efforts to preserve the social structure of rural Algeria, retaining close connections with the rural home and attempting to preserve their traditional social roles. The young, denied even this illusory security, are caught in a half-world between the rural and the urban, expressing their frustration and hopelessness in extreme irrationality and outbursts of violence. The fact of independence changed none of their circumstances. 'The men of the *bidonville* could thus point out with reason that independence had satisfied none of their claims and that the old order of things, against which they had risen with so much violence, remained unchanged.'[17] Completely at the mercy of external forces, forced into unemployment or at best casual labour, ill adapted to an urban economy which has little to offer them, the sub-proletariat exists without a past or future in a present that continually escapes their grasp.*

The world view of the sub-proletariat is expressed by a rejection

---

* The collapse of their past is demonstrated by the fact that eighty-two per cent did not know the profession of their grandfather; in traditional rural areas most could tell their family tree back five, six or even seven generations. (Pierre Bourdieu, '*La hantise du chômage chez l'ouvrier algérien*', *Sociologie du Travail*, October–December 1962.)

of facticity and rationality, by an encapsulation within a system that is felt to operate as a result of a maleficent will of its own. Because poverty and misery must be endured as an inevitable part of things, rather than as a possibly alterable result of the economic or social system, the individual trapped in this belief system is denied the opportunity of becoming conscious of his own alienation. Politically this means that the sub-proletariat can never become conscious of itself as a class. Certainly it can participate with overwhelming effect in a revolutionary upheaval, as the experience of the black riots in the United States shows. Its participation is spontaneous and its violence apocalyptic. But lacking in historicity or class consciousness, it is incapable of a sustained revolutionary effort, unlike the true proletariat, and continually subsides back into apathy.

Since Algeria's independence, this disinherited mass, one-third of the total population, has, like the peasantry, remained outside the whole ferment over the modes of social, political and economic organization. Because of its size and the smouldering potential of its violence it is alternately feared and wooed by the other elements in society. The workers who have jobs fear the competition of this mass for those few jobs that are available. Yet objectively the sub-proletariat is the ally of the working class in their struggle against the new bureaucracy. This bureaucracy knows that the desperation of the unemployed for employment is an important factor in compelling the workers to curb their demands. Yet the new rulers of Algeria dare not unleash a force that might well entail their own downfall.

THE WORKING CLASS

Historically, the Algerian working class is of fairly recent formation. The European near-monopoly of skilled jobs before independence meant that a large percentage of Muslim workers were unskilled. This meant that the division between sub-proletariat and working class was by no means clear-cut. Those in unskilled employment one day might be unemployed the next. In fact the lower paid and less educated sections of the workers shared many of the attitudes of the sub-proletariat; while symptoms of this value system appeared even higher up the occupational ladder. The relatively recent rural background of many of the less skilled engendered feelings of disorientation in relation to the expressed value system of a more modern mode of economic organization. Only those with a longer urban and industrial history (and higher skill and educational levels) were capable of orientating to some of the values and beliefs inherent in industrialized production.

In 1960 Bourdieu, and associates, tried to determine the evolution of attitudes to modern economic organization among the Muslim workers, taking income and educational levels as their variables.[18] They found a widespread absence of both trades-union consciousness and class consciousness. When asked how they would try to achieve higher wage levels 88·6 per cent of all permanent workers and 55·1 per cent of white-collar workers chose to work harder rather than to press for higher wages for equal work. Taking the criteria of literacy, they found that only 1·3 per cent of illiterates chose higher wages for equal work; while those with the *brevet* or higher qualifications who chose higher wages for equal work numbered fifty per cent.[19] Thus, even among permanent workers, it was only those with high occupational and educational levels who could conceive of changing their relative position within the economic system by acting on it rather than existing within it.

The inability of many workers to grasp the possibility of changing their material and social status within the colonial economic system was stressed even further by the small percentage of those who expressed 'rational' hopes for bettering themselves. Among agricultural workers and unskilled and semi-skilled industrial workers 33·9 per cent expressed no hope of bettering themselves; while a further 43·8 per cent expressed what the authors termed 'fantasy' or 'dream-like' hopes; that is, hopes which could not be fulfilled within a possible future, capitalist or socialist. The level of what were termed 'rational' hopes ran at twenty-six per cent for production workers, forty-five per cent for white-collar workers and seventy-seven per cent for *cadres*.[20] The survey tried to relate attitudes to income level in the belief that only material security provided a basis for a 'rational' grasp of life. It concluded that, below a family income of 300 NF a month, aspirations remained 'magical'; between 300 and 600 NF material security was attained and rational attitudes began to appear, above 600 NF a general change in economic attitudes and conduct was reached, based on a rational grasp of the future.[21]

The high level of 'irrationality' among the less skilled, less educated and less well paid workers can be partially ascribed to the cultural confusion stemming from their fairly rural background. The transformation from a society with a traditional value system to the value system of an industrial economy inevitably creates disorientation. Life within such a system is felt to be irrational because it is based on a set of values that have not yet been internalized. But it is important to remember that the economic system itself may deviate from its formal values and thus be irrational in its operation. Bourdieu found that, under colonialism, the elementary fact of finding a job did not, as in the West, depend on skill or qualifications.[22] It depended, instead, on chance or status entirely unconnected with professional skill. Of the workers interviewed, sixty-two per cent got their jobs through friends, relations or 'chance' and only twelve per cent got them through official channels such as employment offices. Sixty-seven per cent felt that something other than technical skill was needed to get a job. This something ranged from the influence of friends and relations, through bribes to the foreman, to the 'will of God'. The feeling that professional qualifications were inadequate by themselves varied with occupational category: sixty-three per cent of white-collar workers felt that skill was enough to get a job; while only forty per cent of unskilled and semi-skilled workers felt this was enough by itself. A final comment on the relative irrelevance of qualifications was that forty-three per cent of those interviewed took the job that they were in because they could find no other.[23]

If the struggle to obtain employment and thus some material security was the main preoccupation of the mass of Algerian workers, the attempt to retain it was certainly a close second. Of those interviewed seventy-two per cent did not like their job, being dissatisfied with either low pay or dangerous work.[24] But two-thirds of these would not have attempted to change jobs because of the near impossibility of finding another. For them employment, and the wage it brought, was the pre-eminent factor in work, not any satisfaction intrinsic to the job. Their attitude was instrumental.

The move from one mode of economic and social organization to another creates disorientation in internalized value systems so that the external is experienced as irrational. This may be emphasized by the actual irrationality in the operation of the new mode. Modern industrial organization depends, in part, for its efficiency on the existence of a stable and skilled labour force. The colonial economy operated in a situation of colossal unemployment and high labour turnover. For the unskilled and semi-skilled not only did it appear irrational in the context of their internalized value system, but it was irrational: employment and income did not depend on any capitalist ethic of hard work but on a series of chance events. Only those who had achieved the usually synonymous positions of higher educational and skill levels had the material security and access to the values of that system on which depended their ability to grasp it as a system and not as the operation of chance. As a result of his work, Bourdieu tried to describe the existential problems of the Algerian worker:

Before the subject can begin to make his future, he must be conscious of having a future. Because the objective future of individuals or groups depends strictly on their material conditions of existence it is clear that the free project and calculated foresight are privileges inseparable from a definite economic and social position: interiorization of the objective future and a planned life are reserved for those whose present and future life has already been torn from incoherence.[25]

From this analysis it is clear that the lower end of the working class, the unskilled (and semi-skilled), shared many of the attitudes and beliefs of the sub-proletariat. They experienced the world as irrational in its operation and effect: they were unable to act on it and could only exist within it. For Bourdieu it is material security and education that make it possible for the individual to grasp the external and act on it. This explanation ignores one central fact: the worker's relationship to the means of production. Without this it is impossible to explain their action in occupying the farms and factories of the *pieds-noirs* in 1962.

The individual who is unemployed, or at best irregularly employed, has only a negative relationship to the means of production. He has only a negative social identity, frozen in a half world between the traditional and the modern. The peasant has a social identity within the traditional social structure and value system. The full-time worker in a modern industrial system has a social identity defined by his role as worker. Subjectively, he may experience this role as an individual, alongside other individuals. Objectively, the fact that the modes of production in a non-traditional economy create groups exterior to the individual or family means that the worker has a social identity; is a member of a class.

Class and Ideology in Algeria

The worker's objective situation as a member of a class does not necessarily assume consciousness of this. Bourdieu's portrait of the Algerian worker in 1960 definitely depicts the absence of class consciousness. Most of his interviewees experienced themselves as individuals or in terms of the other-determined *colon* definition of Muslim. Their solutions to their problems of material existence, when rational as opposed to magical, were couched in individual or racial terms. Yet the action of seizing the means of production at independence can, objectively, only be described as a class action. As I have already discussed in Chapter 3, these actions can be ascribed to the motivations of material self-interest – to the need to continue production in order to earn wages. But the way in which the occupations were carried out makes it clear that individual or racial motivations were subsumed under a class action.

The official explanation of the FLN, that the workers were acting in accordance with the internalized values of cooperation stemming from traditional rural society, must be dismissed as both facile and wrong. Not only does the existing social structure and value system of Algerian traditional rural society make this highly unlikely but, more relevantly, these workers were not members of that society. They were permanent industrial and agricultural workers proletarianized by their relationship to the means of production. What 1962 witnessed was a solidary action based not on 'peasant communalism' but on an identity of class interest. It represented the emergence of a working class capable of acting in class terms; which had already begun to create a separate self-definition.

The development of this self-definition as class consciousness can only be partial. The very material conditions that drove the Algerian workers to seize the means of production also serve as a brake on the development of their consciousness. The economic uncertainties of life create an instrumental attitude to work that can lead workers to sacrifice gains in terms of economic or political control if the material conditions of existence are threatened. Economic self-interest brought the Algerian working class to the threshold of consciousness; it has also, at times, dragged them away from it. But the very fact of independence has accelerated the conditions for the development of consciousness. The simple opposition between Algerian and *colon* is no longer possible. The existence of a bureaucracy with political and economic power, whose members are themselves Algerians, has destroyed the simple, Manichaean identities of pre-independence. The hostility of this bureaucracy to *autogestion* and, therefore, to the achievements of the workers, has fostered the development of class consciousness. Politically, this emerging consciousness has been expressed in a struggle with the state over economic organization, over the control of the means of production.

THE MIDDLE CLASS

The economic structure of Algeria before the French conquest was not conducive to the development of a classical entrepreneurial bourgeoisie. Outside the rural areas, economic activity was confined to trade and artisan production. Large towns like Tlemcen, Oran, Constantine and Algiers were basically trading and religious centres; the largest – Algiers – was also the administrative centre of the Turkish *dey*. The absence of mercantile capital on any large scale and the restrictive practices of the artisan corporations placed a block on the emergence of entrepreneurial capitalism. In fact, the indigenous middle class of traders and artisan workshop-owners was only narrowly separated from the poorer elements of the towns in terms of wealth and social status.[26] This middle class was almost totally ruined during the French conquest.

The European monopoly of economic activity effectively circumscribed the development of an indigenous Muslim entrepreneurial bourgeoisie. The Muslim middle class under colonialism was confined to a small number of semi-feudal land-owners, descendants of tribal chiefs loyal to the French, small traders, owners of artisan workshops, minor officials in the administration and members of the liberal professions. The commercial section of this middle class was characterized by under-capitalization and was a by-product of the colonial economy in that it was confined to areas considered unprofitable by the settlers. It was not involved in industrial production and lacked the capital to become so. In many ways it could hardly be termed a class. *Révolution Africaine* commented:

> The Algerian national bourgeoisie was reduced to a caste, with no precise economic role, composed of traders and intellectuals who were essentially defined by their permanent desire for identification with the Western bourgeoisie.... What they lacked above all was capital, the basis of any true bourgeoisie.... It was therefore essentially a parasitic structure.[27]

Class and Ideology in Algeria

This identification of their values is not strictly true. One section retained a strict allegiance to traditional socio-cultural values; the other, mainly members of the professions and minor administrative employees, did develop a conscious identification with Western values. It was this group that became politically active in the 1930s in the *Fédération des Élus* and later in the UDMA, both under the leadership of Ferhat Abbas.

Since independence this middle class has been characterized by its political and economic ineffectuality. Although Ferhat Abbas and his fellow-liberals eventually rallied to the FLN, the political character of the nationalist movement had little patience with their liberal reformism. Ben Bella's political victory in September 1962 virtually removed the Westernized liberals from the Algerian political stage forever. Economically, the existing commercial bourgeoisie were unable to take advantage of independence by replacing the *colon* bourgeoisie. Not only did the formation of *comités de gestion* pre-empt any action they could have taken but their marginal position in the economy as a whole gave them no opportunity to move into industry. The lack of a true national bourgeoisie made it impossible for Algeria to develop in a strictly capitalist direction after independence.

The small number of medium to large land-owners should be included in an analysis of the traditional middle class. If the criteria of owning fifty or more hectares of land is used, this group numbers around 25,000. Its composition, economic influence and political attitudes are extremely heterogeneous. Many of the largest land-owners, descendants of tribal chiefs loyal to the French, sided with the *colons* during the war. At independence, those who escaped retribution followed the *colons* into exile in France. Of the remaining land-owners, a large number hold land in the mountains or the south where productivity is so low as to restrict economic influence to the surrounding area only. To a large extent the land-owners have opposed agrarian reform; but so too have the small peasants. As opposed to the commercial and intellectual bourgeoisie, their values are marked by a distinct rejection of things Western. Thus, although not a coherent political force, they did, objectively, form part of the bloc opposed to Ben Bella and have given implicit support to the Boumédienne régime. Their relationship to the mainstream of Algerian politics has, however, remained tenuous.

Of far greater importance for the political and economic development of independent Algeria is the new middle class entrenched in the politico-administrative machine. The specifically Algerian form of colonialism prevented the emergence of an incipient indigenous entrepreneurial bourgeoisie. It was also hostile to the training of indigenous administrative cadres, except at the lowest levels. Until de Gaulle's accession to power in 1958 there had never been any real commitment to the idea of eventual independence in the metropolitan government let alone among the *pieds-noirs*. In this situation there was virtually no consideration given to the question of training cadres for the eventual Algerianization of the administration. The cadres that did exist can be divided into two categories. In the outlying rural areas the colonial administration made use of the remnants of the traditional political system. Indigenous officials, such as the *caïds*, represented the artificially perpetuated remains of the pre-colonial system of tribal (and feudal) political authority. These officials were picked with a view to their loyalty to the colonial régime and kept loyal by appropriate rewards. In the central administration the lowest echelons were partially staffed by Muslims from lower-middle-class families. Under colonialism this represented the only channel of upward mobility outside the severely circumscribed capitalist sector. Neither of these groups was involved in the struggle for independence: their status and privileges in relation to the rest of the Muslim population depended on the maintenance of the colonial order.*

During the struggle for independence the FLN set up a political and administrative wing to the military guerrilla struggle inside the country. The *Organisation Politico-Administrative* (OPA), as this was called, was smashed by the military success of the French army and many of its members were killed. In this way the FLN lost a large number of its best educated and politically aware cadres. At independence the flight of the *pieds-noirs* stripped the administration of most of its middle and upper levels, leaving metropolitan civil servants seconded to the Algerian administration and the existing indigenous members. With the destruction of the OPA the FLN was faced with the problem of finding the personnel to fill the administrative machinery of the state.

In the event Ben Bella was forced to rely heavily on the existing

* These groups had their counterparts among the indigenous Algerians who served in the ranks and lower officer grades of the French army.

Class and Ideology in Algeria

personnel in the administration. The extent of this reliance is revealed by the following table.[28]

Members of Algerian administration early in 1963	
category	percentage of members in colonial administration
A	43
B	77
C	12
D	3

Only half the senior administrative level (A) was filled by those who did not cooperate with the colonial administration during the war. In general these were the political and administrative chiefs of the FLN and GPRA who had spent the war outside the country and had little experience in national administration. The second level (B), largely responsible for routine decisions and execution, was almost entirely composed of members of the colonial administration. These were the members of the lower echelons of that administration who, by default, now achieved a rapid acceleration in status. The lower levels (C and D) of the new administration to a large extent consisted of the personal followers of FLN leaders, placed in the administration as a reward for personal loyalty rather than political orientation. Generally the most active FLN militants felt that their role lay, with the masses, in local reconstruction rather than at the centre.

Thus at independence not only were the structures of the colonial administration preserved but the majority of the middle and upper echelons were also formed by its members. Inevitably the orientation of the revolution towards socialism meant that considerable economic and political power would accrete to this administration. The *décrets de mars* took *autogestion* as the specific form of Algerian socialism but failed to take into account the problem of its administration. The rather vague ideas on the supervisory role of the administration were immediately called into question by the composition and ideological orientation of the existing administration. In trying to create a dynamic partnership between the *comités de gestion* and the state agencies the authors of the decrees failed to take into account the relatively weak organization and political consciousness of the *comités* and the ideological and structural hostility of the bureaucracy to anything that threatened its position. Very rapidly this partnership developed into a struggle for political and economic pre-eminence.

The growing power and hostile nature of the administration was recognized by left-wing members of the FLN in the *Charte d'Alger* in early 1964. In their preparatory theses they stated: 'Since independence, a new social grouping of a bureaucratic bourgeoisie has been developing rapidly in the state administration and the economy, thanks to the feeling of power engendered by the exercise of power.'[29] 'This force, through its position in the state machinery and the economy, could prove more dangerous to the democratic and social evolution of the Algerian revolution than any other social force in the country.'[30] On a political level this development could be seen as part of the struggle between two conflicting forms of socialism. As one commentator assessed it: 'Everything has happened as if there was a struggle between a self-management conception of socialism and state socialism, and everything has turned out as if, in the first stage, state socialism has won over self-management.'[31] On one level this formulation is correct. However, it ignores the growing tendency of the bureaucracy to act in the pursuit of definite sectional interests that can only be defined as class interests.

The majority of this bureaucracy were either lower grade members of the colonial administration or placemen. All were upwardly mobile; and in the absence of an entrepreneurial bourgeoisie the only channel for upward mobility lay through the ranks of the administration or party. In view of their background and present position the members of the administration had no overt ideological orientation to socialism. State socialism, however, tended to correspond with their interests in that it situated political and economic power with them as members of the administration. Their life style set them apart, distinctively, from the mass of the people.

The end of colonial domination has allowed certain people to occupy positions augmented by numerous privileges – villas, cars, salaries, influence. These people no longer share the lives of the people; they are separated from them. Very often they have taken the place of the *pieds-noirs*. Their standard of living has risen considerably. Their only desire is to preserve their position against all comers.[32]

Class and Ideology in Algeria

This bourgeois life-style characterizes a large part of the upper levels of the administration; the lower levels are characterized by their desire to attain it.

The foundations of this life-style are based on the possession of political and economic power. Not only do their consumption patterns betray the existence of an ideology of upward mobility but their control of the means of production defines them, economically, as a class. This dual formulation of an élitist life-style and objective relation to the means of production and political power has close parallels with the class characteristics of the Russian bureaucracy.[33]

The party and state bureaucracy cannot be described as a homogeneous class. It contains its own internal conflicts. There is an opposition between those with overtly upwardly mobile characteristics and those with a genuine desire to institute state socialism. It is also the scene of struggles for power and influence between members of regional or 'tribal' groupings and between individuals and their protégés. Despite these internal conflicts, the objective attitude of the bureaucracy as a whole is consistent in its opposition to *autogestion*. Its close and growing identification with the control of the means of production places it in a position of conflict with the urban and agricultural working class. The eclipse and defeat of *autogestion* can only be understood if the simple conflict between two forms of socialism is amplified by the objective definition of a class struggle between two emerging classes: the working class and the middle class centred round the bureaucracy. This struggle has been masked by the embryonic nature and consciousness of these classes and the ill-defined character of their ideologies.

7

THE POLITICAL STAGE, 1963-8

THIS chapter deals with the main facets of Algerian history between 1962 and 1967 in the context of the struggle over *autogestion*. Many of the political clashes of this period grew from personal antagonisms and wartime political differences; but the volcanic and often violent course of Algerian politics since independence may be objectively characterized as a struggle over the mode of political, economic and social organization best suited to the Algerian reality. Specifically, it was the question of economic organization that dominated the formative years of the state and eventually dictated the official ideological stance on all other matters. These years represent a period of confused class struggle during which the definition of the content of the Algerian revolution hung in the balance. The struggle was confused because the classic antagonism of bourgeoisie, proletariat and peasantry was rarely expressed in overt class terms. Objectively, and in retrospect, this period can be seen to represent the evolution of a new bourgeoisie and the development of its consciousness.

Parallel to the development of class consciousness grew the new ideology of state capitalism – the ideology of the hegemonic class. Ultimately, this class was bound to clash with the nascent proletariat whose interests at every level were hostile to those of the bureaucratic *élite*. This incipient class war was waged under the guise of disagreements over economic organization: whether *autogestion* or state control was best suited to the interests of the Algerian people; which would bring the largest and fastest increase in living standards. Although expressed in terms of modes of economic organization, this was, in fact, a struggle for control over the means of production. The gradual stifling of *autogestion* between 1962 and 1967 and the elaboration of the whole machinery of state control represented a victory for the new bourgeoisie. The following pages trace the course of their victory as it appeared on the political stage.

With the elections for the Assembly and the formation of a new

The Political Stage, 1963–8

government in September 1962, Ben Bella consolidated his personal position as head of the government. The banning of the *Parti de la Révolution Socialiste* (PRS) and the *Partie Communiste Algérien* in November and the dismantling of the wartime *willaya* organizations in December further consolidated the position of the FLN as the sole representative national organization. At this point, only the UGTA remained outside the direct control of the FLN, representing an incipient threat to its national hegemony. The UGTA leadership had opposed the fratricidal strife between the various factions after independence and condemned the actions of the *chefs historiques*. Now they wished the UGTA to remain an autonomous organization representing the interests of the working class.

This desire for autonomy stemmed from two sources: firstly the experience of many of the officials who had been involved in Western-style union movements; and secondly their ideological differences with the new political leadership. An agreement to respect the autonomy of the UGTA was signed by the government on 21 December in an attempt to avoid an overt clash. But the conflict broke out again at the UGTA's first congress held in January 1963. In their report, the union leadership, which had been instrumental in promoting the spread of *comités de gestion* in August and September, expressed their opposition to a state socialism which 'allows the petit-bourgeois spirit to persist and allows the exploiters to profit from the situation in reinforcing their privileges and consolidating their political positions'. They also advocated the creation of small-scale industries to solve unemployment, rather than the immediate construction of a capital-intensive industry. Finally they asserted that 'certain party officials who are not unionists and probably have personal motives have tried to take over the structure of the UGTA and its constituent organizations'.[1] The FLN reacted to this barely masked hostility on 21 January when its general secretary, Mohammed Khider, packed the congress with his own supporters, excluded UGTA members and voted out the leadership. Lassel and Bourouiba were replaced by Rabah Djermane who accepted the control of the *Bureau Politique*. A statement was issued announcing that the UGTA would 'mobilize their [the workers'] energy, devotion and technical skill in the service of the nation through the rapid and conscientious execution of the orders of the party'.[2]

The conflict was not only over the question of the UGTA's autonomy, but over its policy and membership. This reflected the controversy over the relative revolutionary roles of the peasantry and proletariat in underdeveloped countries. The UGTA leadership stressed the fact that the proletariat represented the most revolutionary force in Algeria. This was opposed by Ben Bella, who said at the UGTA congress: 'Today's scene will be more convincing when eighty per cent of those present are peasants, when the peasantry are organized in agricultural unions.' His attitude, which was typical of the majority of the FLN and ALN leadership, stemmed partly from the conviction that the peasants as the most dispossessed must be the most revolutionary. It also reflected a political need to play off the two classes against each other – a mode of action which became typical of Ben Bella's style of government.

The FLN was reinforced in its desire to curb the power of the UGTA when, at the congress, the workers' right to strike was defended. This attitude was castigated by the FLN as ouvrierist and out of place in a country where the government had chosen socialism. The hostility to strikes, expressed both by the government and the new tame UGTA leadership, eventually led to the total isolation of the *union centrale*.* Many workers were prepared to strike for higher wages and better conditions and in the end they were actively supported by the *unions locales* and national federations. The resulting split between the official leadership and local militants paralysed the UGTA as an effective political instrument until its second congress in 1965.

With the imposition of FLN control over the UGTA, the government and party had finally established their authority. The moment was therefore opportune to declare *autogestion* as the main form of economic organization and the most important component of the ideology of the revolution. The effective muzzling of the UGTA and left-wing opposition made it possible for the state to consecrate *autogestion* as its own. As we have seen, the *décrets de mars* represented a compromise between those who feared that decentralization would lead to ouvrierism and anarchy, who wanted greater state control,

---

* The UGTA consists of a number of separate National Federations organizing separate areas of employment. At a national level these are unified in the *union centrale* of the UGTA and at a local level by the *unions locales* of the UGTA.

The Political Stage, 1963–8

and those who wished for the minimum of state intervention in the *comités de gestion*. Critics of Ben Bella have never hesitated to state that the *décrets de mars* mark the beginning of the growth in power of the state bureaucracy. Boudiaf, the leader of the PRS, said the decrees were 'the occasion of a generalized administrative interference in the *comités de gestion*';[3] while another critic noted: 'With the official consecration came state control.'[4] However, as I have already discussed, the real contradiction inherent in the decrees was not so much the attempt to create a rational economic and financial superstructure for the *comités* as the total misunderstanding of the social content and ideology of the existing bureaucracy. As Gérard Chaliand, one-time editor of *Alger Républicain*, said:

The essential contradiction lies in the co-existence of *autogestion* with a state apparatus with bourgeois ideology, origins and aspirations, tending, little by little, to create state capitalism. The aim of part of this state apparatus is to liquidate *autogestion* in order to control and integrate this sector into its own sector.[5]

The bitter conflicts over *autogestion* were not, however, in evidence in spring 1963. As a result of the decrees, Ben Bella achieved an immense, if temporary, national and international popularity. From this moment, officially at least, *autogestion* was Algeria's '*option irréversible*'.

Almost immediately the FLN was faced with a crisis involving its ideological conceptions and their application in practice. On 16 April Mohammed Khider, the party's secretary general, went into exile, where he kept control of the party funds entrusted to him before independence. The exact details of the disagreements between him and Ben Bella have never been fully revealed; but it is clear they were based partly on the correct nature of a revolutionary party and partly on the personal power struggles that have marked Algerian history. At independence, the FLN was not a national political party in any sense, but a heterogeneous alliance. At the top, its leaders were co-opted for their political importance, at the base it rested on local notables rather than real militants. Khider wished to form a mass party, open to all Algerians, that would educate and involve the mass of the people in its actions.* Ben Bella, despite his

---

* Khider was to remain abroad till his murder in Madrid in January 1967. It has been suggested that the Boumédienne régime wished to prevent him handing over the FLN funds in his possession to the opposition groups in exile.

populism, was prompted by his close supporters, like Mohammed Harbi, to create an *avant-garde* party.

We were militants for ten years before being revolutionaries. We need a revolutionary *avant-garde*, a party of militants. . . . I could easily form a party of four million Algerians in a month but it would be a party unable to assume its essential functions. I prefer to have a hundred thousand militants, real militants, and then we could build for twenty years hence.[6]

The controversy over the role and content of the FLN has continued. The need for a single party was not only attacked by the PRS and the growing number of opposition parties, but also later by many officials in the UGTA. The supremacy of the party was established in the 1963 constitution. This states that the party 'defines the political stance of the nation and inspires the action of the state, controls the actions of the National Assembly and government . . .'. Under Ben Bella, who became party secretary general as well as prime minister and president, there was a total identification between party and state. The FLN was never reconstituted either as a mass or *avant-garde* party. Its close identification with an increasingly bourgeois administration lost it any pretensions to being a revolutionary party.

The consolidation and isolation of Ben Bella's régime continued through the summer and autumn of 1963. In June the leaders of the PRS, including Boudiaf, were arrested and imprisoned.[7] This alienated a number of left-wingers who had till then given tacit support to Ben Bella in the interests of national unity. In the autumn it was the turn of the right wing: liberal elements from the old UDMA, like Ahmed Francis, were dismissed from the government and Ferhat Abbas was excluded from the FLN. The arrest of Boudiaf drove another of the *chefs historiques*, Hocine Ait Ahmed, to declare his open opposition to Ben Bella. In the National Assembly he had already attacked the government for its totalitarian tendencies and in 1962 had refused to join the *Bureau Politique*. In July he withdrew to Michelet in the Kabylie and founded the *Front des Forces Socialistes* (FFS). At the end of September he was joined by a popular ex-*willaya* leader, Colonel Mohand Ou el-Hadj, and declared a rising against the government.[8] The rising failed but the FFS continued to exist in illegal opposition.

Both Boudiaf and Ait Ahmed had been arrested and imprisoned

The Political Stage, 1963–8

with Ben Bella in 1956. They had long-standing personal differences with him, stemming from his assumption of the leadership of the FLN, despite the accepted principle of collegiality. They and the assassinated Abane Ramdane had represented the socialist current within the FLN during the war. As Marxists they opposed Ben Bella's pragmatic populism, believing instead in a democratic revolutionary socialism. Ait Ahmed tended to take a Maoist perspective, regarding the peasantry as the basis for revolutionary action; Boudiaf had a more orthodox vision of the proletariat as the class from which revolutionary organizations would emerge. This, to a certain extent, explains why they never formed a coherent opposition within Algeria. They failed to gain any mass support at this point because both the peasantry and the working class still identified Ben Bella with revolutionary authenticity. Thus, although their opposition was based on profound ideological differences with Ben Bella, it appeared as yet another purely personal clash over the sharing of power in independent Algeria.

In face of the growing opposition of political leaders and the discontent of the people over continued unemployment and low wages, Ben Bella embarked on another round of nationalizations in an attempt to establish his revolutionary authenticity. At the end of October, the rest of the *colon*-owned lands were nationalized. In November the transport companies, SATAC, SATAS and MORY, and all the tobacco companies were nationalized. During the year a host of other small concerns, cinemas, cafés and shops had been nationalized. Despite the propaganda value, many of these nationalizations formed a sector that was difficult to organize and was of no great economic importance. Boudiaf talks of this as the '*fuite en avant*', saying that most of these nationalizations were

> completely justified in principle but made with no preparation or organization to digest them. They are losing or risk losing all technical efficiency and could lead to economic chaos. Some of them were purely and simply the result of local account settling.[9]

This type of nationalization was typical of the Ben Bella régime. The lack of any precise plan, the uncertain content and strategy of the official socialist ideology, meant that nationalization, except in agriculture, continued to be piecemeal. The host of petty confiscations which took the place of attempts to nationalize important sectors of industry was symptomatic of Ben Bella's demagogic style of socialism. It had direct repercussions on *autogestion* which was confined to concerns that were of marginal economic importance.

The first time that workers in the self-managed sector were able to meet outside the limits of their own enterprises was the *Congrès des Fellahs* (agricultural workers) in late October 1963. Although the workers criticized some of the machinery of administration, the open hostility that characterized later congresses was not yet manifest. Ben Bella's speech at the close of the congress foreshadowed one of the ways in which the state was to undermine the basic economic appeal of *autogestion* for the Algerian workers. He warned that the state would have to take part of their income to provide capital for the rest of the country, saying:

In the course of the year to come, the Algerians who have until now been very privileged in the division of the national income will have to make important sacrifices for their less well served brothers. The workers in the agricultural sector [*of autogestion*] will not see their standard of living improve very rapidly.[10]

Although admirable for its egalitarianism, this speech questioned one of *autogestion*'s fundamental attractions for the worker. The economic necessity that had driven the workers to occupy farms and factories still existed. For many of them the promise of a share in the distribution of profits was certainly as important as the democratization of management.[11] On the level of everyday politics Ben Bella was seeking to secure the support of the peasants and unemployed by depicting the workers in *autogestion* as privileged rather than stating a definite policy.

This question of the distribution of profits came to a head in January 1964, when the *comité de gestion* of COBISCAL voted to reinvest their profits rather than share them out among the workers. They were supported in this by the UGTA leadership who claimed that 'the essential idea of *autogestion* is economic and political power' and that the distribution of profits was a form of 'paternalism'. This attitude succeeded in still further isolating the leadership from the mass of workers in the self-managed sector. At the conference of the socialist industrial sector in March the delegate of SOTRAPPA remarked: 'The question of financial stimulus exists even if certain people want to ignore it. Production must be raised by this means. Otherwise it will be slowed down. By ignoring it certain people

The Political Stage, 1963-8

seek to liquidate *autogestion*.' In the end Ben Bella had to intervene on the side of the workers and promised 230 DA to each worker in enterprises that had made a profit and 110 DA to those in the other enterprises. In fact, the workers in only sixty enterprises received this promised share of their profits and it was the last time that profits were ever distributed. Apart from general administrative interference, the question of profit-sharing became one of the main grievances of the workers in both the industrial and agricultural sectors of *autogestion*.

It was at the first conference of the socialist industrial sector in March 1964 that the hostility of the workers to the administration was voiced openly. The conference was called as a prelude to the FLN congress the next month in an attempt to allay the growing hostility among workers and political leaders. There was a widespread dissatisfaction over the continuing economic crisis and Ben Bella's increasingly personal and authoritarian mode of government. At the conference the workers were outspoken in their criticisms of the bureaucracy. The delegate of the *Coopérative Frantz Fanon* said: 'The state apparatus does not correspond to our socialist option. It has to be changed from top to bottom,' and estimated that eighty per cent of all officials were hostile to *autogestion*. The delegate of the *Usine Gabet* at Rélizane echoed this: 'The reactionaries who are impeding our revolution in the highest spheres of the administration must be swept away.'[12] To the workers' increasing hostility to the administration must be opposed the hard line being developed by Boumaza as Minister of Economics. In January he had called for a 'phase of organization'[13] and at a press conference called at the time of the March conference he repeated this call:

It must be repeated continually that the success of the policy of socialization will not be clear and profitable to everyone unless the workers in our nationalized and self-managed enterprises become conscious of their *avant-garde* role, which they can only perform if they extirpate anarchy and develop a spirit of discipline and hard work.[14]

Despite the hardening of its attitudes, the government itself, as opposed to the bureaucracy, was still committed to *autogestion*.

The main event of 1964 was the first, and so far only, congress of the FLN, which was held between 16 and 21 April in Algiers. In face of the growing dissidence of almost all the historic figures of the liberation struggle, Ben Bella was forced to accede to the reiterated demand for a representative meeting of all the opposition factions. By now these included left oppositionists like Ait Ahmed (in the *maquis*), Boudiaf (in exile) and Bachir Hadj Ali of the PCA; liberals like Ferhat Abbas; members of the old GPRA like Ben Khedda, Boussouf and Ben Tobbal; ex-*willaya* leaders like Mohand Ou el-Hadj and Saout el-Arab; and the religious leaders of the Association of the 'Ulemas. Even the army, which had originally supported Ben Bella, was rapidly becoming hostile in face of his attempts to subordinate it to stricter party control. In this situation it was imperative for Ben Bella to hammer out some kind of compromise between himself and the various factions. Otherwise it was likely that he would be faced by an open insurrection far more serious than the FFS rising of the previous year.

However, the crux of the conflict did not lie in these long-established personal animosities and wartime differences. The real political issue facing the Algerian revolution was the deepening class struggle between the emergent bourgeoisie and proletariat. The basic split was over the content and identity of the revolution: between those who believed in a radical Marxist solution to the country's problems and those who emphasized Algeria's specific Islamic and Arabic identity[15] and the need for some form of strict central control. In this struggle Ben Bella was no more than a figurehead. Mohammed Harbi, one of the major theorists of the left-wing group, has been quoted as saying: 'The problem is not what Ben Bella thinks. The problem is whether the congress will be swayed by the army or by us. Ben Bella will then rally to the winning side and be used as a symbol by it.'[16]

Harbi was one of the main authors of the document that was placed before the congress and which, after its acceptance, became known as the *Charte d'Alger*. The *Charte* in its entirety contains a definite internal contradiction. The first sections emphasize the importance of Islam and denounce the impregnation of Arabic culture by Western values. These are implicitly contradicted by the core of the *Charte* which is firmly Marxist and internationalist. The first sections represent a temporarily successful attempt to placate the right-wing factions and lull them into accepting the overt Marxism of the later sections on political, social and economic organization. With the *Charte*, the left wing reached the high point

The Political Stage, 1963-8

of its official influence.* Despite its acceptance by the congress as the theoretical basis of FLN policy, this recognition remained largely formal. Its recommendations were never reflected in government policy under either Ben Bella or Boumédienne. Within Algeria its importance lies in its position as a theoretical rallying point for the opposition to the new middle class. Internationally, it stands as a milestone in the controversy over the development of socialism in the third world.[17]

The *Charte* first takes capitalism in its classical form and analyses it in a traditional Marxist fashion. It then goes on to point out that capitalism has evolved significantly since the nineteenth century. 'It must be analysed according to new categories. It is unthinkable that a historical reality should be eternally submitted to the same analysis. In place of the anarchy of its [capitalism's] origins has been substituted an illusion of rationality.' This new form of capitalism 'is not condemned to death because its machinery must inevitably break down one day'; nor is it any longer characterized by increasing pauperization but instead by the need to increase consumption in order to expand and survive. In fact:

The deepest tendency of modern capitalism leads it, through an ever-increasing concentration of productive forces, to make private property no longer the sole and fundamental economic contradiction. Liberal capitalism has passed and given place to a capitalism where the state plays the greatest role.

This new form of capitalism has created a new social division; one which corresponds to its bureaucratic complexion. This is the separation between those who actually produce and those who manage.

The worker is an anonymous fragment of the machinery of production. He is a person who performs tasks [*exécutant*], from whom the whole significance of his activity has escaped because he has no access to a total vision of the society and because he is excluded from its management.

The orthodox Russian model of socialism is condemned because it has not been able to solve this problem.

It [true socialism] is not purely defined by the nationalization of the means of production. It is mainly defined by self-management: the

* The term 'left wing' here applies to the group responsible for the *décrets de mars* and who used Ben Bella to push through their demands. It does not refer to the PRS or FFS.

Workers' Self-Management in Algeria

only real solution to the double contradiction of private property and the separation between decision-making and decision-execution.

In view of this analysis, *autogestion* is chosen without question as the basic economic and political form of the Algerian revolution.

Autogestion is the basic principle of this society. With it is reached the end of exploitation, and the understanding by each worker of the meaning of his actions because economic and political activities will become inseparable: it is the direct involvement of the producer in production, i.e. the complete opposite of wage labour. With it is realized the beginning of the reign of liberty.[18]

Despite this decision to make Algerian socialism a truly democratic socialism, the authors of the *Charte* warn that the revolution is not yet complete. The means of production are not yet fully socialized and the revolution is not strong enough to achieve this. They envisage a transitional period of watchful toleration of the private sector, similar to the Russian NEP period, while detailed plans are made for total socialization. Inevitably, during this time, it will be necessary to preserve the state as a managerial rather than a fully democratic organ.

The primary task of such a state is to preserve the existing socialist experiences and help them to overcome the inevitable difficulties, to intervene in the private sector to speed up the process of socialization, to make good the lack of direct [workers'] management where it is not yet possible, without ever losing sight of the fact that this exceptional managerial role which it has to assume is only a temporary phase in the preparation of full self-management.[19]

In this discussion the *Charte* rests squarely within the historical argument over the role of the state in a revolutionary society. Its Trotskyist-influenced authors accepted the need to preserve some aspects of the bourgeois state in order to consolidate the revolution – a clear Leninist position, as expounded in *The State and Revolution*. At the same time, in view of the lessons of Stalinism, they were aware of the dangers of the emergence of a bureaucratic and élitist 'caste' in the state and party machinery during this period. This 'caste' not only existed in Algeria in 1964, it was also in the process of becoming a class.

While accepting the premise of the necessity to keep some aspects of the bourgeois state in order to consolidate the revolution, the *Charte* warns of the ever-present danger of the bureaucracy which had already made its appearance since independence.[20] During the transitional phase the 'new society' must continually ask itself certain questions.

Who controls and sanctions the obligation to work? Who establishes the norms? Who controls production? If the solution leads to a separation between the social group [*catégorie sociale*] charged with controlling the work of others and the producers, then socialism is compromised. Only the organized collectivity of the workers can assume this task. Only it can establish plans that are more than artificial schemes only capable of realization on paper. Only it can give a collective solution to a collective problem. That is the meaning of *autogestion*.[21]

To avoid this separation and the consequent erection of a bureaucratic state, the *Charte* demands 'a radical administrative reorganization with the aim of making the commune the basis of political, economic and social organization'.[22]

The authors stress that the main instrument for realizing all these objectives must be the party. They reject 'multipartyism' as a liberal capitalist mystification which submerges and diversifies the interests of the workers by creating a multitude of false problems and divisions.

The choice of a single party system must be made with a clarity and precision that removes all doubts as to its objectives, its social composition and its principles of operation. Lacking this there is a great risk of creating, sooner or later, either a petit-bourgeois dictatorship, or the development of a bureaucratic stratum [*couche*] that will turn the party into an instrument serving its own interests, or a personal dictatorship using the party as a political police.[23]

The party must be an *avant-garde* party based neither on the masses nor on an *élite* of intellectuals and professional politicians. It can only be revolutionary and democratic if it is based on 'the collectivities directly related to production and essential economic activities: the factory, the self-managed farm'.[24] Not only must the party be based on the most advanced sector of the masses – the proletariat; it must also be separated from the state.

To avoid being absorbed by the state the party must be physically distinguished from it. The majority of party cadres must be outside the state machinery and consecrate themselves exclusively to party work. In this way we can avoid the suffocation of the party and its transformation into an administrative auxiliary or an instrument of coercion.[25]

Workers' Self-Management in Algeria

In the context of the controversy over the best mode of economic development for ex-colonial countries, the *Charte* comes down firmly on one side. It sees the immediate solution to unemployment as of paramount importance: for this reason it supports the widespread use of labour power rather than the use of foreign capital for long-term projects involving an advanced technology and using little labour.[26]

Despite its acceptance by the congress, the *Charte d'Alger* remained a dead letter. The Harbi group had no political or social power base from which to push through their programme. They failed to appreciate that, in the absence of the revolutionary *avant-garde* they wished to create, the fulfilment of their programme lay in the hands of the very state and party bureaucracy that they attacked. The fate of the *Charte d'Alger* was to be enshrined alongside the *décrets de mars* as a testament to the endeavours of a small group of intellectuals to donate a radical Marxist theory with Trotskyist overtones to the Algerian revolution. As the official programme of the FLN, the bureaucracy paid it lip-service while quietly ignoring every one of its recommendations.

The congress achieved a temporary unity between the Ben Bella group, Boumédienne and his supporters, and the ex-*willayists*. In return for Boumédienne's continuing support Ben Bella had to accept that nine out of the seventeen members of the *Bureau Politique* should be army men, and that there should be no party cells in the army. To counterbalance the growing power of the military he brought a number of the ex-maquisards, who were hostile to the army, on to the party central committee.

This calm did not last long. In July Colonel Chaabani led his troops at Biskra into armed revolt and Khider, still in exile, openly declared his support for the guerrilla struggle still being waged by Ait Ahmed and the FFS.* The same month, the PRS, FFS and other opposition groups established the *Comité National de Défense de la Révolution* (CNDR) in Paris. In October another of the *chefs historiques*, Rabah Bitat, issued a denunciation of the Ben Bella régime from Paris. The capture of Ait Ahmed and Colonel Chaabani temporarily brought the armed internal resistance to a halt. But Ben Bella was yet again in the position of being isolated from nearly all the original leaders of the FLN, most of whom were in exile, prison

* He declared that the régime was 'slipping dangerously towards fascism and totalitarianism' (*Le Monde*, 8 July 1964).

The Political Stage, 1963–8

or hiding. All his overt opponents had also been eliminated from the second National Assembly elected in September in the face of widespread popular abstention. The summer also marked the end of the influence of the Harbi group when Harbi himself was removed from the editorship of *Révolution Africaine*.

This period also marked a rapid advance in the encroachment of the state on *autogestion*. The regulations of 8 June which reorganized the socialist industrial sector placed the *comités de gestion* under strict financial control. The consolidation of the sector into an effective economic unit which the workers had demanded in the March 1964 conference was undertaken but in such a way that the *comités* lost a significant amount of freedom. The most profitable concerns were put under the direct supervision of the Ministry of the Economy while the others were left to languish. The reorganization marked Boumaza's attempt to impose a more orthodox version of socialist economic organization.* In line with this attitude, large enterprises like the steel plant ACILOR and the glass plant VAN were placed under the direct management of the state and their *comités* reduced to mere consultative organs.

The growing hostility of the workers in *autogestion* towards the administration was stated more clearly than ever before at the founding congress of the *Fédération Nationale des Travailleurs de la Terre* (Agricultural Workers' Federation) in December. Despite the fact that 300 out of the 700 delegates were ONRA officials, the workers' delegates attacked the administration and demanded the correct application of the *décrets de mars*. One demanded that 'the *comités de gestion* be allowed to play their role in complete liberty; and that the officials of ONRA confine themselves to their role of advisers and do not impose themselves as managers of farms'. The final resolutions contained a clear statement of the growing consciousness of the class nature of the struggle with the bureaucracy: they call on the workers to:

Denounce the manoeuvres and plots of the enemies of the working class who are sabotaging the construction of socialism by impeding the operation of *autogestion* either by refusing the socialist sector the cadres it needs or by not allowing self-managed concerns financial autonomy.

Protest against bureaucratic methods which are concentrating the powers of management in the hands of state functionaries, which ought to be in the hands of the organs of self-management.[27]

* See Chapter 4 for a discussion of these regulations.

This experience was repeated at the second congress of the UGTA in March 1965. The split between the base and the leadership imposed by the FLN in January 1963 finally erupted into the open. The report of the leadership on its activities over the previous two years was rejected out of hand. Then, ignoring Ben Bella's wishes, the delegates elected a new, and more representative, leadership. They went on to attack the administration of the self-managed sector, calling for the firm application of the *décrets de mars* and demanding autonomy for the *comités de gestion*. For some sectors of both the urban and agricultural working class this congress marked the dawn of a conscious class opposition to the state. They were becoming aware of the bourgeois nature of the administration and that the FLN, which was closely involved in this administration, was impotent to represent the interests of the workers. From this point the UGTA began to emerge as a shadowy opposition party that was far more representative than personal creations like the PRS and FFS.[28] But there was still a gap between the leaders of the UGTA *centrale* and the base. Because of their exposed position the leaders dared not express the opposition to the growing power of the state that the militants demanded. By 1967 they were as much resented as their predecessors.

The fall of Ben Bella and the creation of the *Conseil de la Révolution* headed by Boumedienne on 19 June 1965 stunned Algeria. The immediate cause of the final breach between these two dominant figures of the Algerian revolution was Ben Bella's dismissal of Foreign Minister Abdelaziz Bouteflika, a close associate of Boumédienne, a few days before the Afro-Asian conference was due to be held in Algiers. This marked the culmination of a series of actions by Ben Bella aimed at excluding Boumédienne's civilian supporters from the government. In the previous July Ben Bella had forced the resignation of two of these supporters – Ahmed Medeghri, Minister of the Interior, and Kaid Ahmed, Minister of Tourism. This was followed by the reduction in the powers of another Boumédienne supporter – Cherif Belkacem, Minister of National Guidance, and in charge of Information, National Education and Youth. In face of this obvious onslaught on the army and its supporters, Boumédienne and a small group of close supporters had Ben Bella arrested and spirited away to an unknown prison.

But to gain any clear understanding of the meaning of Ben Bella's

The Political Stage, 1963-8

fall it is necessary to reject the vulgar interpretation of the popular radical socialist hero deposed by a right-wing militaristic *coup*. In the years following independence Ben Bella had succeeded in clearing most of the original figures of the independence struggle from the political field. His ability to do this lay in his control of the government and the FLN, well established by early 1963, the implicit support of Boumédienne and the army, and in the obvious disunity of his opponents. The losers in this struggle lay on the left (Boudiaf and the PRS, Ait Ahmed and the FFS, Hadj Ali and the PCA), the centre (Khider) and the right (Ahmed Francis, Ferhat Abbas, Ben Khedda). The wide ideological spectrum of the eliminated groups means that this process cannot be taken solely as part of a class-based struggle. It represented the continuation of the factional struggles that had shaken the FLN since its inception. Apart from the moderate right-wing groups, none of the factions had an explicit class base. By centring official revolutionary authenticity on himself as head of the government and party Ben Bella was able to exclude his opponents in the name of this authenticity. With no mass basis of support the various factions were quite unable to oppose this process.

The elimination of nearly all the historic civilian political figures left Ben Bella in a situation of considerable formal power. By the beginning of 1965 he was president of the republic, party secretary general, prime minister, Minister of the Interior, Finance and Information; with the dismissal of Bouteflika he became Foreign Minister as well. This accretion of power left him totally isolated in face of Boumédienne and the army, the only national organization that had so far escaped his control. The gradual exclusion of Boumédienne's supporters from the government gave clear warning of Ben Bella's desire to impose his authority on the army as well. This would have marked the culmination of the elimination of all the original leaders of the FLN.

The purely factional appearance of the disputes leading up to the *coup* must be clearly related to their class nature and that of the *coup* itself. The question must be asked whether the *coup* represented a direct assault by the emerging bureaucratic bourgeoisie on the working class, as many left-wing observers suggested, or whether it was more complex than this.

Among the petit-bourgeoisie and the small classic bourgeoisie, hostility to the overt socialist content of government policy had long been apparent. This group had suffered directly from the sporadic nationalizations of small concerns which Ben Bella had undertaken rather than face a clash with the much more important foreign-owned concerns. Not only was this classic bourgeoisie hostile to socialism but it was closely related to the religious organizations in its condemnation of the West and its emphasis on traditional Islamic values. The economic doctrine of the bourgeoisie had no popular appeal but the emphasis on the traditional culture did, especially when it was taken up by the 'Ulemas. In a clandestine tract issued by Rachid Brahim, president of the Association of the 'Ulemas, in April, this emphasis is made clear:

> The hour is grave. Our country is sliding nearer and nearer to hopeless civil war, an unprecedented moral crisis and insurmountable economic difficulties. Those governing us do not seem to realize that what our people aspire to above all is unity, peace and prosperity, and that the theories which should inspire their actions are to be found not in foreign doctrines but in our Arab-Islamic roots. . . . The hour has at last come for the children of Algeria to gather together to build a city of justice and freedom, a city where God will have his place.[29]

This appeal to a traditional national identity played an important part in the ideology surrounding the *coup* even if these essentially conservative elements were foreign to it.

The prime aim of the leaders of the *coup* was to restore the revolution to what they saw as its original path, emphasizing the role of the peasantry and guerrilla fighters as the real bearers of revolutionary authenticity rather than civilian political figures. They wished to restore the tradition of leadership by a college of equals which had been neglected by the increasingly dictatorial Ben Bella. In terms of its expressed ideology, the *coup* was clearly not anti-socialist; but it shared the 'Ulemas' emphasis on the national specificity of Algeria.

> Algeria is not communist. In neglecting this truth, the previous régime, seeking, for reasons of expediency, the support of the renegades of the PCA before being devoured by them, committed a grave error of judgement. In building the socialist edifice, we will not neglect the support of Marxism. In fact it does not seem possible that a developing country can afford to ignore the economic and scientific aspects of Marxism. But to ignore the inherited traditions of our Arab-Islamic past, to ignore certain aspects of our national culture is to cut Algeria

The Political Stage, 1963–8

off from all that gives her originality, from that which will enable us to realize an authentically revolutionary socialism.[30]

The simultaneous orientation of the *coup* round socialism and nationalism allowed Boumédienne to gain the tacit support of socialists like Boumaza who, as Minister of the Economy, had opposed the radical Marxism of the *pieds-rouges*, as the Harbi group came to be known. The support of the army and most of the bureaucracy, who were similarly opposed to any form of radical socialism, was already a foregone conclusion.

Overt opposition to the *coup* inside Algeria was small and confined mainly to the FLN youth and the students of the *Union Nationale des Étudiants Algériens*. These groups had been fired by Ben Bella's populism and had not experienced the underlying character of his régime. Of far greater importance was the attitude of the UGTA. After eight days of silence it finally issued a statement of lukewarm and conditional support for the *coup*. It noted that Ben Bella's régime had been marked by 'the non-application of democratic centralism, the absence of collegiality, the use of anti-democratic methods'. But it pointed out that 'the way opened up by the events of 19 June is compromised by the presence or return to the political scene of arrivist and opportunist elements who are just as responsible [as Ben Bella] for the non-respect of our institutions'. Beneath the inevitably guarded tones, the UGTA's statement expressed the feelings of the majority of the workers. Under Ben Bella they had experienced the gradual whittling away of the powers accorded them by the *décrets de mars*; nor had their economic situation improved in any way that could compensate for this loss of control. On an immediate level the *coup* had little to do with the class struggle: it was merely a change of leadership while the bureaucratic administration remained unchanged.

Apart from its stunning suddenness, the lack of immediate resistance to the *coup* must be explained by the absence of any organized mass support for Ben Bella. The working class had come to identify him with the state apparatus that was responsible for the erosion of their liberties and had expressed this hostility clearly at the UGTA congress in March. The FLN, although officially headed by Ben Bella, was in no position to come to his defence. It had never been reorganized, either as a mass or *avant-garde* party, and remained largely an adjunct of the state apparatus. The Algiers, Oran and

Annaba sections were fairly loyal to Ben Bella but they had no mass support.* The organized working class had already expressed their extreme disillusion with the FLN. The rest of the population, the unemployed masses and the peasants, were locked in a grinding poverty. Ben Bella's early promises of land and work, which had won him such popular acclaim, had worn thin in face of his total failure to fulfil them. In this situation open opposition was small and the success of the *coup* was never in doubt.†

The 19 June *coup* was not a counter-revolution in a classic sense. It marked a point of rationalization and acceleration of a counter-revolution that had been under way since soon after independence. Under Ben Bella the new middle class had already become firmly entrenched in the state and party apparatus. The achievements of the workers in 1962 had already been eroded significantly. The *coup* was part of a class struggle that was already under way. In this struggle Ben Bella represented a populist mystification; his removal clarified and sharpened its lines.

The new régime took a deeply ambivalent stand over *autogestion*. In its first statements there was a marked hardening of attitudes over economic performance:

> The era of paternalistic *autogestion* is over. . . . No more favouritism. The workers in *autogestion* must pay their enterprise taxes: they will get no more loans; they must pay for the amortization of their capital goods; in a word, they must, in future, run their sector rationally. Only after an experience of this sort can we make a definitive and rational judgement on *autogestion*.[31]

This marked the increasing application of solely economic criteria to *autogestion*. Yet at the same time, Boumédienne was forced to recognize that the workers' grievances against the administration were justified.

> No, the system, such as it has been applied, is nothing but a caricature of *autogestion*. The workers have not in fact been able to participate in management and their financial involvement in production has not passed the stage of promises.[32]

In face of demonstrations and student strikes against the régime in

* Most of the open opposition to the *coup* occurred in Oran and Annaba.
† Hervé Bourges estimates that only fifty people were killed in the immediate aftermath of the *coup*.

The Political Stage, 1963–8

Algiers in January and February 1966, Boumédienne again intervened to allay the fears of the workers.

> We must organize, give more initiative to the workers. *Autogestion* is not only a matter of wages but also the means of involving the workers. For that, we must have the courage to decentralize to the maximum. As for the government, we promise to place more credit and material at the disposition of this sector.[33]

These interventions of Boumédienne became reminiscent of those of Ben Bella. Both heads of state made similar pronouncements designed to demonstrate disapproval of the actions of the state bureaucracy and head off criticisms by the UGTA and workers. They had little relevance to, or effect on, the policy or actions of the administration itself.

One of the most immediate decisions in relation to *autogestion* was the denationalization of a number of small workshops, hotels, cafés and shops. In economic terms this rationalized the socialist sector but it was a clear warning to the workers of what they might expect in the future. It was also a political move, recognizing the implicit support of the petit-bourgeoisie for the *coup*. In fact, despite Boumédienne's promises, little was done to aid the self-managed sector in industry. The creation in April 1966 of the *Banque Nationale d'Algérie* (BNA), as a specific organ of finance for *autogestion*, instead of aiding the *comités de gestion* merely increased the weight of the administrative apparatus.

The ideological orientation of the new régime began to emerge clearly in 1966. In May, with the nationalization of mines, began a series of nationalizations which have led to a state monopoly in transport, banking, insurance, oil distribution, textile production, steel, chemicals and most of the export–import trade as well as a substantial share in oil and natural gas production. These nationalizations were carried out in an orderly spirit far removed from Ben Bella's demagogic denunciations of capitalism, both Algerian and foreign. They were inspired not so much by an explicit ideology of socialism as a nationalist desire to own and control the country's major economic resources. The absence of any large-scale indigenous entrepreneurial bourgeoisie meant in any case that hte economy had to be controlled either by foreign capital or by the state in some form. For the new régime state control was a foregone conclusion, not so much because they were socialists, but because they were nationalists.

Workers' Self-Management in Algeria

It was in the way in which the nationalized or newly created enterprises were organized that the attitude of the new régime became most apparent. They were not formed into *comités de gestion* or directed by the state in the orthodox socialist manner that Boumaza, among others, had advocated. Instead they were formed into *sociétés nationales* patterned closely on the structure of French nationalized enterprises like Renault or the mines. Although the director generals are nominated by the ministry and the *sociétés* are financed by the state (through the *Caisse Algérienne de Développement*) they have juridical autonomy and are free to develop their own investment, production and marketing policies. There is no question of self-management in the *sociétés nationales*; the workers' participation in the management is confined to purely consultative *comités des travailleurs* in each separate production unit and in some of them a central *conseil des travailleurs* which meets once a year to offer advice to the director general.

The summer and autumn of 1966 saw the consolidation in power of the group that firmly believe in this form of state capitalism. In July a number of trade-union leaders were arrested, temporarily putting a stop to open demonstrations of hostility to the régime. In August Hadj Smain, ex-Minister of Reconstruction and Housing, went into exile, followed in September by Ali Mahsas, Minister of Agriculture, and in October by Boumaza, Minister of Information since the *coup*. All of these men, though holding posts under Ben Bella, had acquiesced in the *coup* in the hope that they would be able to continue with their orthodox socialist policies. But after a year it had become apparent that the new group in power under Boumédienne's umbrella had not the slightest sympathy for socialism as an ideology. This new group was composed of Boumédienne's closest supporters – the Oujda group of Boutefika (Foreign Affairs), Medeghri (the Interior), Kaid Ahmed (Finance) and Belkacem (head of the party executive); allied to this group were a number of ex-members of the GPRA, such as Ben Yahia, Lamine Khan and, most importantly, Belaid Abdessalem, the Minister of Industry and Energy. Following the flight of the ministers, Slimane Rebba, the national secretary of the UGTA, also went into exile, in October.

With the elimination of most of the orthodox socialists from the government the way was now open for the state capitalists to open a frontal assault on *autogestion*. A number of large enterprises under

The Political Stage, 1963-8

self-management, such as the *Huileries Modernes d'Alger*, were turned into *sociétés nationales*. Firms under self-management in the construction sector were incorporated into SONATIBA (*Société Nationale des Travaux d'Infrastructure et des Bâtiments*), those in the transport sector were taken over by the SNTR (*Société Nationale des Transports Routiers*). In each case the *comité de gestion* was shorn of all its powers and was reduced to a purely consultative capacity. No official justification for these moves was ever issued, but in a private conversation with a senior official of SONATRACH I was told: '*Autogestion* is a child's dream. The workers will have *autogestion* in twenty or fifty years as a reward for their hard work in the present.' In agriculture the demands of the workers were apparently realized in the disbanding of ONRA which they had long opposed as a bureaucratic monstrosity. The functions of ONRA were distributed among a series of regional and departmental offices of the Ministry of Agriculture. The day-to-day supervision of the *comités de gestion* was handed over to the CCRA which already managed their finances. This was not a decentralization in the interests of democracy, but in the interests of economic efficiency. In fact, despite the disbandment of ONRA, the same officials continued to control the *comités* and were encouraged to do so with even greater thoroughness.

This total rejection of all the tenets of the *décrets de mars* and the *Charte d'Alger* provoked militants of the UGTA and FLN into open opposition. A pamphlet issued by some of these militants early in 1967 criticized the whole administration's attitude to *autogestion* in industry:

The texts relative to the industrial sector [the decrees of 8 June 1964], as well as limiting *autogestion* in this sector, were never even applied. Thus industrial concerns restarted on the workers' initiative were completely abandoned without even a minimum of organization, or technical and financial aid. . . . Thus industrial *autogestion* foundered in agony and gave a pretext for the creation of the *sociétés nationales* which are likely to strangle *autogestion* completely.[34]

In this confrontation with the architects of state capitalism the UGTA had some allies in the government still. One of these was Abdelaziz Zerdani, Minister of Labour. In a speech to the Algiers *locale* of the UGTA in January 1967 Zerdani declared: '*Autogestion* has never been seriously applied: it has even met with a more or less clearly defined hostility among certain organs officially charged with organizing this sector.'[35]

The clash reached a high point in the summer of 1967; a clash totally unmitigated by calls for national unity in face of the Arab-Israeli conflict. In June Abdessalem, the Minister of Industry and Energy, called a conference of the socialist industrial sector without inviting the FLN, the UGTA, workers' representatives or the Press. Complaints about the undemocratic nature of the conference resulted in Abdessalem sacking the top fourteen officials of BERI, Algeria's principal organ of industrial development. A few days later he accused the executive committee of the union in SONATRACH of subversion and dismissed them. This heralded a sustained attack on union officials in the *sociétés nationales*. A general strike was only averted by Boumédienne's personal intervention and the UGTA's reluctance to have recourse to an open struggle. When Zerdani, as Minister of Labour, sent in officials to investigate the trouble he too was accused of subversion by Abdessalem.

Despite the party executive's attempt to stop it, the Algiers *locale* of the UGTA held its own regional conference of the socialist industrial sector in August. Here the total breach between the workers and the party and state became clear. One union official said of the creation of the *sociétés nationales*:

This has alerted the unions not only over this event, which is bad enough in itself, but also over the structure of the *sociétés nationales* which totally ignores the producers. Thus we have a duty to consider an ideological problem: in face of the systematic sabotage of *autogestion* by the administration, the state and the party, the workers must seize back their own rights. We maintain that, in view of the difficulties that we and the workers have experienced, both with the party and the state, we must fall back on our own resources and redress this situation ourselves.[36]

At this point the prospect of the UGTA becoming a clandestine workers' party, rather than just a union which had first emerged at its 1965 congress, had become a near reality. With the party and state in the hands of the new bourgeois *élite* they were forced to fall back on themselves.

With this realization came a redefinition of *autogestion*. It was realized that the restriction of *autogestion* to the economic sphere, and in particular to production, had made it easier for the bureau-

The Political Stage, 1963–8

cracy to seize control of the party and the state. Rather than an explicit form of economic management, *autogestion* became a symbol of the way in which a truly revolutionary society should be organized in its totality. 'In effect, they [the political leaders] saw only the economic side of *autogestion*; while *autogestion* can only be conceived of in its widest sense as a total vision of all that the life of a people ought to be in all its political, economic, social and cultural institutions.'[37] This concept of self-management was further clarified by another delegate at the August conference.

Autogestion is a state of the spirit. It must not be restricted to our economic enterprises. It must flourish in the whole of our activities. It is the development of the human personality in all its diversity and unity. It is a way of thinking and acting, of posing and resolving problems in common at every stage.[38]

This restatement represents a move away from the economistic Marxism that characterized its early protagonists. It became a revolutionary symbol rather than an organizational prescription.

The political tensions of 1967 reached their culmination in a military rising against Boumédienne in December. In the autumn, Ali Yahia, the Minister of Agriculture, had resigned over the refusal of Kaid Ahmed, the Minister of Finance, to give financial aid to the *comités de gestion*. In this growing atmosphere of crisis the ex-*willaya* leaders who had initially supported the *coup* demanded a meeting of the *Conseil de la Révolution* to explain why the Oujda group and the ex-GPRA politicians held a monopoly of political and administrative power in the state and party. This was refused as the guerrillas were in a majority on the *Conseil*. On 11 December Kaid Ahmed was put in charge of the FLN replacing the old executive that contained several ex-*willaya* leaders. In face of the obvious intent to exclude the former guerrilla leaders from power, Colonel Tahar Zbiri, army chief of staff, led an armed rising against the régime in the Mitidja on 14 December, but by the 16th it had been contained. The majority of the ANP was loyal to Boumédienne and all the key posts were held by the younger professionals. Zbiri escaped and was joined in hiding by Zerdani, the Minister of Labour. Other former guerrilla leaders, like Mohand Ou el-Hadj, Salah Boubidner and Katib Youcef, also went into hiding.

Zbiri's defeat and the elimination of the guerrilla chiefs from the party marked the end of an era in Algerian politics. By the beginning of 1968 all the original civilian and guerrilla leaders of the revolt against colonialism had been excluded from power and were in exile, prison or hiding.* Besides Boumédienne himself, the political victors of the factional struggles that had shaken the country since independence were those who had made their early careers with the ANP† or who had held subordinate posts in the GPRA. But in terms of the class struggle which had replaced the fight for independence, the real victors were the bureaucratic *élite*. This new middle class had finally triumphed over the early radical achievements of the revolution. Control of the means of production, as well as of the party and state apparatus, now lay firmly in their hands. *Autogestion* existed in name only. The *'option socialiste'* had been reduced to state capitalism. The losers in this phase of the struggle were not only the working class but the unemployed and the peasants. The working class, enfeebled by its small size and its cultural and economic isolation, was driven back into a purely defensive posture in the face of the sheer strength of the bureaucracy and army. The counter-revolution that had been accelerated by the 1965 *coup* was now, to all intents, complete.

The final event in this process came at the third UGTA congress in May 1969. In October 1968, Kaid Ahmed, the general secretary of the FLN, called a conference of union cadres to discuss a new party document on the reorganization of the unions. This document was the long-awaited assault on the policies, actions and leadership of the UGTA.

The leading bodies of the trade unions have been under the influence of elements imbued with out-of-date principles based on a narrow concern with wages and working conditions and class struggle.[39]

It accused the post-1965 leadership of the UGTA of openly flouting the FLN's authority and of frightening away foreign capital rather than encouraging it to come and participate. It emphasized that the task of the unions was to support the government without reserve and demanded that the old leadership should be thrown out at the coming congress. In relation to this, the events at the 1963 congress, when Khider threw out the then UGTA leadership, were referred to.

* None of the original members of the CRUA held any position of power in Algeria at this point.
† Bouteflika, Kaid Ahmed, Cherif Belkacem, Medeghri.

The Political Stage, 1963–8

The party had to intervene to prevent a syndicalist deviation which would have had serious consequences. In the conditions of the time there was no democracy it [the party] was bound to respect except that based on revolutionary legitimacy and the higher interest of the nation.[40]

In the 'higher interest of the nation' the 1965 leadership was duly thrown out by a congress packed by Kaid Ahmed's 'gorillas' and the document was adopted in full. The UGTA centres at Algiers and Skikda, both traditional centres of militancy, were dissolved. The UGTA itself was once more under firm state and party control.

8

THE BUREAUCRATIC EMPRISE ON THE *COMITÉS*

IN the previous chapter I outlined the public and political conflict over the form and content of the Algerian revolution, describing it as a class struggle ending in victory for the bureaucratic *élite*. Apart from the personal aspects of this conflict, it centred on the question of the control of the means of production, of the party and of the state. With the seizure of the means of production by the workers, the creation of *comités de gestion* and their formal institutionalization in the *décrets de mars*, the revolution committed itself to the management of the means of production by the workers. Despite the formal acceptance of the *Charte d'Alger*, this principle was never extended to the administrative superstructures of the economy, to the party or the state. There was thus an innate contradiction between a system of production formally controlled by the workers and an administration that totally escaped their control: an administration which, as we have seen, was largely composed of officials who had served under colonialism and by arrivist and opportunist elements who had used independence to achieve rapid upward mobility. Nor was this bureaucracy effectively counterbalanced by an *avant-garde* party. The FLN and the state administration rapidly became homogeneous in both content and ideology.

The elaboration of the administrative superstructures of *autogestion* played directly into the hands of this bureaucracy. The architects of the *décrets de mars* felt that if *autogestion* were to be successful economically it needed to be organized and unified at a level higher than the individual enterprise. They also feared that the *comités* were not strong enough, politically or economically, to combat either the development of an indigenous entrepreneurial bourgeoisie or the possible return of the settler bourgeoisie. To solve these problems they aimed to strengthen the *comités* by placing them under the protective guidance of the state. Objectively, this coincided with the

The Bureaucratic Emprise on the Comités

desire of the more orthodox socialists, like Boumaza, for greater central control to combat the alleged ouvrierist tendencies of the *comités*. Neither of these groups can be accused of actively wishing to suppress *autogestion*. The Harbi group accepted it implicitly but wished it to develop under the guidance of a revolutionary *avant-garde*; while Boumaza wished to place it under the temporary control of the state until full socialization had been achieved.

The immediate effect of both of these theories was to contain *autogestion* in the sphere of production. In the absence of any radical reconstitution of the party or state this containment placed the *comités* firmly under the control of the existing bureaucracy. The ensuing unequal struggle between the *comités* and the bureaucracy ended in victory for the new middle class. We have seen how this struggle developed in terms of the public clashes on the political stage. It is now time to look at some of the ways in which, almost from the very beginning, the administration was able to contain, control and subordinate the *comités*.

ELECTORAL MANIPULATION

One of the clearest ways in which self-managed concerns lost their independence was by widespread manipulation in the formation of *comités de gestion* and the election of their members. This was directed to ensuring the existence of *comités* that owed their primary loyalty to the administration rather than to the workers.

In the original occupations of the summer and autumn of 1962 the *comités de gestion* were formed by mutual consent rather than through the process of a formal election. The workers continued to operate their concerns much as they had been under colonialism. The *comités* were not well-defined bodies with specific structures and responsibility. They were *ad hoc* gatherings of the most skilled or experienced workers. Often they included all the workers who wished to participate in the discussions. While many of them were extremely democratic, inevitably some were controlled by an oligarchy of senior workers, representing the hierarchy of authority that had existed under private ownership.

Faced with the existence of *comités* in a large number of agricultural and industrial concerns, and having no immediate alternative means of management, Ben Bella's government introduced legislation to place a *comité* in every abandoned European concern (the decrees of 22 October dealing with agriculture, and 23 November, dealing with industry and mining). Even before this the government had tacitly recognized their existence. On 10 October the Ministry of the Interior had sent telegrams to all prefects, asking them to ensure priority for ex-combatants in any elections to the *comités*. This was the first step in the long series of administrative interventions in the operation of the *comités*. The government acted on the reasoning that the ex-combatants were not only more seasoned militants but also deserved some reward for their sacrifices. As we have already seen, in Chapter 3, this gave rise to an intense hostility between the permanent workers and the ex-combatants.

It is clear that the intermediate elections in October and November 1962 were extensively interfered in by the administration. Daniel Guérin gives evidence of an agricultural estate – Domaine Sainte Louise – at Ameur-el-Ain where the election was manipulated by the army and the local prefect.[1] Estier emphasizes that the *comités de gestion* set up after October were not elected but appointed by the local administration.[2] Temmar goes even further and states that those enterprises which did not have *comités* by October were managed by the *sous-préfectures* until May 1963.[3]

Thus, at the point when the *décrets de mars* were introduced, the *comités* had already experienced administrative interference. The government was aware of this and began a campaign for new and proper elections in May 1963. In a speech inaugurating the 'National Campaign for the Democratic Reorganization of Self-Management Bodies' Ben Bella acknowledged this problem and promised reforms.

Today, with the campaign we are launching for the reorganization of self-management bodies, we offer yet another proof of our determination not to let the *décrets de mars* 1963 become dead letters or self-management a ritual, empty of all democratic and effective content. Up to now, some *comités de gestion* have, by force of circumstances, been nominated from above. There have often been bogus *comités* that the workers do not accept but reject. We are determined to remedy that.

He went on to urge workers to 'elect those brothers and sisters that have your confidence, whom you consider the most fitted, the most energetic, so as to get the farms and factories running at their best'.[4]

Even after this campaign the number of democratically elected *comités* in agriculture remained low. Many of the new *comités* were,

The Bureaucratic Emprise on the Comités

in fact, appointed by local officials of the newly created ONRA.[5] Out of forty-one estates in the Dar el Beida district only six had elected *comités*; while in the Mitidja only forty out of 250 estates had real elections.[6] One observer was driven to remark: 'The conditions of the election allow us to state that in reality at most 10 to 15 per cent of the *comités de gestion* have been elected in a democratic manner by the *assemblée générale*.'[7]

In the rural areas the local branch of the FLN, the *sous-préfet* and ONRA officials very often worked together to secure the formation of a *comité* that would accept their control. They were able to do this for several reasons. The high level of illiteracy cut the vast majority of agricultural workers off from the campaigns to explain the *décrets de mars*. Not only was their level of consciousness generally lower than that of the workers in the towns but they had not yet been organized into a union by the UGTA. Owing to the physical distances involved, UGTA and FLN militants who were trying to ensure democratic elections were unable to reach all the farms. In the absence of any alternative the workers succumbed to the traditional local authorities. In the towns a much larger percentage of the *comités* were correctly elected. The greater political awareness of the workers and the presence of the UGTA kept administrative interference to a minimum. But even here there were a large number of cases of manipulation. Two cases, of which I have personal knowledge, will suffice as examples.

In December 1964, four abandoned road haulage firms were amalgamated into one concern, *Transports Sidi M'Hamed*, based in Algiers with some 100 employees and fifty vehicles. The *comité de gestion* was appointed by the *Office National des Transports* (ONT). In August 1967 when all the self-managed firms were incorporated into a *société nationale* (the SNTR) this body of five men was still the *comité de gestion* and continued to be the *comité d'entreprise* under he SNTR. The case of the *Coopérative Frantz Fanon* is even more revealing of the methods employed by the administration. The cooperative, which included several painting, decorating and printing concerns run by a central *comité*, ran into financial difficulties in 1965. On investigation this proved to be mainly due to a debt of 600,000 DA owed it by various government departments. However, the situation was used by the Ministries of Finance and Industry to put in their own financial and technical 'experts'. The old *comité* was charged with being incapable of fulfilling its responsibilities and a new election was ordered. In this, only one list of candidates, drawn up by the administration, was put before the workers.

The *décrets de mars* stipulated that one-third of the *conseil des travailleurs* and the *comité* should be re-elected every year. Technically the responsibility for holding elections lies with the *préfectures*, but they have not acted. Since the original campaign for elections in May 1963 very few elections for the renewal of *comités* have ever been held. Thus the majority of concerns have the same *comité* as they had when they were placed under *autogestion*.

One example of this in industry is COBISCAL, a cooperative of twelve production units producing biscuits, cakes, etc. in the Algiers region. It contains eight separate *comités de gestion* whose presidents, the state-appointed director and his assistant, form a central *comité d'administration*. The particular *comité de gestion* in question groups three production units with 160 workers. The main unit was sabotaged and then abandoned by its European owners. In 1963 it was re-opened by five men who had repaired the machines with a small government grant. These five became the *comité de gestion*. With the exception of one who had resigned, the same men were still in office in the summer of 1967. There had never been any elections nor had a *conseil des travailleurs* been formed, as stipulated by the *décrets de mars*. Despite the undoubted economic success of the *comité* (between July 1966 and 1967 they raised production by eighty per cent) their continued occupation of the functions of management represented a common problem for *autogestion*.

The *décrets de mars* stipulated partial annual elections with the intention of avoiding the development of a self-perpetuating bureaucracy within *autogestion*. (The implications of the development of this 'factory bureaucracy' are discussed in the next chapter.) It was also felt to be important that as many workers as possible should have experience of management problems so as to raise their consciousness and technical skills. In the case of COBISCAL the workers felt that they could not elect a better *comité*. But there are a large number of self-managed concerns where the workers actively desire the renewal of *conseils* and *comités*, especially where these were not elected in the beginning. The fact that *comité* elections have not been held on a national level since May 1963 allowed the administration to strengthen their hold over many *comités*. It has also

The Bureaucratic Emprise on the Comités

meant that many workers have become disillusioned with the whole concept of *autogestion*. The UGTA, while calling for new elections, could not be sure whether the growing strength of the administration might not make it even easier for it to manipulate elections.

There are even more glaring examples of the abuse of the spirit of the *décrets de mars*. In some cases the local administration was strong enough to render the *comité* completely superfluous to the management of the enterprise. The *Entreprise de Filature et Tissage de Tlemcen* was nationalized in 1963. Its previous owner, an Algerian, was then appointed as state director. Although formally under *autogestion*, the firm continued to be managed in exactly the same fashion as previously. The *comité* was powerless to effect any real changes in the organization of the firm or even to fulfil its legal role.*

The appointment of the original owner as director is unusual; but it does show the extent to which the socialist ideology contained in the *décrets de mars* was being deformed even as early as 1963. A more common abuse was that concerning the decree on *biens-vacants*, which states that they should be managed by a *comité de gestion*. However, as the administrative opposition to *autogestion* increased the formation of *comités de gestion* became a rare occurrence. The more usual course of action was to place the firm under state control and manage it in the same way as before. An example of this is the firm *Éts Veuve Cote*, one of Algeria's largest paint and household chemical manufacturers with wholesale and retail outlets in the Algiers region. The workers, prompted by the UGTA, carried out a series of strikes aimed at forcing the European owner to leave. When the owner finally left in 1966, the workers were promised that the firm would re-open under *autogestion* and they elected a *comité de gestion*. Instead, the ministry appointed a *commissaire* to run the firm and demoted the *comité de gestion* to a *comité d'entreprise* with purely consultative powers. The *commissaire* continued to run the firm as it had been under the ex-owner and refused to deal with the *comité* or even to allow a trade-union committee (*section syndicale*) to be formed.

Since the Boumédienne *coup*, an infinitesimal number of concerns have been placed under *autogestion*. Those that have are small and under-capitalized and hence of no great economic importance.

* In 1967 this firm was amalgamated with other textile firms into the *société nationale* SONACO.

Placing them under *autogestion* enables the government to abnegate any responsibility for making them profitable. As I described in the previous chapter, the policy since 1966 has been to create *sociétés nationales*, incorporating newly nationalized concerns, those originally under *autogestion*, and new factories built by the state. I have already outlined the general extent of workers' representation in the *sociétés nationales*, but there are great variations in this scheme. Almost invariably these variations represent the strength and determination of the workers and unions to oppose the bureaucratic encroachment on their liberties. They represent a defensive rearguard struggle to prevent all the achievements of 1962 being swept away.

In most of the *sociétés nationales* formed to manage newly created industries like textiles (SONITEX) there is no workers' representation in the organs of management. There is only a rather weak *section syndicale* or union shop-floor committee. In these new industries there were no extant organs of participation or self-management which could form the nucleus of any organized representation. The creation of even a *section syndicale* in many of the new industries is extremely difficult. The factories are often built in rural areas, employing landless ex-peasants for whom this is often the first experience of industrial employment and where there are few traditions of this basic type of class organization. The existence of a vast mass of unemployed in the surrounding areas also effectively reduces the likelihood of any real militant action by those who have employment.

The *Société Nationale des Tabacs et Allumettes* (SNTA) was created in 1964 to manage tobacco and match production which had just been nationalized by Ben Bella. Because the sector was felt to be of national importance it was not placed under self-management, an example of the early deviation from the spirit of the *décrets de mars*. There are no organs of direct workers' participation in management. Instead, the workers are represented by elected union delegates on the *conseil d'administration*, the central management body for the various factories that make up the SNTA. In each separate factory the union delegates meet the director every week for formal discussions. The delegates who are elected, under UGTA supervision, by the workers each year, have the right to be informed on all aspects of managerial decisions: profits, sales, investments,

The Bureaucratic Emprise on the Comités

redundancies, etc. The union was already in a relatively strong position before nationalization and was able to maintain this. The UGTA, after 1965, felt that the direct connection of the delegates with the union meant that they were less likely to be intimidated than purely worker representatives.

The *sociétés nationales* created out of the amalgamation of enterprises under *autogestion* generally contain a *comité d'entreprise* in each unit and a *conseil des travailleurs* at the centre. The *conseil* plays the mainly consultative role accorded it under the French law of 22 February 1945. Here, as for example in building (SONATIBA) or road transport (SNTR), it was impossible for the administration to reduce participation below this level. The workers had experienced up to five years of self-management and opposition to any reduction in their powers was very strong. Where the administration attempted to disband the *comité de gestion* completely without allowing any measure of participation they met with serious opposition. At the *Verreries de l'Afrique du Nord* (VAN) the government attempted to do this and the management was faced with a long series of strikes. Eventually they had to capitulate and agree to the formation of a *comité d'entreprise*. In these cases, although the workers and the union had no hope of preventing the disbandment of self-management, they were strong enough to maintain some degree of participation in management decisions.

The highest degree of participation in any *société nationale* is in the SNCFA (*Société Nationale des Chemins de Fer Algériens*). Before independence, the railway workers, organized by the CGT, had been one of the best organized and most militant sectors; this tradition was continued by the *Fédération des Cheminots* of the UGTA. The scheme of participation in operation in the SNCFA is called *cogestion* (co-management) by union officials. The SNCFA is divided up into three services corresponding to its technical and financial organization: permanent way and buildings, rolling stock and locomotives, and the actual operation of the system. At the local level, each service has a *comité local*, made up of three workers' representatives, three administration representatives and a chairman who is the local manager of the service. At the regional level there is a *comité régional* for each service with six representatives from each side and the regional manager as chairman. The workers' representatives for both these committees are elected at the same time by a secret ballot organized by the union. At the centre there is a *comité central* for each service with twelve representatives from either side and a chairman. The workers' representatives on the central committee are elected at the union's regional congresses but are not full-time union officials. This high degree of participation is due both to the strong traditions of organization in the industry, maintained by the *Fédération des Cheminots* after independence, and to the fact that it was set up in 1963 in the period of official enthusiasm for *autogestion* and participation.

During the rapid demise of *autogestion* after 1965 the ability of the workers to wrest some degree of managerial control from the state depended largely on the strength of their organization. In almost every case this came to mean the strength of union organization. In the *sociétés nationales* and firms run directly by the state the union began to assume the functions of representing the workers as the conflict began to develop into a straight clash between two classes. This process is illustrated by the case of the *Société Algérienne des Boissons* in Algiers, in 1967 the only large state-owned manufacturer of soft drinks and beer. In 1966 the French owner of the firm left the country, owing 2·5 million DA in unpaid taxes. This device has been employed by many of the European capitalists to realize as much profit as possible before leaving. Often in such cases the government, since 1965, has sold the enterprise in order to recoup the taxes. Here the workers, who were well organized, demanded nationalization. The state acceded to this and appointed a state director who refused to consider any form of workers' participation. Faced by this, the workers operated a go-slow and demanded a new director. Specifically they asked for a man who had been a UGTA official until he was implicated in the 1963 FFS rising. In face of a reduction in production from 60,000 to 5,000 bottles a day the state gave in to this demand.

As the state refused to allow the firm to become self-managed, the new director, with the full support of the UGTA, turned the *section syndicale* into a form of *comité de gestion*. The *section syndicale*, consisting of five members, is elected by all the workers. It meets every week with the director to discuss and decide on all management questions. This form of management by the union is unusual but, like the formation of *sections syndicales* in other state-controlled firms, it represents a tactical improvisation by the UGTA. Unlike other

The Bureaucratic Emprise on the Comités

forms of representation it is under direct union supervision and cannot be manipulated by the administration so easily. Forced by the increasingly overt class character of the administration and its evident desire to put an end to *autogestion*, the UGTA was seeking to replace the isolated *comités* of separate concerns by bodies which received their coherence through being organized in class terms.

Firms under *autogestion* have not only been integrated into *sociétés nationales* or placed under direct state control; there are numerous cases of denationalization or the complete disbandment of the machinery of self-management. In some cases denationalization was a result of the widespread corruption prevalent in the administration; in others it stemmed from a desire to subordinate the political connotations of *autogestion* to the demands of a technocratic economic rationality.

A well-documented case of attempted denationalization due to corruption is that of the *Entreprise Ben Badis* at Rouiba, a firm making agricultural machinery.[8] A *bien-vacant*, the firm re-opened under *autogestion* in August 1964; but it was in competition with the private, French-owned firm SACRA. In March 1966, the director of Ben Badis asked that his firm be merged with SACRA as a mixed, state–private concern, because he could not compete with it. In November 1966, a government enquiry found that the managing director and sales director of SACRA had bribed Ministry of Agriculture officials and the director of Ben Badis in an attempt to get hold of the firm. (The extent of corrupt practices in the administration is described more fully in the next chapter.) The paper of the PRS – *Sous le Drapeau du Socialisme* – gives another instance.[9] Ministers Medeghri, Abdesselam and Bouteflika tried to give some farms under *autogestion* in the Oranais to some middle-class friends early in 1966. The public outcry raised by the UGTA forced Boumédienne to intervene and return the farms.

Denationalization immediately after the 1965 *coup* affected some quite large concerns such as the *Coopérative Ouvrière Aissat Idir*, which was centred round Blida. In Blida itself the cooperative contained a butcher, a fruit market, furniture shop, ironmonger, stationer, chemist, a garage, a hotel, a soft-drinks factory, a brick works and several small farms. At Boufarik, twenty kilometres away, there was a building concern and a paint workshop; fishermen at Bou Harroun, Chifalo and Castiglione were also members of the cooperative. In all, the cooperative involved some 1,500 workers. There were four *comités de gestion*, one for each sector – agricultural, food, mechanical and building – headed by a *conseil d'administration*, elected by the *comités*. In strict economic terms the cooperative was unwieldy, embracing so many activities. As a political experiment in social and economic integration it was one of the most successful examples of *autogestion*. On state orders, many of the small concerns were sold or returned to their original owners; the rest were integrated into the various state sectors for agriculture, industry, building and fisheries. The breaking up of the cooperative, which had been founded on the initiative of the UGTA, gave clear evidence of the administration's fear of the implications of the successful local organization of production and distribution by workers acting entirely outside the state. As a political and social experiment it threatened not only the power of the administration but, implicitly, its whole *raison d'être*.

Another organization that was disbanded and suffered from denationalization or integration into the state sector was the *Comité de Gestion des Hôtels et Restaurants* (COGEHORE). COGEHORE was composed of some fifty-five hotels, restaurants and cafés, with a central food and equipment store, distribution organization and administrative offices employing, in all, 800 workers. There was a central *comité de gestion*, elected by a *conseil des travailleurs*, composed of one representative from each establishment. In 1964 Kaid Ahmed, then Minister of Tourism and one of Boumédienne's close supporters, had tried to supress COGEHORE but had been prevented by Ben Bella and forced to resign. In 1966 it was finally disbanded, the smaller concerns sold and the larger, like the Hotel Albert Premier, put under the direct control of the Ministry of Tourism. The internal organization of COGEHORE was not specifically democratic and did not accord with the *décrets de mars*. But this deviation was not a motive for its disbandment. As in the case of the *Coopérative Aissat Idir*, a strictly economistic argument was applied and relatively unimportant units returned to the private sector. But again, objectively, the existence of an integrative organization of even a minor sector by workers' representatives undermined the role of the administration.

In agriculture, apart from a few scandals like the one mentioned above, there have been relatively few denationalizations as such;

The Bureaucratic Emprise on the Comités

while the successful manipulation of *comité* elections and strict financial control by the administration has avoided the need for any overt state control. However, in an undisclosed number of cases estates under *autogestion* have been broken up and distributed to ex-combatants, particularly after 1965. An example of this is the Domaine Zair Houari at El Ançor, which was placed under *autogestion* after the nationalization of the remaining European lands in October 1963. In the autumn of 1966 it was taken over by the army and turned into a *Coopérative Agricole d'Anciens Moudjahidins* (ex-combatants). The *comité de gestion* was dissolved and most of the permanent workers forced to leave. The estate was then split up into smaller units, each of which was given to an ex-combatant. The way in which the army took over farms at independence has already been described in Chapter 3. Since the Boumédienne *coup* the army has had a relatively free hand in this type of operation. The underlying rationale is that the *anciens moudjahidins*, who fought for independence at the cost of losing their land in the traditional sector, should be rewarded for their services. Economically, the dismemberment of large integrated estates into small units has meant a loss in productivity. Politically, it has involved the strategic placing of groups whose first loyalty is to the army.

Aside from imposing its control first by electoral manipulation and then by the outright dissolution of *comités de gestion*, the administration was able to circumscribe the operation of self-management by the use of economic mechanisms. The main charge levelled against *autogestion* was its apparent economic failure. As this was used as the rationale for imposing state control or reducing the powers of the *comités* it is necessary to look at the realities of the situation. This is not to share the economistic ideology of the new bureaucratic *élite* but to examine how far the *comités* can be held responsible for any economic failure, and how far it was, in fact, the responsibility of the administration itself.

We have already seen how the colonial economy was characterized by increasing stagnation in terms of output, under-capitalization, a sectorial imbalance away from industry and an almost total reliance on the metropolis. Independence, on its own, did not change any of these basic characteristics. The socialized sector of the economy was faced not only with these problems but also with competition from an internal private sector, financed from abroad and with competition on a world market dominated by international capitalism. This sector, which in the beginning was represented by the *biens-vacants*, was extremely ill-fitted to meet such competition. The almost total absence of liquid capital made it difficult to exploit the capital represented by plant, buildings and labour force. The enterprises under *autogestion* were also faced with a widespread disruption of the normal commercial circuits and a desperate lack of trained technical personnel.

The administrative and economic superstructures created in an *ad hoc* fashion out of the ruins of the colonial mechanisms were aimed at offsetting some of these problems by providing capital, financial and technical expertise, and by organizing the supply of raw materials and the sales of finished products.* In terms of the stated ideal to create a planned socialist economy it was also felt important to integrate the individual *comités* into a coherent national economic structure. In their ideal form the superstructures were supposed to prevent any tendency to ouvrierism. Harbi referred to this when he wrote: 'In the beginning and in the spirit of the decrees [the *décrets de mars*] this element of state property was destined to avoid the appearance of economic units turned in on themselves and acting independently of the general economic context. In sum, it was necessary to close the way to all group egoism.'[10] In this schema the *avant-garde* elements in the administration would benevolently guide the *comités* into the right economic and ideological paths, only actively interfering if state laws were broken.

The reality was very different. At first the economic supervisory organs were merely incompetent. But as time went on they arrogated so great a degree of control as to make the economic independence of the *comités* derisory. The exact nature of the administration's role and its relationship to the *comités* was never clearly defined. As a result the bureaucracy was able to extend its control unchecked by any legal considerations. Economically, their stranglehold over *autogestion* appeared in three main sectors: finance, marketing and provision of raw materials.

I have already described how, in agriculture, the accounts of the *comités* were first of all held by the *Sociétés Agricoles de Prévoyance* (SAP), then by the *Centres Coopératifs de la Réforme Agraire* (CCRA) and since the dissolution of ONRA by the *Caisses Régionales*

* See the description of these superstructures in Chapter 4.

The Bureaucratic Emprise on the Comités

de Crédit (CRC). In industry, funds were first held by the local prefect, then by the *Banque Centrale* (BCA) and then by the *Banque Nationale* (BNA). Practically, this has meant that the administration not only holds all the funds, but keeps the accounts and itself pays for all financial transactions of the *comités*, including, at times, wages. The *comités* are allowed a small amount of petty cash for day-to-day needs only.

The administration often justified such a total control of finance by pointing out the absence of trained book-keepers in the *comités*. However, this control led to the *comités* having no real idea of their financial position and even to the loss of the idea of value – so essential in what is still a market economy. Under ONRA it was even known for the CCRA to refuse requests by *comités* to see their accounts.[11] As one commentator stated: 'The workers will never have effective control without any objective, detailed, complete and almost day-to-day knowledge of the accounts of the enterprise.'[12]

In financial terms, this strict control by the administration means that the economic future of the enterprise is no longer in the hands of the workers. This is especially true in the field of credits or loans to individual enterprises. Most of the *comités* in the re-opened *biens-vacants* were faced with two immediate problems: sabotaged machinery and lack of liquid capital. There was a great need for credit, not just to finance long-term programmes but merely to make immediate production possible. The *comités* were allowed to borrow from state or private sources, but the continued refusal of the state to agree to loans forced many *comités* to borrow from private sources at high rates of interest. In 1965, only ten out of 400 *comités* applying were given loans from the BCA or CAD.

The effect this can have is illustrated by the case of a small furniture factory (ex-Caramelino). The European owner left Algeria in January 1965, leaving 150,000 DA in unpaid taxes and having illegally transferred all the liquid assets to France. In February 1965 a *comité de gestion* was formed under the guidance of the UGTA. They asked for a loan from the BCA but were informed that they must present accounts showing a profit or near profit for three years of operation. The lack of liquid capital meant that they were often unable to purchase raw materials, and more importantly, could not give credit to customers who naturally turned to the private sector. In addition, although their speciality is bunk beds for institutions, the state has given its contracts to private firms. They were also refused permission to join the *Union Départementale des Industries du Bois* (UDIBA), the 'horizontal union' for their sector (see Chapter 4) which would have provided an integrated purchasing and marketing organization. The reason for this was that, after 1966, only profitable firms were incorporated into UDIBA. By July 1967 their debt to the state had risen to 300,000 DA as they could not afford to pay taxes.

This case exposes the situation of many of the smaller firms under *autogestion*. The *comité* was caught in a total impasse: unable to make a profit without a loan and unable to get a loan without a profit. By applying abstract financial criteria the administration effectively blocked the development of whole areas of the socialist sector. The short-sightedness of this economic rationale is shown by the fact that the enterprise is still a cost to the state in respect of the unpaid taxes.*

Besides this crippling financial control, many self-managed firms in industry suffered from a lack of state aid in competing with the more highly capitalized private sector. A clear example of this was the *Huileries Modernes d'Alger* (ex-Tamzali) which produced olive oil. This self-managed firm was in competition with a French-owned firm, Lesieur, which also had a near monopoly in imported soap. Lesieur managed to get wholesalers to stock their olive oil rather than HMA's by offering cheap soap as well. HMA asked the Ministry of Industry for permission to produce soap in order to meet this competition. But in March 1966, after two years, the Ministry allowed Lesieur to produce, as well as import, soap and become the official government supplier. In 1967 the *comité de gestion* at HMA was dissolved and the firm put under central control as a *société nationale*.

The experience of HMA was repeated with ALUMAF, the only firm in the socialist sector producing aluminium goods. It produces aluminium disks and household articles using imported Russian aluminium. ALUMAF was in competition, in terms of finished goods, with a private firm, ALLAL, which used to buy the blanks produced by ALUMAF. In 1966, ALLAL started to buy blanks from Canada, even though the price difference was marginal. The government, despite repeated requests, refused to make use of its

---

* The fact that ex-Caramelino held annual elections for its *comité* and *conseil* added a political tone to its victimization.

The Bureaucratic Emprise on the Comités

import controls to force ALLAL to buy from ALUMAF, which, as a result, had to lay off workers. In both these cases the government was clearly favouring foreign-owned private firms at the expense of the socialist sector.

The administration's financial stranglehold over the *comités de gestion* was repeated in the organization of sales and the provision of capital goods and raw materials. This was especially true in agriculture where the *comités* were, and are, totally dependent on the state marketing organizations to realize their income. The *Office National de Commercialisation* (ONACO) through its subsidiary offices, the *Coopératives Régionales Agricoles* (CORA), is responsible for marketing all the agricultural produce of the *comités*. In the beginning, these organs manifested such incompetence that many *comités* were driven to sell their products to private buyers, which led to the realization of vast profits at the *comités*' expense. In the summer of 1963, a *comité* at Pérégaux, seeing that its vegetable produce would rot while waiting for the administration to deal with it, organized an auction. This was attended by European buyers who set up a ring, bought the products for 46 million AF and later sold them for 200 million AF.

After experiences of this kind, sales to the private sector were technically forbidden. The workers demanded that they be allowed to control the marketing organizations. 'We, the peasants and workers in *autogestion*, are convinced that we shall not be able to get out of our present difficulties and go forward unless the CORA and ONACO are in our hands, as production is already.'[13] This radical demand for direct workers' control of distribution as well as production was inevitably refused, and despite criticism of ONACO from all sides of the country, their difficulties remained unsolved.[14] In 1966, the UGTA paper *Révolution et Travail* noted that when products were delivered at the CORA they were often invoiced for less than was in fact delivered, resulting in a loss of income to the *comités*.[15] In 1967, the situation was so bad owing to low fruit prices paid by ONACO (far lower than world prices) that *comités* were forced to mortgage the next year's harvest in order to pay workers' wages. Some *comités* were even led to risk selling products on the black market in the attempt to raise money for wages and immediate expenses. In July 1967, 100 workers from one self-managed estate were arrested for this offence.

Workers' Self-Management in Algeria

The administrative control over the provision of machinery and spare parts caused great difficulties in agriculture. The problem was not so great in industry since the administration had no direct control over such matters. One perennial problem was the provision of tractors which were often held by the administration and hired out to *comités de gestion*. At the October 1963 congress of agricultural workers, the delegate of the Chena M'hand *comité de gestion* at Akbou stated: 'The SAP holds all the machinery and finances. We hope that the enterprise will be given its own machinery and have money to make its own purchases. The SAP hires us tractors at exaggerated prices.'[16] The provision of spare parts was another problem. In August 1965, one show farm, El Djoumhouria, on the outskirts of Algiers, had one-third of its tractors out of commission because ONRA had not ordered spares from England.

Another factor, with equally disastrous effects for *autogestion*, must be mentioned in this review of the economic subordination of the *comités* to the administration: the question of profit-sharing and production bonuses (*primes*). In the *décrets de mars* the net income of the enterprise was to be divided into three parts: state, enterprise and workers; and annual bonuses were to be awarded for high productivity.* Workers in *autogestion* are paid time rates rather than piece rates, so the incentive for high productivity was to come from the annual distribution of profits and productivity bonuses. I have already mentioned the first occasion when this question came up, in January 1964. Here Ben Bella decreed that workers in profitable enterprises should receive 230 DA and the rest 110 DA. This was, in fact, the only time that such a distribution of profits has been made.

The distribution of profits in agriculture and industry has been blocked consistently by the administration, and even the January 1964 payments were not widely received. Under conditions where the accounts of the *comités de gestion* are managed by the administration it is not very difficult for payment of profits to be withheld. It is also impossible for the *comités* to establish the exact profit-or-loss situation of their enterprise. The administration's usual rationalization for the non-distribution of profits was that workers in *autogestion* were already privileged in relation to the rest of the country; and that their profits were to be used to help the under-privileged sections of the community. However, the general opinion of both the

* See details given in Chapter 4.

The Bureaucratic Emprise on the Comités

workers and the UGTA is that what profits there have been in *autogestion* have been used to finance the costs of the administration.

Absorption of profits by the state has had serious consequences for *autogestion*, both in terms of the economic position of the individual enterprise and the attitudes of the workers to the system. The average income of workers in the self-managed sector of industry is lower than that of workers in both the private and state-controlled sectors, as the following table shows.[17]

	autogestion	*private*	*state-controlled*
		(April 1961 = 1·00)	
un- and semi-skilled	1·51	1·62	1·74
skilled	2·13	2·49	2·55

The non-distribution of profits has encouraged workers, particularly skilled workers, to move into either the private or state sectors. A delegate from the paper factory at Saida summed up the problem in the March 1964 conference of the socialist industrial sector when he said: 'For a year now we have told the workers, "You'll have your share of the profits." If we deceive them – goodbye to the workers! They will go and work in private firms.' The discrepancy in salaries between the self-managed and private sectors was even more apparent in the case of administrative and technical staff.[18]

	autogestion	*private*
	(monthly salaries in dinars)	
technical/engineering	2134·39	2680·83
upper administrative grades	1046·30	2172·06
middle and lower grades	839·41	1541·42

The low salaries paid by the self-managed sector also encouraged trained administrative and technical staff to seek employment elsewhere.

The control of every financial transaction by the administration amounted to the virtual imposition of a wage freeze in the self-managed sector. The existence of a free market in labour and a private and state sector that paid higher wages meant that there was an automatic tendency for skilled labour to drift from *autogestion* in industry. In agriculture, despite the imposition of a state-controlled national wage, there was no parallel drift as there was no real alternative employment in agriculture and the industrial labour market was only open to skilled workers. The effect of this relative economic deprivation on the workers' attitudes to *autogestion* is discussed in the next chapter; but in pure economic terms it resulted in bleeding the *comités* of skilled manpower they could ill afford to lose.

The freezing of profits by the administration affected reinvestment as much as it did wages. The *comités*, in general, did not receive the one-third of the profits destined for reinvestment, while the workers were unable to use their share for extra income or reinvestment. This meant that even the most profitable enterprises were continually starved of reinvestment capital that could increase productivity. The refusal of the state to invest in deficitory firms has already been described. The net result of this situation, in both industry and agriculture, was that the capital assets of self-managed firms were allowed to deteriorate to a point where production began to be seriously affected.

The concept of economic independence within the general terms of national planning was thus a purely juridical fiction for the *comités de gestion*. Almost from the beginning, the administration removed the ability to take any really meaningful decision on the economic future of the enterprise from the hands of its workers. The profitable areas of self-management were used as a milch-cow, while the rest were allowed to stagger on towards increasing debilitation. As one commentator put it: 'For these enterprises, in the majority of cases it is the socialism of poverty; it is not a question of development or constructing a socialist economy. The owners have gone, no one condescends to replace them. The workers try to organize penury in order to keep their jobs and not die of hunger.'[19] On a strictly economic level it is quite clear that the charges levelled against *autogestion* by its opponents had no real foundation. The economic success or failure of self-management lay entirely in the hands of the administration. By restricting the *comités de gestion* to a managerial role purely in the area of day-to-day production, the *décrets de mars* removed from the workers any possibility of seriously affecting the country's economic development. The *comités* were handed over to an administration that actively interfered in their day-to-day operation and totally circumscribed their economic activity. The charges of economic failure are charges against the administration itself.

The Bureaucratic Emprise on the Comités

The onslaught on *autogestion* did not become part of an open state policy till the creation of the *sociétés nationales* in 1966 and 1967. But behind the scenes of public professions of attachment to the principles of *autogestion* lay the realities of a sustained and insidious bureaucratic counter-attack. Each one of the cases cited in this chapter is a record of the gradual and largely unrecognized organization for a political counter-revolution. Long before Ben Bella's fall, the future of *autogestion* had been mortgaged to the administration. The new middle class had instituted its control of economic organization long before it felt politically powerful enough to announce this as a reality.

9

WORKERS AND MANAGERS

So far, we have witnessed the class struggle for political and economic control of independent Algeria in its broad historical outlines and in the context of the structural factors which formed the context within which *autogestion* emerged and which eventually moulded its defeat. The colonial prehistory, the fight for independence, the revolution of 1962, the economic and social structures, have all deeply affected the modes of political and economic organization. We have seen how the eventual political victory of the new bourgeoisie reflected a pre-established hegemony over the means of production. In view of the seizure of part of the means of production by the workers in 1962 it has been necessary to explain how they lost this control. In handing over the supervision of *autogestion* to an unreconstituted administration the *décrets de mars* clearly allowed this bureaucracy to control the economic activities of the *comités de gestion*. Equally, it enabled them to practise widespread manipulation and intervention in the composition of the *comités* and their day-to-day functioning.

The *de facto* administrative control of the machinery of *autogestion*, the failure of the revolution to extend any further than a change in the direct management of production, the restriction of the principles of *autogestion* to the point of production, all explain, on an external level, the eventual defeat of the revolution. What they do not explain is why many *comités de gestion* and their workers accepted this counter-revolution; how in face of the gains of 1962–3 it was possible for the new bourgeoisie to impose its control so rapidly. To understand this we have to look at the way *autogestion* operated within the majority of the enterprises under self-management; in other words, how the component parts of the system – director, *comité de gestion* and workers – grasped the concept of self-management. It is here that we come face-to-face with the question of the

Workers and Managers

extent and nature of the consciousness of the Algerian working class. A large part of the success or failure of the Algerian revolution depended, in the last analysis, on the ability of the working class to grasp the political implications of *autogestion*.

THE DIRECTOR AND THE 'COMITÉ DE GESTION'

Any discussion of the role of management in workers' self-management involves the identification of two main groups: the non-elected director and administrative staff, and the elected management committee. The relative powers of these groups to affect decisions depends to a large extent on the relation between the state and the enterprise. In the Yugoslav experience of self-management the influence of the director was at its highest when state controls over the enterprise were greatest. The slackening of state controls led to the erosion of directorial power and the appearance of a 'factory bureaucracy'. Although the managerial powers of this bureaucracy are similar to those of the director, its composition is heterogeneous. The exact composition of this group has to be related to the social, political and economic structures of the country concerned.

In Algeria, although the *décrets de mars* created the post of director, the number of people trained in the appropriate technical skills was extremely low. The organization of the FLN was too fragmented, its ideological content too eclectic, to create a homogeneous body of loyal cadres as had been possible for the Communist Party in Yugoslavia. In this situation the government could not always rely on the director to represent the interests of the state. The administration had to evolve other means of control over the economic and political actions of the concerns under *autogestion*. As I have already described, the two major means used in this process were electoral manipulation and strict economic control.

Economic independence was effectively reduced by the administrative control of sales, profits and credit. The overt success of the directors and the administratively manipulated *comités* was less apparent in containing *autogestion*, economically or politically. The way in which these two elements succeeded in deforming the original concept of *autogestion* lay less in the fact that they were a transmission belt for state policy than in the class values they possessed and developed. In other words, it is necessary to identify subjective expressions of class interest rather than a conscious exposition of an objective political policy.

The administrative cadres of independent Algeria were largely composed of lower-middle-class elements or, more correctly, the petit-bourgeoisie of the colonial period. Apart from a small minority of genuinely revolutionary militants this was the only class with sufficient opportunity and educational background for it to become upwardly mobile. Those who became directors in nationalized enterprises, whether state-run or self-managed, formed part of this social group. The almost complete absence of trained Muslim management under colonialism meant that enterprise directors (or *chargés de gestion*) were generally not appointed on the basis of technical qualifications. In agriculture a certain number of directors were appointed from the minor officials of the colonial SAP; in industry a few who had had minor experience in France were encouraged to return. Apart from the possession of the *Certificat d'Études Primaires*, the only qualification required by a director was the appropriate connections: most obtained appointments through the clientèle system. In some cases the most blatantly reactionary elements were made directors, such as the director of one large estate outside Algiers who had been a member of the hated Muslim section of the Paris police during the independence struggle. Like the majority of the administration, this group was identifiable by its lack of commitment to the ideas expressed in the *décrets de mars* and the *Charte d'Alger*.

The absence of ideological commitment, the stresses of mobility and the lack of any immediate conscious class orientation created an anomic situation for the majority of the administrative cadres. In the absence of any ethical code or explicit class structure with which to identify, the new bureaucrats sought, not unnaturally, satisfaction in material terms. The only life style which they could emulate was that of the *pieds-noirs*. In view of the early strict 'official' morality on salary differentials, the only access to material enrichment was through corruption. Corruption, in the sense of the appropriation of social property for personal ends, became an accepted mode of material advancement within the administration.

The effect of this type of corruption on *comités de gestion* is shown by the following instances. The iron-mining complex of Zaccar, Miliana, was placed under *autogestion* in July 1963. The first director was imprisoned after selling the complex products for his own profit. The second director hired his own friends as the administrative staff. He kept the profits made by an eighty-hectare farm attached to the complex for his own use. He used the repair shops to repair private cars and again took the proceeds. Finally, he sold machinery, destined for the complex, to private industry, again taking the profits.[1] Another case concerns the *Société d'Entreprise de Routes en Algérie*, controlling four concerns in Algiers and two in Oran. The European owners left in 1963 and, after six months' stoppage, during which the army tried to take over the road-mending machinery, a government *commissaire* was appointed. The *commissaire* dismissed many of the original workers, even framing some of them for theft. In 1965 he disappeared and the workers set up a *comité de gestion*. They found that there was only 560 DA left in the firm's account and that the *commissaire* had drawn out 140,000 DA before fleeing the country.[2] Yet another case of corruption concerned the *Coopérative Laimeche Ali* in Tizi Rached, in the Kabylie. This firm, making building materials, started work in September 1963 having raised money from a bank and the local population totalling some 8·5 million AF. By 1964 the cooperative had doubled its work-force to over 400 and had bought modern machinery. But by the end of the year it had shut down almost completely when the accountant, appointed by the state, fled abroad with all the liquid assets.[3]

Corruption was not usually as flagrant as this. It was mostly confined to petty embezzlement. In recent years it has become less frequent. The administration, initially in an anomic situation extremely conducive to deviation, became consolidated in a class. It came to possess a value system and ideology that confirmed individual members in their status as part of a hegemonic class, which had begun to establish its own system of rewards. There is a growing identification with the technocratic ideals expressed by the group in power, even though financial rewards, now officially condoned, are still important. The growing homogeneity in terms of values and consciousness has created a greater coherence in the activities of the state organs and their subordinate administrators. The bureaucracy has moved from utilizing the situation for their own immediate personal ends to using it for class ends.

The role of the director within the enterprise is intimately related to the composition and attitudes of the *comité de gestion* and its president. The vagueness of the original decrees created an implicit jurisdictional conflict between director and *comité*. Within this arena of possible conflict the ability of the director to impose either his own or the state's goals lies in several factors. The strength of his position rests on his connections with the administration (party and state), his technical knowledge and the relative inability of the workers to assert their formal rights through illiteracy, lack of technical expertise or a low level of political training.

Except in the larger enterprises in industry, the factor of the director's technical competence enabling him to dominate *comités de gestion* did not play a large part. The lack of trained technical or managerial cadres often meant that directors were less competent to take decisions on production than the more experienced workers. A far more important factor was the workers' own uncertainty as to their rights. There was no really effective campaign to explain the *décrets de mars*, and the overwhelming level of illiteracy meant that few workers could read the published texts. As Juliette Minces points out, although the Press in the early days was in the hands of left-wing elements supporting *autogestion*, few could read it and most relied instead on the radio which did not display the same enthusiasm.[4] In agriculture, the director, or *chargé de gestion*, was often the only literate member of the concern and was thus usually called upon to explain the decrees. In the large towns, the UGTA made great efforts to create a clear awareness of the content and meaning of the decrees and kept a close watch on the activities of directors.

Despite the opportunities, the directors in *autogestion* played a relatively minor role in deforming the original purposes of the decrees. Certainly they were able to manipulate the activities of many *comités*, but the state's success in containing *autogestion* lay largely in the external controls. Much more serious for the future of self-management as a mode of political or economic organization in countries like Algeria are the attitudes among the workers themselves.

Technically, the *comité de gestion* is responsible to the *assemblée des travailleurs* which elects it. But even disregarding the fact that many *comités* were appointed by the local administration, the form of the original decrees gave the *comité* the means of asserting its independence. The *assemblée* was not allowed to make and pass amendments or counter-proposals to those elaborated by the *comité*. These had to be sent to the *comité* which only had to send them back for a vote by the *assemblée* if it thought fit. The length of time formally needed to re-elect a *comité* – three years – also contributed to its relative immunity. But these purely technical considerations, allowing the *comité* a large measure of independence from its electorate, had only a marginal effect in the development of some *comités* into a 'factory bureaucracy'.

The emergence of authoritarian and undemocratic tendencies within the internal organs of *autogestion* was rooted in the political and social conditions at the time of their formation. The widespread manipulation of the original elections meant that many *comité* members were chosen in view of their relations with the local administration, the FLN, the army or the supervisory organs. As we have seen, since this time there has been no general renewal of *comités*. Not only did many *comité* members owe their position to these external groups, but they also derived power and prestige from them. The resulting evolution in the attitudes and actions of such *comité* members was described rather simplistically by Juliette Minces: 'The local administration named the management in *autogestion*, many of whom, in consequence, take themselves for the new owners.'[5] But the process whereby *comités* or their presidents objectively participated in the deformation and containment of *autogestion* is not so straightforward. They have rarely consciously subscribed to the class ideology of the new bourgeoisie. Temmar cites the cases of three members of separate *comités* who, besides this position, were also small-time capitalists in rural areas.[6] But this duplication was a relatively minor occurrence.

In the outlying rural areas the *comité* members who exerted personal or autocratic control over their enterprises were often fulfilling a traditional role in Muslim rural society. The remains of the indigenous local leadership, in the shape of the *caïds*, was annexed by French colonialism as part of their system of local political control. The *caïds*, chosen and suitably rewarded for their loyalty to colonialism, dispensed patronage, adjudicated in disputes and acted as informers for the state. In view of their close identification with colonialism, many of the *caïds* were killed during the war or at independence, while others were imprisoned or fled to avoid retribution. But as independence failed to bring any alternative system of local government or any widespread change in social structure, their political and social role was filled by others. When the UGTA stated: 'The presidents of *comités de gestion* are often just new *caïds*', they were accurately describing not only their mode of action but the social role they fulfilled.[7]

The so-called 'new feudalism' of the *comités* was, in part, merely the expression of one of the few forms of social solidarity to survive colonialism. In the absence of other social links, such as class, and in the absence of any clearly based ideology, the concepts of cooperation inherent in *autogestion* were often, in the outlying rural areas, translated into traditional forms of social solidarity. The nepotism prevalent among some rural *comités*, and bitterly denounced at several congresses, was the expression of the normal values of traditional society. A case cited by Krieger is a clear example of the way such norms continued to operate. The president of a self-managed estate brought his friends and relatives from a village 100 kilometres away and enrolled them as permanent workers, forming thirty per cent of the total permanent labour force.[8] The workers' acceptance of the authority wielded by *comités* or their presidents is similarly rooted in the norms of traditional society. In the past it had been customary for men of local eminence, such as the *caïds*, to establish their position through the distribution of favours, like employment. In accepting the personal autocracy of some presidents the workers were expressing a sense of reciprocal obligation.

The close identification between the *comité* and the organizational chain of command reinforced these traditional obligations. As Lazarev pointed out: '... the organs of *autogestion* tend to be limited to the *comité de gestion* and this tends to be confused with the normal hierarchy of the organization of work.'[9] Very often the president, whether a political appointee or not, was the foreman or senior Muslim worker under the colonial management; while the *comité* members were the most senior or most experienced workers. At times this identification between the *comité* and the hierarchy of production management was total. On one estate, the Domaine Megnouch Mustapha, near Algiers, the individual production units were each managed by a foreman; these same men also formed the *comité de gestion*.

The strength of this duplication of authority roles rests on the workers' acceptance of a status hierarchy internalized before independence. This hierarchy was compounded both of the ascribed status of traditional society and the achieved status of industrial society. The ability of *comité* members to capitalize on the accepted norms of authority roles in two cultures rendered their position doubly strong. Only the internalization of a third ideology, such as that contained in *autogestion*, which challenged the value system of the other cultures, could render workers conceptually capable of challenging the authority of the *comité*.

In the large estates in the coastal areas and the industrial units under *autogestion* the autocratic and illegal behaviour of some presidents and their *comités* must be ascribed to different causes. The breakdown of the structure and values of traditional society in these areas made it impossible for *comité* members to fulfil traditional authority roles based on ascribed status. When not political, their authority was based on their role in the organization of production. The attitudes of some presidents and the extent to which they misused their position were severely criticized at the 1964 conference of the socialist industrial sector.

There are still the remnants of neo-colonialism in their heads. They waste the property of the people. They have the same disdain for the workers as the old owners. They make fat provision for themselves. They give themselves apartments and take other privileges without justification. They drive round in Peugeot 404s.*

These criticisms are similar to those levelled at state-appointed directors and, in fact, the position and attitudes of a number of presidents and *comité* members were similar to those of directors.

Comité members in industry, like those in agriculture, were often the foremen and senior workers under the previous colonial management. Their delegated authority as members of a *comité* thus coincided with their organizational authority based on achieved status. One of the clearest examples of this coincidence was in COGEHORE, the *comité de gestion* managing hotels and restaurants in the Algiers area, which I have already mentioned. Here the manager of each unit was also the unit's representative on the *conseil des travailleurs*. Besides this duplication of functions, the *comité* collectively or the president individually were often filling the organizational role of the director, because of the shortage of trained cadres for that position. Many of them had achieved a position of authority with no

* The Peugeot 404 was the status car of the Algerian bureaucracy at that time.

well-defined social value system. Unlike those in the outlying rural areas, they were unable to cloak their new-found authority in the values of traditional society. The absence of a generalized socialist 'culture' meant that there were few who had internalized the values implicit in such a culture. A large number of *comité* members were thus unable to achieve any gratification from the roles prescribed for them in the ideal type of *autogestion* as laid down in the *décrets de mars*. In this situation they turned to the other value system most available to them – that of the previous *pied-noir* management.

The failure of many *comités* to fulfil the role allotted them in the original decrees must be seen in the light of cultural as well as political and economic factors. Strict financial control and electoral manipulation were definite political decisions aimed at reducing the independence of the *comités*. The authoritarian, nepotistic and corrupt nature of some *comités* was not the result of any overt manipulation by the administration. It was the product of the social and cultural superstructures of the pre-existing colonial society. These, whether based on the traditional rural economy or colonial capitalism, were carried over into post-colonial Algeria because the fact of independence itself was not enough to change the prevailing systems of values. The partial imposition of a socialist economic organization, whatever its form, does not imply a *de facto* modification of cultural norms. Only those who had implicitly internalized the concepts involved in *autogestion* were fully capable of identifying with its norms.

THE WORKERS

The formation of *comités de gestion* and the elaboration of *autogestion* in Algeria created a radical departure from the pre-existing capitalist mode of organization of the means of production. In assessing the role of the workers, as distinct from the *comités*, in this process the key question is whether in fact they grasped it as a radical departure. The worker's attitude to self-management, in any form, is determined by the cultural values of his society and class. This attitude is essentially circumscribed by the worker's subjective relationship to the means of production, and consequently, work itself. In order to assess the ability or desire of workers to participate in management, the role played by work in their lives must be gauged.

Workers and Managers

The means of production and work may be grasped by the worker in different ways. Work may be a means of providing the income necessary to satisfy material or status needs. It may provide a source of intrinsic satisfaction in the process of the job itself or in the status connected with it. Alternatively, the worker may see his own relationship to the means of production within the totality of economic, political and social organization. In other words, the worker may be conscious of the social context of his individual relationship to the means of production. All of these determining attitudes are to be found among workers in the industrialized West.

In a society such as Algeria, where un- or under-employment is the norm, work takes on a meaning that is radically different from that in advanced industrial countries. 'In such a context, competition for a job is the foremost form of the struggle for existence; a struggle which, for some, begins each morning in anxiety and uncertainty.'[10] Under colonialism and after independence the less skilled, lower paid worker was faced with the alternatives of accepting an unsatisfactory job, in terms of income, or no job at all. I have already discussed the effect this situation had on preventing the development of a basic trade-union consciousness. I stated that, in 1960, 88·6 per cent of all permanent workers when faced with low wages chose to raise them by maximization of effort rather than fighting for higher wages for the same amount of work. It was only among the better educated, more skilled and consequently higher paid workers that any form of trade-union consciousness appeared. Only these workers had the conceptual ability to grasp the economic system as a rational entity that could be acted on rather than the operation of a capricious fate that had to be accepted.

The struggle for employment and material survival, the relative inability to grasp the economic system as a social totality, are both crucial in their effect on the worker's attitude to self-management. *Autogestion*, whether conceived of as a form of production management or as the basis of a socialist organization of economy and society, is not confined to the provision of employment and wages. It demands that the new managers, the workers, should be aware of a whole complex of economic and social problems. It implies, not only that they are capable of solving these problems, but also actively desire to do so. Self-management, if it is not to be an empty formalism, demands a high level of class consciousness, an ability to grasp the meaning and content of class conflict. In Algeria the majority of workers were, and still are, deeply immersed in an everyday struggle for material survival where the next job or the next wage packet becomes the limit of their horizon. Their attitude to self-management is radically circumscribed by this context. The life situation and belief system of the vast majority of Algerians is inimical to the development of that form of consciousness implied by self-management.

We have already seen how the occupation of factories and farms in 1962 was spurred on by basic economic necessity. Despite the attempts by the UGTA, and some FLN militants, to give a political content to these actions, the majority of workers were impelled to form *comités de gestion* by the demands of material survival, rather than by a coherent revolutionary consciousness. In the breakdown of normal social structures following independence the workers re-created a classic socialist form of organization because at that juncture it was the only form open to them. The absence of a state, or an entrepreneurial bourgeoisie, left them face-to-face with the problem of organizing their own survival. They were driven by material necessity to give actuality to their objective situation as the negation of capitalism. But it was not a conscious seizure of the means of production by a class fully aware that they were engaged in a class struggle.

The authors of the *décrets de mars* and the *Charte d'Alger* conceived of a system whose success depended on the existence of a working class with a sufficient degree of consciousness to grasp the revolutionary content of *autogestion*. The demand, so often voiced by the Harbi group, the PRS and other left-wing groups, for an *avant-garde* party represented their fears that the workers had not developed a sufficient level of consciousness to combat the bureaucratic tendencies of the state. Orthodox socialists like Boumaza criticized what they termed the ouvrierist tendencies of the workers. 'The great difficulty in *autogestion*, an essentially evolutionary formula, is to find the right mean between the anarchic, ouvrierist tendency at the base and the centralizing, bureaucratic, *étatiste* current at the top.'[11] Foreign observers also noted the existence of this ouvrierist attitude among the workers. 'In practice it happens that the *comité de gestion* appears to face the director or supervisory organ as an organized trade union, more ready to obtain particular advantages than to improve production.'[12] This identification of the workers' attitudes, which provided yet another rationalization for imposing greater central control, is too simplistic.

The struggle for material survival was, for many workers, of greater importance than fulfilling the wider economic role allotted them by the *décrets de mars*. They tended to visualize their job in an instrumental fashion, according to the equation: work equals money and security. *Autogestion* as a mode of organization capable of solving the political and economic problems of a revolutionary society was not only a concept foreign to their experience but was felt as marginal to their immediate needs. This basic concern with survival in the immediate present is clearly reflected in the statements of two workers from farms where no wages had been paid for two and a half months in September 1965. One worker from the Domaine Hassamène said: 'My children have only maize to eat, they have not tasted this season's fruits . . . every new day is a burden for us; how can we work on empty stomachs?' The other, from the Domaine Amirouche, complained: 'We have lived like wolves for seventy-five days . . . we are in a situation of misery without escape. Everywhere we are ignored; for them we don't exist; they want to take the fruits of our work without repaying the producer.'[13]

The workers did not form *comités de gestion* in 1962 and thus implicitly seize control of the means of production for purely political reasons. They did so because not to work meant to starve and because elimination of the capitalist owner would mean higher wages. This material and instrumental involvement of workers in the *comités* was explicitly recognized by the *décrets de mars* in their recommendations for the distribution of profits. The workers were given a direct economic incentive to participate in the management of their factories and farms. Yet, apart from Ben Bella's formal distribution of profits in 1964, these incentives failed to materialize. Thus, one of the main motives for involvement in *autogestion* was never satisfied. Particularly in agriculture, with fixed wages and no profit-sharing, there is not much to show that anything has changed since colonialism. As the president of a self-managed farm said to me in 1965: 'In this situation, how can we persuade the worker that he is no longer working for a capitalist exploiter?'

It is not surprising that, with their basic economic needs remaining unsatisfied, the workers should experience disillusion. The imposition of strict financial control by the administration served to channel the hostility and despair of the workers. For them the state clearly had taken on the role of the ex-owners and they responded accordingly. 'Their attitude remains the attitude of paid employees, all the more clearly manifested as they feel state supervision as if it were the authority of a private owner. It is the state that pays them, so it is to the state that wage claims are made.'[14] With the imposition of state control on the *comités de gestion* the workers had no alternative but to treat the state as if it were an employer.

Continuing economic deprivation has provoked various reactions among workers in self-management. In 1964 the director of COTEINTAL, a self-managed cooperative laundry, had to call the police to stop the workers forcibly redistributing their own profits. In agriculture, as we have seen, a common means of increasing wages has been for *comités de gestion* to sell produce on the black market. The more conscious translated their continuing deprivation and despair into a clear hostility towards the state, as was witnessed in the barrage of denunciations at every congress. In 1965 a worker in a self-managed transport concern noted: 'The revolution pulled up a few big trees and let lots of little ones grow instead. At least the *colons* put something back. The new rulers just consume and do not reinvest.'

Conditions of material insecurity and the absence of any well-defined national ideology of socialism act, at times, as a positive disincentive to become involved in *autogestion*. This can be seen in a simple and direct way in agriculture. Tractor drivers get paid 12 DA a day, the other workers get 7·5 DA a day. Many tractor drivers, who are usually the more skilled workers, refused to become members of *comités de gestion* because this would have meant accepting a wage cut of 4·5 DA a day.[15] At COBISCAL, a concern I have already mentioned, the workers refused to elect a new *comité* or share the responsibilities of management. They wanted to keep the same president because under him they made good wages and felt secure. As one of the workers said: 'Wages are more important to us than politics or management.' The director of another, state-owned, firm felt that workers preferred a private owner because they could demand wage increases without worrying about profitability.

The criteria by which many Algerian workers judge management is economic rather than ideological. Yet this involvement with

Workers and Managers

material self-interest is not in itself evidence of a hostility to self-management or even an incapacity to take responsibilities within it. The concern with wages and security of employment creates an ideology which judges an economic and social system by its material results. The extreme exploitation of the colonial system led to the struggle for independence and the formation of *comités de gestion* in the attempt to construct a freer and more materially secure future. By these acts the Algerian workers showed themselves capable of grasping the possibility of creating their own future. Despite continuing economic deprivation there remains a preparedness to work for this future. 'We have our responsibilities to our families, but we must learn to take them on in other areas if we are to make Algeria a better place to live in.'*

The revolution contained in the formation of *comités de gestion* created a heightening of consciousness among the workers. The 'anarchic, ouvrierist tendency of the base' criticized by orthodox socialists represented a consciousness that the worker has a right to the 'fruits' of his labour. It represented a clear consciousness that the economic system is not the result of blind fate but something that can be acted on. In assuming ouvrierist positions *vis-à-vis* the state the workers were not rejecting the chance to control their own future through *autogestion*. Chaliand claims that the absence of a true revolutionary socialist *avant-garde* led the workers to draw the maximum immediate profit from the situation.[16] But this *avant-gardist* formulation is not clear enough. The imposition of state control over the *comités* through electoral manipulation and economic mechanisms meant that, even though formally involved in self-management, the workers were not in fact in control of their individual or class futures. For many workers their consciousness lay in the recognition of the bureaucracy in the party and state as part of a class that was preventing them from achieving the material benefits of their labour and disposing of them as they themselves saw fit.

The years following independence witnessed the development of a class consciousness among industrial and agricultural workers. To most, the fight against the settlers had been against colonialism rather than against capitalism, for independence rather than for socialism. After 1962 little changed for the peasants, the vast rural

* Said by a worker at the *Société Algérienne des Boissons* in July 1967.

and urban sub-proletariat, and many of the lower paid workers in private industry. They remained immured in a world of unending struggle for daily survival. For the workers on the larger agricultural estates and in the socialist sector of industry, the dispossession of the *colons*, the formation of *comités de gestion*, the *décrets de mars*, the *Charte d'Alger* created a vision of socialism; a vision that was every day controverted by continuing poverty, by bureaucratic control, by cynical manipulation and corruption. The ouvrierist response to this situation, the demand for immediate benefits, was objectively the individual and collective expression of an implicit class conflict. To many of the workers the state had merely replaced the *colon* bourgeoisie. For the more politically aware, grouped round the UGTA, the situation was one of explicit struggle against a bureaucratic form of socialism in which *autogestion* assumed the role of an ideal of economic and political liberation.

The division between the proletariat and the mass of the Algerian population lies at the point where the involvement with survival leads to the assumption that the present and future may be acted upon. The consciousness of the possibilities of action as a means of solving economic deprivation is the beginnings of a class consciousness. This consciousness becomes explicit when the individual is brought to identify himself as a member of a class. Classically, in Algeria, it was the experience of revolution allied to economic deprivation that created the rudiments of this consciousness. Its development was partial and hesitant. In the early years the official position that there were no classes in Algeria, and the socialist language used by the state, obscured the realities of the situation. It was only after 1965 that the bourgeois class composition and ideology of the state and party became increasingly clear through their political and economic policies. The establishment of its hegemony found only a minority of the working class, itself a minority among the mass of the population, fully conscious and prepared to oppose the new *élite* openly.

10

THE LESSONS OF ALGERIA: WORKERS' COUNCILS IN ADVANCED ECONOMIES

IN just over five years the Algerian revolution had been recuperated, institutionalized and then emasculated by a new bourgeois *élite* firmly entrenched in the state and party. The *comités de gestion* had been suppressed or existed in name only. *Autogestion*, once so proudly proclaimed as Algeria's contribution to the construction of revolutionary societies in the third world, had given way to a banal state capitalism. The original leaders, of whatever political complexion, had been replaced by previously unknown careerists and bureaucrats. Abroad, the revolution that had fired so many failed to live up to their expectations and their attention drifted to other areas of struggle, spectacularized in their turn by the media. Algeria became yet another revolutionary failure.

The question of the actual nature of the Algerian revolution and, hence, the reasons for its defeat remained largely unanswered. The lessons to be drawn from the experience, and its relevance to revolutionary struggle as a whole, were not widely discussed except in terms of sectarian preoccupations. At this point the Algerian experience must be reinserted into the historical and analytical process with which this book began. We are faced not just with the specific problems of Algeria but with the continuing dilemma of revolutionary authenticity in relatively underdeveloped societies and ultimately with the basis of authority in any revolutionary society.

The immediate misconception that must be corrected is that of the nature of the Algerian revolution. Many saw the violent resistance to colonialism and the ultimate achievement of independence as revolution. This is a profound error which can only lead to a misunderstanding of the subsequent events. What began in 1954, with the formation of the FLN and the declaration of armed struggle, was not revolution; it was the development of the fight for national independence on to an intense and violent plane. To term the struggle against colonialism as revolution is to mistake the nature and aspirations of this struggle. It is to confuse the identity of revolution as a class struggle aimed at the overthrow of pre-existing social, political and economic structures with the attempt to replace them with structures more closely related to specifically national aspirations. Although a small section of the FLN in 1954 was influenced by socialist ideas, the aims of the majority were circumscribed by nationalism; their aspirations were rooted in traditional Arab, Berber and Islamic culture. Algerian nationalism reflected the social and cultural Manichaeism forced on the country by a specific colonial enterprise. The appeal of the FLN, for the masses, was its aim to restore a historical, cultural, social and political entity that had been destroyed with the defeat of Abdel Kader.

The extreme violence of the struggle gave expression to the violence already implicit in the relations between colonizer and colonized: a violence that was itself a product of the process and mode of colonization. It is this violence that largely created the myth of the revolutionary nature of the fight for independence. Fanonism, in particular, was responsible for the widespread misconceptions over the nature of the struggle. As we have seen, the struggle was seized in racial and cultural terms: the two communities, Muslim and European, faced each other as more or less homogeneous blocs. Apart from a few exceptions, class alliances between the communities did not exist; and where they had existed the war served to sever them almost completely. This gave rise to the attempted elision of a national with a class struggle through the identification of the European settlers as the oppressors and the indigenous population as the oppressed. Such reductionism had widespread appeal because of its apparent simplicity. But, despite the political and economic hegemony of the *pieds-noirs*, it is not possible to describe the war as a class war because of the existence of parallel class structures in the two communities. Although the settler proletariat were distinguished from the Muslim proletariat by their social and economic privileges, objectively they were in a similar relationship to both colonial and metropolitan capitalism.

Certainly the war contained overtones of a class struggle as a rising of the underprivileged and dispossessed. Mass support for the FLN in the early days came extensively from the traditional rural areas and its leaders were at pains to describe their struggle as peasant-

The Lessons of Algeria

based. It was in the countryside, with its consciousness of a past destroyed by colonialism, rather than in the towns that the FLN based both its military and political organizations. Despite this emphasis on the peasantry, dictated by tactical as well as ideological considerations, the struggle was national in orientation and extent. Members of all indigenous classes were fired by and, in varying degrees, took part in the revolt against colonialism. In seeking to overthrow French colonial hegemony the FLN was demanding the re-establishment of an Algerian national identity. Until the Tripoli meeting of the CNRA in May 1962 there had been no official expression of a socialist conception of the future, and even then it had a national rather than a class definition. The continued refusal of the FLN to accept the existence of classes in post-independence Algeria is a clear witness of an inability to define the social and economic contradictions existing within the indigenous population.

If the achievement of independence was not, of itself, a revolution, the occupation of the means of production by the workers and the formation of *comités de gestion* can be said to constitute the revolutionary aftermath of independence. It was the establishment of workers' management of the ex-*colon* industrial, commercial and agricultural concerns that formed the revolutionary nature of independent Algeria. It was the proletariat rather than the peasantry who broke through the specifically national identifications of race and culture to develop a class action. The class nature of this action raises the question of the situation and nature of revolutionary consciousness both in Algeria and in similar societies.

Since the Russian revolution confused the identification of the revolutionary overthrow of capitalism as developing in advanced industrial societies, the left has been embroiled in controversy over the nature of revolution in non-industrialized countries. The classic, Europo-centric, Marxist thesis has been felt to be contradicted by a series of apparently successful peasant-based revolutions in largely non-industrial societies. This has given rise to an attempted redefinition of the exact class situation of revolutionary consciousness. While not producing a complete answer to this question the Algerian experience is of great relevance.

The rejection or amplification of the classic definition of the proletariat as the sole negation of capitalism has been undertaken where there is a vast peasant majority or where the working class appears to be increasingly incorporated within capitalism. In non-industrialized societies this has led to the identification of a revolutionary consciousness among the peasantry, stemming from their participation in wars of national liberation and, to a lesser extent, class wars against a national bourgeoisie. The Fanonist ideology, as expressed in *The Wretched of the Earth*, identified the most dispossessed as the most revolutionary. Fanon, like Marcuse,[1] appeared to be able, at one stroke, to cut through the problem of the continuing absence of revolution in advanced industrial societies. By opposing the industrialized and colonizing to the underdeveloped and colonized, the class struggle assumed global proportions. The working class of the West became the bourgeoisie of the dispossessed of the third world. The appeal of this Manichaean division lay in its simplicity. For the 'wretched' it subsumed all local contradictions within a global contradiction; it removed the necessity for any critical analysis. For the intellectuals of Europe and the U.S.A. its attraction lay in the way in which it played on the guilt mechanisms of liberalism. The sordid abasement of Sartre in his introduction to *The Wretched of the Earth* has been paralleled by the stampede of American intellectuals to prostrate themselves at the altar of black power.

In discussing the value systems and consciousness of the peasantry, sub-proletariat and working class of Algeria, I have attempted, in this specific case, to unmask the absurdity of this type of reductionism. Neither the peasantry, nor the truly 'wretched' – the sub-proletariat – can be said to have played an objectively revolutionary role in Algeria. The involvement of the population of the traditional rural areas in the independence struggle must be clearly separated from their passivity in face of its revolutionary aftermath. The peasantry were fighting for what they regarded as their inheritance: a heritage firmly rooted in the Arab, Berber and Islamic past. Their consciousness was rooted in the values and traditions of this past and their aim was its re-creation. Revolution, as a concept, is alien to the peasant consciousness while their relationship to the environment remains one of passive endurance rather than active transformation.

The true disinherited mass of Algeria, as in the rest of the third world, is the rural and urban sub-proletariat. They exist in a half world that is neither the traditional nor the modern. They are denied the uneasy security either of the traditional values of rural society or

The Lessons of Algeria

of employment in the industrial economy. This mass, spawned by demographic growth, changes in agricultural methods, by industrialization, war and poverty, is involved in a desperate daily struggle for existence. For Fanon and for Marcuse it is this desperation and hopelessness which should drive the masses to revolt. Yet, as I have described earlier, it is this very desperation and extreme aculturation which deprives them of the ability to act on the external in a conscious manner. Subjectively, the sub-proletariat is not conscious of itself as a social organization: its total deprivation of social or economic self-identity makes of it a series.

Fanon, in particular, is at pains to emphasize the effect that participation in revolt has on the development of consciousness. For him, this experience breaks the chains of the psychological and social alienation forged by colonialism: the catharsis of violence liberates the individual and the society from the passivity engendered by the death of traditional cultural and social relationships. In *L'An V de la Révolution Algérienne*, he prophesies that the participation of Algerian women in the struggle against colonialism foreshadows their liberation from traditional male dominance. The fact that this liberation was not achieved after independence is symptomatic of the underlying fallacies of Fanonism. Neither the peasantry nor the sub-proletariat played any other than a purely negative role in the events after independence. Involvement in the revolt against the French did not transform their consciousness. Fanonism, with its abstract Manichaean division of the world, is pure ideology. It lacks a critical and dialectical analysis of the process of the formation of consciousness.

As ideology, Fanonism must be placed in a different context from the purely tactical or strategic identification of rural areas as a suitable operational base for guerrilla activity. The FLN, in Algeria, eventually achieved independence, not because the peasantry emerged as a successful revolutionary class but because France could only hold the countryside by an unacceptable expenditure of effort. Depending on their physical nature, rural areas can provide a suitable base for guerrilla activity. This does not mean that the rural population is involved as a conscious revolutionary force. As we have seen, the nature of their involvement is clearly dependent on the nature of the struggle. In Algeria the peasantry was deeply immersed in the attainment of national liberation because it promised a re-creation of a glorious past to which all their values were intimately related.

The desperation that drove the Algerian industrial and agricultural working class to seize the means of production must be qualitatively separated from that of the peasantry and sub-proletariat. The motivation of the workers in occupying and managing the *colon* farms and factories was extensively based on the purely immediate necessities of material survival. Despite the fact that they shared the same desperation as the mass of the population, the objective result of the workers' reaction to this situation was revolutionary. It cannot, however, be described as a conscious assumption of the historical revolutionary role of the proletariat. This fallacious interpretation led many to misconstrue the primitive nature of the seizure of the means of production as a sophisticated and mature revolt against capitalism.

It is in the objective relationship of the Algerian working class to the means of production that the key to their action lies. Unlike the peasantry and sub-proletariat, their relationship to the means of production was social rather than familial or individual. The social basis of the peasant economy is defined by a restricting relationship that pre-exists and encompasses the means of production – the extended family. Thus, although the peasant economy is apparently cooperative, the social relationships associated with it are not class-based. An industrial mode of production, despite the separation it engenders between individual workers, objectively creates an identity that transcends the boundaries of traditional relationships. The seizure of the means of production by the Algerian workers represented the subsuming of a series of individual motivations under a solidary, class action.

The contradictions of the Algerian revolution lay in the fact that it was not a conscious praxis. It was the practice of revolution with no concomitant theory. The class initiative of the workers must be considered in relation to their relative lack of revolutionary consciousness. Although able to embark on a class solution to their common desperation, they were not, at that point, capable of fully apprehending the meaning of their action. They were accustomed to using the self-definitional concepts of race and culture and not of class. The rapid imposition of bureaucratic controls on the *comités de gestion* and the development of an authoritarian state apparatus

The Lessons of Algeria

stems from the inability of the Algerian working class to grasp the immediate necessity of extending their revolutionary initiative further than the point of production. By the time this became apparent they had lost the initiative.

Besides the absence of a hegemonic consciousness, the Algerian working class was deeply inhibited by the contradictory nature of the party and state. For the mass of Algerians the FLN and the state under Ben Bella were cloaked in the mystique of the struggle for independence. They were vested with the authority and authenticity of success in the fight against colonialism. The Algerian working class found extreme difficulty in separating the nature of the FLN and its leaders during the war from their role after independence. The majority failed to see the full implications of their own actions: that the formation of the *comités de gestion* implicitly challenged the authority of the party and state. The tensions implicit in the tripartite division of workers' councils, party and state in any revolutionary society were immeasurably increased in Algeria by the simple fact that the party and state were not products of the revolution.

Apart from some UGTA officials and some FLN militants, the Algerian nationalist movement was singularly unprepared to deal with the question of the country's future. During the war the heterogeneity of the FLN made agreement on anything outside the achievement of independence almost impossible. Despite its wide popular support, the FLN was never more than a loosely co-ordinated front for a wide assortment of political tendencies and personalities. It was not a socialist or a revolutionary party. Once independence was achieved it fell apart into a whole series of competing factions. The extent of its irrelevance to the immediate problems of Algeria was revealed during the summer of 1962. While the political and military leaders of the front were engaged in near civil war the working class was objectively turning independence into revolution. On his victory in September 1962, Ben Bella was forced to acknowledge that in many respects the Tripoli Programme had already been surpassed in actuality.

Many observers of and participants in the Algerian experience have located the failure of the revolution in the absence of an *avant-garde* capable of creating a theory and unifying this with the actions of the working class in a revolutionary praxis. The structure, function and policies of the FLN in 1962 quite clearly defined it as other than an *avant-garde* party. After the factionalism of the summer it was patched up to represent more or less the same tendencies as before. In fact, at this point, no such *avant-garde* existed as a coherent force. Its elements were located in several centres: in the UGTA, in Boudiaf's PRS, the PCA and in the FLN itself. Apart from the leaders of the UGTA, few of these potential elements had played any real part in the formation of the *comités de gestion*. The conditions of the war had in any case separated them from contact with the working class. Essentially they were split between those who saw that the front had become outmoded with independence and those who wished to use its national status as a vehicle. The banning of the PRS and the PCA and the defeat of the UGTA leadership in January 1963 effectively removed the immediate possibility of developing a legal political *avant-garde* outside the FLN. The establishment of the FLN as the single, official, authentic, national party faced the *avant-garde* with the dilemma of opposition or entrism. Many, most notably the Harbi group, chose entrism.

The revolution at this point was incomplete. A sizeable proportion of the means of production had been seized by the workers but the state and party remained outside their control. This contradiction between the economic and the political manifested the underlying contradictions of the revolution. The *décrets de mars* and the *Charte d'Alger* were at one and the same time the measure of the success and failure of entrism. The *avant-garde* within the FLN could produce programmes and legislation but they were utterly incapable of carrying these through into practice. They did not control the party or the state and had no mass base among the working class or peasantry. As the counter-revolution gathered strength they were swept aside and only their texts remained as a memorial.

The public image of the Algerian revolution, created by the institution of *autogestion*, the *décrets de mars*, the *Charte d'Alger* and a revolutionary foreign policy, masked the deeper realities of the unfinished nature of the class struggle. The Trotskyist-influenced *avant-garde*'s attempt to create the revolutionary tripartism of councils, party and state was meaningless as long as the party and state remained in the hands of a bureaucracy not only totally separated from the working class, but having different class origins. The lack of critical analysis of the modes of class formation stems,

The Lessons of Algeria

once again, from Fanonist-inspired simplifications. During the war, the internal class contradictions of the indigenous society were largely subsumed under the wider definitions of race and culture. To a large extent, the only social formations recognized as separate from the mass of Algerians were the remnants of the tribal–feudal leadership and the Francophile bourgeoisie. Through the identification of independence with revolution it followed theoretically that these feudal and bourgeois elements had been largely dispossessed and had become peripheral to Algerian social reality. The *Charte d'Alger* recognized the existence of social divisions within Algerian society but did not use the term class to characterize them. The bourgeoisie, the petit-bourgeoisie and the bureaucracy are all defined as strata (*couches*) and not as classes.

This failure to identify the class characteristics, not only of the bourgeoisie but also of the new national bureaucracy, underlines the absolute necessity of rejecting the Manichaean vision of a global class struggle. It meant that the *avant-garde* within the FLN were unable to define the contradictions between the *comités de gestion* and the administration as part of an internal Algerian class struggle. In subordinating the *comités* to the administration, the *avant-garde* placed the whole revolution in jeopardy. The vision of the *avant-garde* was obscured by two analytical mystifications. Firstly they tended to accept the definition of the indigenous population as an undifferentiated mass in terms of its opposition to colonialism. Secondly, and more erroneously, they equated the seizure of the point of production with the seizure of the state. In their analysis, the fact that the means of production were largely in the hands of the workers prohibited the development of a national middle class. They were able to identify the emergence of a bureaucracy in Russia with interests opposed to the working class. But their answer to this problem lay in *autogestion* which, of itself, would remove the separation between the managers and the managed.

It is essential to the understanding of the failure of the Algerian revolution to realize that the bureaucracy acted as a class. It was sharply differentiated from the peasantry and the working class, and more narrowly from the classical bourgeoisie by the nature of its consciousness and by its relationship to the means of economic and political power. Although under *autogestion* the working class formally controlled the means of production, they did not control the relations of production. The administration through their control of the mechanisms of finance and marketing were, in fact, able to determine the economic life of each enterprise. With the development of the *sociétés nationales* this control became total. The bureaucracy rapidly developed a hegemonic consciousness and within five years had carried through a successful counter-revolution.

The Algerian revolution was unfinished in the sense that the working class never seized the state and that the party was an appendage of this state. Not only did the entrist tactics of a section of the *avant-garde* fail to push the revolution any further than the workers had already objectively achieved in 1962; they also made the task of the counter-revolution immeasurably easier by handing the gains of the workers over to the state.

In respect of this analysis it is possible to identify three stages of class struggle in ex-colonial territories. The first, the struggle for national liberation, precedes the real development of class antagonisms. It is only after independence that the existence of contradictions over and above those of colonialism become explicit. The second is the conflict between the national bourgeoisie and the mass of the population ending in the seizure of the means of production. The third is the conflict between the working class (and peasantry) and the state and party bureaucracy, ending in the seizure of the state. The specific conditions of colonialism in Algeria made the near temporal elision of these first two stages possible: the third stage was not achieved. The seizure of the state does not depend on the existence of an *avant-garde*, either pursuing entrist tactics or as a party in its own right; it rests on the development of a hegemonic consciousness by the proletariat. Anything short of the full, conscious seizure of the mechanisms of the state and the economy by the proletariat leads to the development of a bureaucratic bourgeois *élite* within the state. In this situation both classic socialism and self-management can only represent both a recuperation of the class struggle and a mystifying obscuring of its very existence.

Before discussing the question of the development of a hegemonic consciousness and the role that *autogestion* may play in inhibiting this, the role of the economy in this process must be identified. In the third world the economic situation of most countries and of their working class and peasantry is deeply antagonistic to the development of a full revolutionary consciousness and to its realization. The

The Lessons of Algeria

problem is situated around two major factors: the global economic dominance of neo-imperialism and the low level of material security of the mass of the population.

For Algeria, formal political independence did not bring economic independence from the metropolis. Not only was Algeria traditionally tied economically to France, but the relation was one of dependence. For most third world countries, the Stalinist and Maoist solution to dependence on international capitalism remains a practical impossibility. They do not have either the manpower, the variety of mineral and agricultural resources or the internal markets to attempt development in isolation. The imperialist expansion of Russia into Eastern and Central Europe after the Second World War and the subordination of the economies of this area is a clear measure of the difficulties of isolated development. At present the only possibility for the vast majority of underdeveloped countries is to maintain relations with international capitalism. It is to Western markets that their raw materials must be sent, and it is from the West that they must buy both industrial and consumer goods.

Clearly this relationship is an obstacle to the revolutionary development of the third world but it is an error to suppose that it necessarily prevents the emergence of certain forms of socialism. Western capitalism will defend its direct holdings in ex-colonial territories and to a limited extent the nationalization of foreign-owned means of production is a blow against this form of capitalism. But the potency of such a step is severely reduced by the fact that it does not alter the overall economic relationship.

Algeria's nationalization of most important sectors of the economy aroused no serious opposition from any neo-imperialist power. The formation of the *sociétés nationales* in fact made relations between large international companies and the Algerian economy far simpler. Henri Alleg noted: 'The *sociétés nationales* are very suitable for dealing with foreign companies. In the recent period, as we have already seen, very many contracts have been signed with American, French and West German firms.'[2] Alleg goes on to enumerate the number of joint companies set up by the *sociétés nationales* and foreign companies. On one level it could be said that the *sociétés nationales* have prevented the large-scale penetration of the Algerian economy by Western capitalism. But the fact remains that substantial profits can still be made by foreign companies either through joint ventures or simple trading agreements with the *sociétés nationales*. American capital has no qualms about economic cooperation with Algeria; indeed the state pays a Chicago firm of consultants one million dollars a year to study the reorganization of the socialist sector.

Similarly, efforts at trade diversification are at best a simplistic view of the relationship with neo-imperialism. Algeria has attempted to break the near monopoly of trade with France and has succeeded in lowering the volume of trade, in both directions, from around seventy per cent to between fifty and sixty per cent. However, the bulk of this diversification has been towards France's other Common Market partners. The signing of contracts with Russia and East European countries has meant a rise in trade volume from almost nothing to five per cent. The logic of this move was expressed by the Algerian Minister of Trade when he announced: 'In fact these agreements are in the tradition of the Soviet government's and Soviet people's firm support for the strengthening of economic independence and the struggle against colonialism in all its forms and against imperialism.'[3] Basically all that this represents is diversification from one form of dominance to another. Soviet aid is largely restricted to the development of particular products which are in short supply within her own economy. Diversification only reveals the continuing subordination of the ex-colonial economy. The idea of exploiting intra-capitalist contradictions can give marginally greater room for manoeuvre but leaves the basic nature of the economic relationship unchanged. Trade with the Russian bloc can be used as a bargaining counter but even this can only mean continued subordination to the needs of other economies.

The global dominance of neo-imperialism and the historical situation of the majority of the underdeveloped territories as part of this system create a series of problems. Given that most of such countries are orientated towards the production of raw materials rather than either capital or consumer goods, any attempt to lessen this subordinate position entails the development of a comprehensive industrial infrastructure. Apart from large political and economic units, such as Russia and China, such an attempt is economic lunacy. National economic self-sufficiency and the concept of the siege economy is deeply reactionary in terms of the international division of labour made possible by advanced technology. A possible

The Lessons of Algeria

solution to the dilemma has been seen to lie in the formation of more comprehensive trade blocs in competition with neo-imperialism. However, this meets with the obstacle that the economies of the potential members of such a bloc are not complementary.

The political effect of economic subordination is seen to entail neo-imperialist support for either a national entrepreneurial bourgeoisie or, in its absence, a bureaucratic bourgeois *élite*, whether in civil or military form. It does not necessarily mean opposition to forms of state ownership and control of the means of production where this does not conflict with the interests of advanced monopoly capitalism. In fact the relationship can act as a positive incentive to the development of such forms of economic organization. The national need to avoid blatant neo-imperialist exploitation makes the creation of a unified form of economic organization a positive necessity. Although cloaked in the language of socialism, the development of such forms is more likely to be an expression of nationalism. Politically and socially, this economic centralism accelerates the development of a heterogeneous coalition of petit-bourgeois and bourgeois elements into a fully fledged class. Thus, in the absence of a successfully concluded revolution, any attempt to reduce global contradictions by creating unified forms of economic organization leads to the intensification of internal class contradictions.

Autogestion, as visualized by the *avant-garde* in Algeria, represented a revolutionary alternative to this process. Vesting control of the means of production and, after a carefully supervised period, of the state, with the workers was designed both to avoid the development of a hegemonic bureaucratic bourgeoisie and to create the conditions for economic independence. The error of the *avant-garde* was, as I have stressed, to misconstrue the nature of the revolution. By identifying the events of 1962–3 as a revolution, rather than as the partial and hesitant onset of one, they were led to simplify the class structures of Algerian society. They also failed to appreciate the true state of the consciousness of the working class. The institution of a unified and unifying politico-economic structure above the point of production played directly into the hands of a petit-bourgeoisie and bourgeoisie already partially seated in that structure. Before it had really taken place the revolution was institutionalized and reified into a series of symbolic forms.

Workers' Self-Management in Algeria

It is at this point that the relevance of *autogestion* as a form of revolutionary organization must be called into question. In the introduction I noted that, apart from those that were crushed by counter-revolution, workers' councils have tended to experience the same history. Thrown up as a basic form of political and economic organization at particular points in a class struggle, they have been rapidly institutionalized and emptied of anything but a purely ritual content. Their fate has been singularly uniform, whether within a formally socialist or capitalist society. They have failed to create any lasting form of political or economic organization external to the point of production and have been eventually confined to this area.

In analysing the role of workers' councils and *autogestion* as a basic form of revolutionary organization the problem of consciousness must be faced. To what extent does a working class actively desire to control the means of economic and political organization? How far is the working class conscious of its historical role as the negation? If class consciousness is intimately connected with the relation to the means of production, even if not totally determined by it, what are the factors in this relationship that create consciousness? In answering such questions the subjective effect that material conditions have both on the individual and the class must be identified. This involves an analysis of quantitative and qualitative differentiation in material conditions.

In this book I have devoted some space to elucidating the interrelationship between culture, forms of economic organization and material conditions of existence and their effect on the consciousness of the main social groups in Algeria. From this, it appeared that while the working class possessed the objective conditions for class conciousness; for the peasantry, consciousness of belonging to a social category was socially rather than economically defined by reference to the network of family, clan and tribe. Before independence only a small proportion of the Algerian working class displayed any consciousness that the economic or political environment could be acted on to create a change in their material or social conditions. Bourdieu, and other French sociologists, were emphatic in establishing a correlation between such a realization and factors of education, skill or occupational level and income, stressing income as the most important variable. This thesis involves the concept that quantitative changes in material conditions create a qualitative change in

The Lessons of Algeria

attitudes and consciousness. Put simply, it states that the worker who is deeply immersed in a daily struggle to survive materially is incapable of conceptualizing the economic system as a social construct and is therefore incapable of envisaging a change carried through by a social agency. Only the worker who has achieved a certain level of material security is capable of visualizing the social nature of economic organization.

The events of the summer of 1962 in Algeria showed that this correlation was too simple. The workers involved in the setting up of *comités de gestion* did not all come from the high education, skill and income brackets indicated by Bourdieu. Earlier, I emphasized the importance of the social nature of the worker's relationship to the means of production: that is the objective categorization of the worker as a member of a class even if full subjective consciousness is lacking. The social nature of this relationship meant that the occupation of the means of production and the formation of the *comités* was a social act expressing a common class interest. This common interest was the necessity of producing in order to consume. Material desperation for the working class, unlike the peasantry or subproletariat, is a factor in creating solidary actions of a class nature.

However, the revolutionary nature of the class consciousness of the Algerian workers must not be over-stressed. The majority did not see the formation of the *comités* as a revolutionary act. Although this act gave witness to the emergence of a consciousness of class identity, rather than one based on race or culture, its nature was corporate rather than hegemonic. The occupation of the means of production was not a direct, conscious frontal assault on colonial capitalism; nor were the seizure of the state and the radical transformation of all elements of Algerian society envisaged. Despite the objectively revolutionary nature of their action, the preoccupation of the vast majority remained the daily struggle for material survival.

It is in this situation that *autogestion* came to form part of a system of mystification. The creation of an official ideology of revolution, both by the *avant-garde* and by the state bureaucracy, made the rapid recuperation of the original act possible. Independence was followed by the sustained erection of a mythology about Algeria which asserted that class conflict, and indeed classes as such, no longer existed; that the revolution had already taken place; and that the conflict had taken on the dimensions of a struggle between a unified revolutionary nation and neo-imperialism. Thus, at the very moment it emerged, class conflict was frozen by the myth of national revolutionary unity. One of the cornerstones of this myth was *autogestion*. The *comités* became symbols of a revolution that had already, in some mystical way, been achieved. The few who attempted to demystify the situation were repressed in the name of national unity. Once the new ruling class had established itself the symbolic form itself could be discarded.

In considering workers' councils or self-management we are facing two connected problems. The first is that if 'control' is confined to the point of production and the political and economic system in its totality escapes the direct control of the proletariat, then councils or self-management become a massive exercise in mystification and containment. The second is the deeper problem of consciousness or, more exactly, the worker's subjective appreciation of the necessity of controlling the means of production.

As is the case for the majority of workers in underdeveloped countries, control of the means of production appeared as largely irrelevant to the immediate needs of most Algerian workers. In the daily struggle, who controls the means of production becomes secondary to keeping the job and gaining the income that allows the worker and his family to survive. The existence of this instrumental attitude to work was implicitly recognized in the *décrets de mars* where, over and above the basic wage, a close connection was made between remuneration, individual effort and the success of the enterprise. The distribution of profits was seen as a direct incentive to the workers to take responsibility in management. The failure to redistribute profits profoundly disillusioned many who had seen *autogestion* as a means of increasing their income.

In an underdeveloped economy the needs of the worker are real in that he exists on the edge of absolute poverty. Although class consciousness will emerge among the working class it remains circumscribed by the conditions of absolute deprivation. The conditions of existence act as a positive disincentive to see work in any other terms but immediate survival. However, the converse is not true in advanced industrial society. Here, within certain parameters, the attitude to work, and thus to participation in the management of, or control of, the means of production is still determined by deprivation, even if this deprivation is only relative.

The Lessons of Algeria

One of the essential differences between an underdeveloped economy and an advanced one is the level of technology. The presence of an advanced production technology makes possible both a greatly increased level of productivity per head and consequently a higher potential income. The effect of advanced technology on attitudes to work and the organization of work is the subject of some controversy. Many sociologists have stressed that the technology of production tends to determine the structure of management and that technical criteria are the prime factors in the arrangement of human work groups.[4] This line of thought would indicate that the decentralization inherent in self-management is in contradiction with the need for continuous centralized decision-making required by a complex technology. It also assumes, implicitly, that the separation between skilled decision-makers and semi- or unskilled subordinates is sanctioned by the logic of technology. In contradistinction to this attitude, Serge Mallet, in *La Nouvelle Classe Ouvrière*, stresses that the high level of integration between previously separated production functions and work roles, caused by advanced technology, actually creates solidarity between all employees of a firm. For Mallet this technologically fostered solidarity could become the basis of a new form of unionism with 'workers' control' as its ultimate aim. Mallet admits that the identity of the worker in advanced industrial society is subject to a schizophrenic dualism centred round the polarization of work and non-work. The worker only feels himself as a worker at work; outside work he is a privatized member of a mass society. For this reason Mallet identifies the workplace as the sphere for the development of a new radical class consciousness based on the solidaristic desire to control the work process.[5]

This raises yet again the question of the relevance of work to the life situation of the worker and hence his consciousness. The key to this lies partly in the extent to which involvement in life outside work, in the achievement of certain consumption patterns, has replaced a culture in which the work situation formed the main preoccupation. Behind this lies the even more significant question of whether alienation continues to be centred round work or whether, as Marcuse would have it,[6] it has been transferred to the endless pursuit of falsely created consumption goals. In fact, is control of the process of production by the working class any more a central factor in the removal of alienation?

Workers' Self-Management in Algeria

Marx, in *The Economic and Philosophic Manuscripts*, developed a clear characterization of alienated labour:

> Labour is *external* to the worker, i.e. it does not belong to his essential being; so that in his work, therefore, he does not affirm himself but denies himself, does not feel content but unhappy, does not develop freely his physical and mental energy but mortifies his body and ruins his mind. The worker therefore only feels himself outside his work, and in his work feels outside himself. He is at home when he is not working, and when he is working he is not at home. His labour is therefore not voluntary, but coerced; it is *forced labour*. It is therefore not the satisfaction of a need; it is merely a *means* to satisfy needs external to it.[7]

Bourgeois sociology has attempted to show that advanced technology is effectively reducing the amount of physical energy expended in labour; that technical and intellectual skills are largely replacing physical skills.[8] An ideology has been developed which stresses that automation, far from degrading the worker still further as a mere adjunct to the machine, actually creates dignity and responsibility in work. The American sociologist Blauner, in a study of various levels of production technology in the U.S.A., tried to show that alienation which finds its peak on the car assembly line decreases once fully automated production is reached.[9] According to Blauner, the vastly expanded responsibilities of the worker in checking the complex process of production in, for example, a modern refinery, give a measure of dignity and importance to his work: attributes which are entirely absent from the mechanical and routinized content of work on the assembly line.

These conclusions have been challenged on an empirical and theoretical basis by recent work in Yugoslavia where it was found that alienation increased in direct relation to the complexity of the technology involved in the process of production.[10] The important difference here is one of meaning. Blauner, and other sociologists, have identified dis-alienation with a sense of intrinsic satisfaction in the work being done; so that as work becomes more responsible the satisfaction achieved from its performance increases. Obradovic, in Yugoslavia, defined alienation as the subjective feeling of loss of control over the process of production and the product. Thus the increasing separation between the worker and the process of production (and the product) inherent in advanced technology was

The Lessons of Algeria

experienced as profoundly alienating. Furthermore, this experience appeared to be entirely unmitigated by the formal existence of self-management.

Technology, however, is not a determinant but only one variable which must be correlated with the worker's own attitude to the place of work in his life schema, and in consequence, with socialized attitudes to work. Serge Mallet's argument, that the workplace remains the centre of potential working-class radicalism and that technology does not affect this identification, depends on the worker's subjective acceptance of such a definition. It depends, as a prediction, on a correct analysis of the links that bind the worker to the enterprise. As we have seen, Mallet characterizes the interdependence created by modern technology as the basis for a new form of solidarity between all workers, whether manual or non-manual. Marcuse, in *One-Dimensional Man*, opposes such a characterization, seeing the process as one of integration with capitalism:

These changes in the character of work and the instruments of production change the attitude and consciousness of the labourer, which becomes manifest in the widely discussed 'social and cultural integration' of the labouring class with capitalist society.[11]

He goes on to state that: 'The new technological work-world thus enforces a weakening in the negative position of the working class: the latter no longer appears to be the living contradiction to the established society.'[12]

What we are concerned with here is the apparent disappearance of the traditional working class and its acceptance of the defined values of advanced capitalist society. The classic proposition for this thesis of *embourgeoisement* is based on the growing subordination of the traditional solidarity of the working class to a privatized life style, characterized by individual consumption; in short, the adoption of a characteristically middle-class way of life that is also manifested in voting habits and political attitudes. Galbraith, and others, have characterized this as the logic of industrialism which will eventually create a uniform pattern of existence in all advanced industrial societies, whether formally socialist or capitalist. As Marcuse emphasizes in the passage quoted above, this apparent logic leads to the weakening of the 'negative role of the working class' and potentially to the disappearance of this specific aspect of the class struggle.

Workers' Self-Management in Algeria

At this point, however, a new concept has been introduced: rather than changes in the character of work or technology it appears that changes in aspirations and patterns of consumption are responsible for the progressive integration with capitalism. The preoccupation of the working class with material benefits has never been in doubt. Marx characterized labour as a 'means for satisfying other needs'. What is in question is whether involvement in the satisfaction of these needs creates a reduction in class consciousness, a disinvolvement with the work situation and a disinvolvement with class politics.

Surveys, such as *The Affluent Worker*[13] in England, have stressed the widespread existence of instrumental or calculative attitudes to work. Work is seen as a means to extrinsic ends and workers will take jobs that are more 'alienating' in order to increase their wages, and therefore their consumption power. For André Gorz this preoccupation with commodities stems from the alienating nature of labour under capitalism. He feels that it is the form and organization of labour that forces the worker into seeing work as a materially supportive adjunct to life outside:

It is precisely because the worker is not 'at home' in 'his' work; because denied him as a creative, active function, this work is a calamity, a *means* solely of satisfying needs, that the individual is stripped of his creative active needs and can find his own power only in the sphere of non-work – the satisfaction of the passive needs of personal consumption and domestic life.[14]

This attitude appears to contradict Marx's original sequence of alienated labour being the result of the necessity of undertaking 'forced labour' in order to satisfy needs.

Self-management has often been advanced as a solution to alienated labour in that the workers are given the opportunity to exert control over the process of production. In the context of Gorz's analysis, forms of self-management should lead both to the worker feeling 'at home' at work and to a reduction in his preoccupation with personal consumption. Leaving aside the question of technology as a determinant, it appears that self-management in any of its present forms has done little to create an intrinsic involvement with work. For example, Otto Neuloh has stressed that workers in *Mitbestimmung*, in Germany, see their participation in terms of material benefits only. Of course, this is not so surprising since the amount

The Lessons of Algeria

of participation is severely limited and the real structures of control and ownership are left unchanged. Of far greater relevance is the situation in Yugoslavia. An extended study in Slovenia showed that, as real wages rose and consumer goods became available, workers increasingly devalued intrinsic work satisfaction, and indeed the importance of work in their life scheme, in relation to the search for satisfaction in their 'private' lives.[15] Workers became widely disinvolved from the organization and management of their labour in favour of the adoption of consumption patterns typical of Western capitalist society. They adopted an instrumental attitude to work which came to be seen as a necessary means in the pursuit of extrinsic goals. Self-management in Yugoslavia cannot be portrayed as being in any way ideal; however, it remains true that the workers there have a greater degree of control over the management of labour than anywhere else. Yet it appears quite clearly that they exhibit similar attitudes towards the work situation as workers in enterprises where they have little or no control.

From this we have a clear indication of the extent to which activities outside work continue to dominate the work-situation, and of the extent to which the worker is prepared to accept alienated labour in face of the possibility of achieving satisfaction of other needs. It does not follow that this involvement with extrinsic goals will necessarily reduce the level of working-class militancy. Traditional communal collectivism aimed at social solutions to social problems may be declining but it is being replaced by an instrumental collectivism.[16] Even if work is seized in an instrumental fashion there is still the necessity for collective action to secure the means (wages) to obtain the goals (commodities), even if the goals are privatized. Such collective action may be translated in political terms as support for whatever group or party appears to offer the greatest material benefits. It may indeed cut through traditional class and party alliances, but it will remain a collective action. Thus forms of organization come to be seen for their extrinsic rather than intrinsic merits. The demand for workers' control may be made, not in order to reduce the alienating nature of labour, but to increase the workers' share in the value of the product of their alienated labour.

Because consumption patterns are tending to become privatized, class goals are correspondingly shifting to individual goals. Paradoxically, the overwhelming similarity of this series of privatized goals creates solidarity in the attempt to attain them; but it is a solidarity based on the correspondence of individual needs rather than class needs. If the relation to the means of production is no longer experienced as the fundamental factor in the process of self-identification with a social group, then the traditional basis of class consciousness is being undermined. The privatized individual instead receives the corporate identity of consumer: an identity which is both active and passive. The struggle to be able to raise levels of consumption is carried through in both individual and corporate action; but such activity is subsumed within the passive acceptance of the dominance of an externally determined hierarchy of consumption values.

Marcuse calls this the perpetuation of obsolete forms of the struggle for existence, the imposition of 'false' needs over 'true' needs. 'The only needs that have an unqualified claim for satisfaction are the vital ones – nourishment, clothing, lodging at the attainable level of culture.'[17] This does not, of course, mean that the desire to possess commodities outside these basic essentials is necessarily false:

'False' needs are those which are superimposed upon the individual by particular social interests in his repression: the needs which perpetuate toil, aggressiveness, misery and injustice. . . . Most of the prevailing needs to relax, to have fun, to behave and consume in accordance with the advertisements, to love and hate what others love and hate, belong to this category of false needs.[18]

This struggle to satisfy 'false' needs is a struggle to achieve a 'false' form of existence. Instead of achieving liberation from material want the individual is faced with the steady accumulation of new mountains of needs which, one after the other, must be scaled in the endless pursuit of a mythical happiness.

If for Marcuse the imposition of these 'false' needs has a function in perpetuating 'toil' and 'misery', for Gorz the process has its function in making humanity forget its misery:

The further it goes in this direction, the more it numbs a stunted mass-produced humanity with satisfactions that leave the basic dissatisfaction untouched, but still distract the mind from it: the more it hopes that these men, preoccupied with the various means of escape and oblivion, will forget to question the basis of the whole system: the alienation of labour.[19]

The Lessons of Algeria

In this way, alienated labour in Marx's original sense has become even more alienated in that it is now imposed for the fulfilment of artificial needs. There can, however, be no strict separation of consumption and labour: alienated labour is supplemented by alienated consumption. Alienated consumption, in fact, becomes the reason for the continued existence of alienated labour.

As the necessity for labour to satisfy basic human needs recedes, both through their fulfilment and the ability of technology to replace human labour, so the need arises to create new forms of labour and new forms of need in order to preserve the existing form of the economy:

> When economic necessity is replaced by the necessity for boundless economic development, the satisfaction of primary human needs is replaced by an uninterrupted fabrication of pseudo-needs which are reduced to the single pseudo-need of maintaining the reign of the autonomous economy.[20]

The contradiction of the 'autonomous economy' lies in its inability to dispense with the labour freed by automation while labour remains a commodity, the source of the commodity and ultimately the means by which the commodity is consumed. This economy manifests itself as an endless spiral of production–consumption that has no relation to real needs; one which demands false forms of labour and false forms of consumption in order that it may continue to expand and survive. The old penury is replaced by a new privation; one which the individual feels just as strongly as the old.

If, in advanced industrial society, we are witnessing the gradual disappearance of an economy based on the elimination of real scarcity and the slow death of the traditional working class, we are by no means seeing the end of the negation outside the realms of theory. The proletariat remains in existence irreversibly. The traditional definition must be expanded to include all those who have no control over their own lives. The proletariat cannot be defined out of existence merely because the old perspectives have collapsed. It remains bound to an alien economy in the way it always has; its labour and consumption are still determined by the needs of that economy. Its continuing subordination to the pseudo-needs of the economy is not indicative of its incorporation but, rather, of the success of its containment undertaken and perpetuated by the superstructures of that economy.

Workers' Self-Management in Algeria

Workers' control continues to be hailed as an important transitional demand. But until the proletariat becomes truly conscious of the interconnected domination of alienated labour and alienated consumption, any type of proletarian organization conceived of as a form of production organization will continue to be seized as a means to the satisfaction of externally determined goals. The same is true of the workers' council. Till now the revolution has remained frozen at the apparent capture of the means of production rather than of the economy itself. Only the subordination of the economy to the conscious and liberated desires of the proletariat will destroy the dominance of the commodity. At this point the workers' council will no longer be, as it has been, a means of organizing alienation. Without this the council can be no more than another link in the chain binding the worker to a system of production and consumption that is alien.

APPENDIX I

THE *DÉCRETS DE MARS*

THE actual text of the second and third of the *décrets de mars* is given below. The first decree – that of 18 March 1963 – is concerned with establishment of the criteria of *vacance*.

DECREE NO 63.95 OF 22 MARCH 1963

Providing for the organization and management of industrial, mining and artisanal concerns as well as for vacant agricultural concerns.

Section I: On the organization of self-management

Article 1. Vacant industrial and mining enterprises as well as agricultural concerns are to manage their own affairs through the following bodies:

(a) The workers' general assembly
(b) The workers' council
(c) The management committee
(d) The director

However, on the decision of the President of the Council [Ben Bella] certain enterprises or undertakings of national importance may be integrated into the public sector and managed by public or semi-public bodies or by *sociétés nationales*.

Sub-section I: The Workers' General Assembly

Article 2. The workers' general assembly is composed of the regular workers of an enterprise or concern, chosen according to the criteria defined in Articles 3, 4 and 5.

The number of its members is fixed annually according to the extent of the development and expansion of the enterprise or concern.

The plan for the development and expansion of the enterprise or concern is to be in conformity with the national plan.

Article 3. To qualify as a member of the workers' general assembly the worker must fulfil the following conditions:

be of Algerian nationality;
be over eighteen years old;

not have been deprived of his civic rights;

perform a useful function for which he is physically fitted;

have no major income except the product of his labour in the enterprise or concern;

be a regular worker of the enterprise or concern;

have been employed without interruption for six months.

However, permanent workers who have left the enterprise or concern for reasons arising from the liberation struggle are exempt from the last condition.

Article 4. Seasonal workers may neither be members of the general assembly nor have the rights and prerogatives connected with that position.

Article 5. The director, on the advice of the competent bodies and of the communal council for the promotion of Self-management (CCAA):

draws up the list of the members of the workers' general assembly and provides them with membership cards;

determines each year the optimum number of permanent workers technically necessary to carry out the economic programme of the enterprise.

Article 6. Each member of the workers' general assembly has the right to one vote only. He may not be represented by proxy. Voting must be by secret ballot. Two-thirds of the members is necessary for a quorum.

Article 7. No worker eligible for participation in the deliberations of the workers' general assembly may be excluded except for a serious offence.

Proof of a serious offence lies with the workers' council or with the workers' general assembly if there is no workers' council.

Article 8. The workers' general assembly must be called by the workers' council or the management committee at least once every three months. It may be convened, extraordinarily, on the initiative of one-third of its members. In enterprises employing less than thirty workers, the workers' general assembly replaces the council.

Article 9. The workers' general assembly:

adopts the development plan of the enterprise within the framework of the national plan, as well as the annual investment, production and sales programmes;

adopts the arrangement concerning the organization of work and the definition and distribution of functions and responsibilities;

approves the final accounts;

elects, if there is one, the workers' council.

The Décrets de Mars

Sub-section II. The Workers' Council

Article 10. The workers' council, chosen from among the members of the general assembly of the enterprise, is composed of a maximum of 100 members and a minimum of one member for each fifteen workers; the minimum being in no case less than ten.

Article 11. At least two-thirds of the workers' council must be directly engaged in the production work of the enterprise involved.

Article 12. The members of the workers' council are elected for three years and one-third of the members come up for election every year.

Article 13. The workers' council meets at least once a month on the decision of the management committee. It may, however, hold extraordinary meetings on the request of one-third of its members.

Article 14. The workers' council:

adopts the internal regulations of the enterprise;

decides on the purchase and sale of material equipment within the framework of the annual equipment programme adopted by the general assembly; always on condition that the firm's original capital value is never reduced;

decides on long- and medium-term loans in the framework of the development plan adopted by the general assembly;

decides on the exclusion of members with the reserve of the right of appeal before the general assembly; .

decides on the admission of new permanent workers within the limits prescribed by Articles 3, 4 and 5 of the present decree. Should the council fail in its duties, the director may assume its functions. In the admission of new workers, war veterans and victims of the repression should have priority;

examines the final accounts before their presentation to the general assembly;

elects and checks on the management committee.

Sub-section III. The Management Committee

Article 15. The management committee comprises three to eleven members elected by the workers' council from among its own members; of these two-thirds must be directly engaged in production.

The management committee designates, each year, one of its members as president.

Elections take place each year at the end of the financial year, for a one-third renewal, as laid down for the council.

Article 16. The management committee assumes the tasks of managing the enterprise and, in particular:

draws up the development plan for the enterprise within the framework of the national plan, as well as the annual equipment,

production and sales programmes;
draws up the final accounts;
regulates the organization of work and the distribution of functions and responsibilities;
prepares the ground for the decisions of the workers' council;
arranges short-term loans within the framework of the annual equipment, production and sales programmes;
decides on the mode of purchase of necessary stocks such as raw materials, seed, etc., on the basis of the annual production programme;
decides on the means of selling products and services;
handles production problems, including the hire of seasonal workers.

Article 17. The management committee meets at least once a month, and also as often as the interest of the enterprise requires, at the call of its president.

It may admit to its meetings, on a consultative basis, members of the council or workers' general assembly who are ready to develop propositions and suggestions concerning the running of the enterprise which have been previously submitted to the management committee.

Article 18. For the deliberations of the management committee to be valid a quorum of two-thirds of its members, including the director, must be present. Decisions are taken by a simple majority of those present.

Where the votes are evenly divided the president has the casting vote.

Article 19. The president of the management committee:
presides over and directs the discussions of the management committee, the council and the workers' general assembly;
countersigns the minutes of the meetings of the management committee, the council and the workers' general assembly;
countersigns documents involving financial commitments and payments;
convenes, on the decision of the management committee, the council and workers' general assembly;
represents the enterprise in external relations and before the law, after authorization by the management committee.

Sub-section IV. The Director

Article 20. The director:
represents the state in the enterprise or concern;
oversees the legality of the economic or financial operations of the concern; in particular:
he opposes any operational or development plans that do not conform to the national plan;

The Décrets de Mars

he vetoes any measure that does not conform with Articles 3, 4 and 5;
he opposes any reduction in the original capital value of the means of production of the enterprise;

undertakes, under the president's authority, the day-to-day running of the enterprise by applying the decisions of the management committee and the workers' council, in conformity with the laws and regulations;

signs documents involving financial commitments and cheques;
holds funds in cash for current expenses;
checks the annual accounts;

draws up and keeps inventories of immovable and movable material and keeps the accounts of the enterprise according to the rules and procedures laid down by the supervisory body;

is the secretary of the management committee as well as of the council and workers' general assembly, keeps the minutes and sends a copy to the supervisory body.

Article 21. The director is automatically a member of the management committee with the right to vote. He may never be president. The management committee may call on him to present reports to the council or the general assembly.

Article 22. The director, who must possess the personal and professional qualities required by his work, is nominated and dismissed by the supervisory body on the agreement of the communal council for the promotion of self-management (CCAA).

He may be dismissed from his post as director only for a serious offence, or for obvious incompetence, or if the communal council for the promotion of self-management withdraws its recognition.

Section II. Bodies for the promotion of self-management

Article 23. A communal council for the promotion of self-management is to be set up in each commune, composed of the presidents of the management committees and the respective representatives of the party, the UGTA, the ANP and the communal administrative authorities.

If necessary, an intercommunal council may be created in place of the communal councils, but it may not take the place of more than five such councils.

Article 24. The communal council for the promotion of self-management:

assists in the creation and organization of management bodies in enterprises;

involves the workers in the problems of self-management;

coordinates the activities of the enterprises under self-management in the commune;

calls on the technical and financial assistance of the supervisory body in matters of management and control;

gives or withholds its recognition of the director appointed by the supervisory body in accordance with Article 22 of the present decree.

Article 25. The communal council for the promotion of self-management elects its president from the presidents of the enterprises under self-management. It meets, on the initiative of its president, at least once every three months.

Article 26. Neither the members of the workers' councils and management committees of enterprises nor the members of the communal council may receive any special payment for the tasks involved in membership, since the time devoted to the meetings and work of these bodies will be considered part of normal working hours and remunerated at normal rates.

Article 27. Members of the above bodies only exercise the functions entailed by their membership during the meetings of the bodies of which they are members; they may not take advantage of those functions outside the meeting of those bodies except with the express permission of the body concerned.

Article 28. Any person who knowingly hinders the functioning of a management committee will be liable to the penalty of one to five years' imprisonment and a fine of between 1,000 and 10,000 DA, or to one or other of the two.

Article 29. The provisions of the present decree come into force on its publication and must be executed in full within a year.

Article 30. The present decree on the organization of self-management of enterprises annuls all earlier contrary provisions.

Article 31. The manner and means of application of the present decree will be defined by presidential circulars.

DECREE NO. 63.98 OF 28 MARCH 1963

Regulating the distribution of revenue in enterprises and concerns under self-management.

Article 1. The annual revenue of each enterprise under self-management is equal to the annual production of that enterprise (i.e. the total output for the year in products and services) less running costs other than labour costs.

Article 2. The annual revenue thus determined is divided into two principal categories:

The Décrets de Mars

levies payable to the national community;

revenue due to the workers of the enterprise under self-management.

Article 3. Payments due to the national community comprise levies for:

the redemption of financial liabilities incurred by the enterprise under self-management. The total and the employment of this levy are subject to official regulations. The enterprise may, however, be partially or totally absolved from this levy by the supervisory authority if internal or external economic circumstances render this necessary;

the national investment fund;

the national fund for balanced employment.

The nature of these funds will be defined by subsequent texts which must provide for the participation of workers in their management.

In making these levies, account will be taken of the practical possibilities of contribution by the enterprise on the basis of normal production.

The totals and payment systems of these levies, the working of the national investment fund and the national fund for balanced employment will be fixed by official regulations.

Article 4. The income due to the workers of the enterprise includes:
  (a) The payment of seasonal workers in enterprises under self-management, in particular the wages and benefits offered to these workers in conformity with social legislation.
  (b) The basic wages of the regular workers, fixed by the supervisory body according to job and based on the norms of minimum productivity.
  (c) Productivity bonuses attributed to regular workers according to individual and team output. These bonuses are fixed by the management committee and must be approved by the supervisory body. They are given periodically in so far as the workers' output exceeds the minima laid down in clause (b) above.

Basic wages and productivity bonuses are paid in cash or in kind (in the form of goods produced by the enterprise, the values of which are calculated on the basis of market prices). The forms of such payments are fixed by the management committee with the agreement of the director.

These basic wages and productivity bonuses are counted in finance and before the law as salaries.

  (d) A remainder to be shared. The workers' council or, if necessary, the general assembly decides on how it shall be divided.

It may decide to deduct from this remainder further sums attributed to:
> the investment fund of the enterprise in question;
> the social fund of the enterprise (towards housing, equipment for education, leisure activities, health, mutual insurance schemes, participation in communal, union or cooperative funds, etc.);
> any reserve fund or provision it may judge necessary.

The surplus balance is shared out at the end of the financial year between all the members of the general assembly of workers in proportion to their respective basic wages plus production bonuses as laid down for the members of that assembly.

The general assembly of workers may, however, at the suggestion of the management committee, take a levy on this surplus balance to be given to the director and members of the management committee as a bonus for good management.

If the funds of the enterprise under self-management are running low, the director may decide that the sum payable to the members of the general assembly of workers shall be paid into the general account of the enterprise until the state of the general funds permits a final payment. This payment must never involve an increase of debts owed by the enterprise to third parties.

Article 5. If the annual income of the enterprise is not sufficient to enable it to fulfil its obligations towards its workers and the national community as defined in Articles 3 and 4 above, the management committee should, on the suggestion of the director, take the necessary measures to right the situation. These measures are submitted to the workers' council and the general assembly.

Article 6. To satisfy this present decree, the director, besides the legal accounts forms, keeps check on the following business documents for which he is responsible:
> an annual production and sales programme or campaign;
> an annual account of running expenses and a budget forecast;
> an investment programme;
> a table of basic wages and bonuses attributed to each job.

Article 7. The annual accounts should include, besides the balance sheet, the accounts necessary for the application of Articles 1, 2 and 3 above.

Article 8. The annual income of enterprises under self-management is liable to tax on industrial, commercial or agricultural profits, as may be appropriate, in conformity with the legislation governing cooperatives. However, the following sums are considered deductible expenses:
> levies for the national community listed in Article 3 above;

basic wages and productivity bonuses to regular workers;
wages paid to seasonal workers and the benefits offered them in accordance with social legislation.

Article 9. A member of the general assembly of workers who, for whatever reason, leaves the enterprise, has no right to the benefits accorded by the investment fund, social fund, sinking fund or by any of the reserves or provisions of that enterprise.

Unless he has been dismissed for a serious offence, he may participate on the basis of length of service in the share-out of the net income.

APPENDIX II

LA CHARTE D'ALGER

As far as I can discover, the texts adopted by the first congress of the FLN (16–21 April 1964), and afterwards known as *La Charte d'Alger*, have never been translated into English; even the original French edition, published in Algiers, achieved only a limited circulation. The full text runs to 176 pages and it is obviously impossible to reproduce it in full here. Some of the passages relevant to the argument over *autogestion* and its relation to the economy, the party and the state were outlined in Chapter 7. Two sections which are of relevance to this discussion are translated in full below. These are 'the ideological foundations of the Algerian revolution' and a discussion on the problems of transition from capitalism to socialism. Implicit in both these sections is an attempt to draw lessons from the fate of the Russian revolution under Stalin. Despite the obvious limitations of the analysis, the *Charte* remains one of the key documents of the Algerian revolution, even if only in terms of its aspirations.

Chapter III Ideological Foundations of the Algerian Revolution

The Characteristics of Algerian Society

1. An understanding of the present state of our country, of the struggles taking place there, and of the contradictions to be overcome demands an exact identification of its characteristics.

Algeria is an Arab and Muslim country. However, this definition excludes all references to ethnic criteria and does not imply an underestimation of the 'stock' existing before Arab penetration.* The division of the Arab world into individualized geographical or economic units has not been able to force into the background the unifying factors forged by history, Islamic culture and a common language.

---

* This refers, especially, to the Berbers of the Kabylie who form a distinct linguistic and cultural group within Algeria. The distinction between Berber and Arab was fostered by the colonial authorities and the fears of the Berber minority played an important role before and after independence.

La Charte d'Alger

The Algerian masses are strongly religious and have fought vigorously to free Islam from all the deviations and superstitions which have suffocated or changed it. They have always reacted against the charlatans who wanted to turn it into a doctrine of resignation and have related it to their own desire to end the exploitation of man by man.

The Algerian revolution has an obligation to itself to give back to Islam its true identity – that of progress.

The Arab and Muslim essence of the Algerian nation has been a solid rampart against its destruction by colonialism. The brutal suppression of institutions, the direct appropriation of land, means of exchange and the state apparatus by a foreign minority, which owed its position to conquest, has not stopped the Algerian people from reconstructing a new social life. All that they have done is to give a specific character to agricultural and cultural problems and to questions of administrative and technical organization.

2. The struggle for the victory of democratic principles has penetrated the masses, given impetus to their actions, and determined their attitude and perspectives. Through the armed resistance to French imperialism they have become conscious of their own strength and ability to solve their own problems themselves.

3. Algeria has just emerged from colonial domination. The compromise peace of Évian* may block the revolution if the terms of the agreement are not refused in the national interest.

The Évian Agreements are the mould which has shaped the rebirth of the Algerian nation and state.

However, the presence of the French army† and still more the nature of our financial and economic relations with France, limit our sovereignty and give particular emphasis to negative phenomena and to the activities of the national exploitative stratum.‡ The national tasks laid down in the Tripoli Programme remain. Imperialism is still the major enemy of our country. The party must fight vigorously against those who wish to undermine our will to disengage ourselves from imperialism by submerging it under the weight of everyday problems; who wish to lull popular vigilance and make our dependence even greater. The struggle to consolidate independence and the struggle for the triumph of our socialist option are inextricably linked. To separate them is to encourage

---

* The Évian Agreements, signed in March 1962, involved a cease-fire and provisions for a referendum on independence as well as stipulating the structure of relations after independence.

† Under the terms of the Évian Agreements the French were to keep a military presence in Algeria.

‡ The word in the original is *couche*, which will be translated as 'stratum'.

Workers' Self-Management in Algeria

the growth and influence of forces hostile to socialism and to water down the leading role of the toiling mass of workers and peasants into a series of groups without any principles.

4. Algeria is characterized by the unequal development of its different regions. This situation, inherited from the past, gives a real significance to the phenomena of regionalism, survivals of feudalism and other forces opposed to progress. Equal rights for all Algerians would be an empty principle if no account were taken of the development of the material base. Only the increase of the general wealth of the country and the development of productive forces in the backward areas can lead to the removal of the obstacles to the integration of these areas and the establishment of the harmony necessary for the normal evolution of the country.

5. National resistance to colonialism and imperialism found its basic support in the mountains. But the immediate advantages of independence have been felt in the towns and the plains. There is a contradiction here. To solve this contradiction we must work to unite the poor peasantry with the workers of the towns and realize one of the most important conditions for the victory of socialism. The accomplishment of this task is all the more vital because the groups most open to the idea of a social revolution (workers, intellectuals, etc. . . .) have at times been less lucid over questions of the national liberation struggle than have other more traditional strata. The country runs the risk that the ideologues in the service of the exploiters will use their relative clarity on the national question to prevent a scientific approach to problems which are now of a revolutionary nature.

6. Colonialism developed habits of consumption among Algerians which are out of proportion to the real possibilities of the country. These habits, aggravated by the war, have created an astounding corruption. The Party cannot accept, without cutting itself off from the masses, the present disparity of incomes. It must combat vigorously the parasitism which developed in conditions of a compulsory exploitation of the working masses. The success of this struggle is linked with the elimination of the privileged strata from the front of the stage and, instead, the exercise of political responsibility and control by the toiling mass themselves. This is the only just and effective way to avoid falling into the trap of pseudo-egalitarianism.

Structure and Tendencies of Algerian Society

7. In our country, the social structure has been determined by the character it acquired under imperialism. This factor has retarded the development of the privileged national strata at the same time as

La Charte d'Alger

promoting the proletarianization and impoverishment of the vast majority of the population.

8. At the end of 130 years of settler colonialism Algeria had only a few relatively important industrialists and a few higher grade cadres and intellectuals. More important bourgeois elements were formed by the larger traders and above all by the medium and large land-owners. In total the bourgeois strata did not exceed 50,000, less than a fortieth of the active population.

9. The petit-bourgeoisie, a potential source of elements with a bourgeois ideology hostile to socialism, filled a more important position in agriculture, retail trade, artisan production and the lower technical, administrative and intellectual grades, etc. . . . In total, about an eighth of the active population.

10. To determine the effective weight of these bourgeois and petit-bourgeois strata in the social conflict we must take account not only of their economic role but also of their ideological, cultural and political influence in a peasant and working-class environment which is very unfavourable to them.

11. Since independence a new and rapidly developing social stratum threatens to appear in the form of the instinctive anti-socialism of the bureaucratic bourgeoisie which is forming in the machinery of the administration, the state and the economy. This is due to the feelings of power brought on by the exercise of power.

12. This force, through its position in the state and economic machinery, may become considerably more dangerous to the democratic and socialist evolution of the revolution than any other existing social force in the country. This is due to the fact that the Algerian state has maintained the administrative structures established by colonialism when it was called, by the historic development of the revolution, to assume an economic role for which the administrative structures were not fitted. In effect, the structures established by colonialism had as their aim the promotion of a liberal economy in which economic organization was left to the owners of the means of production, the entrepreneurs and the intellectuals of the liberal professions.

13. It is because the administrative and economic bureaucracy was led to assume an economic role within the framework of the colonial administrative structures that it may become considerably more dangerous to the democratic and socialist evolution of the revolution than any other existing social force in the country. It can transmit equally well the influence of imperialism and the national bourgeoisie whose aim is to thwart a socialist policy and then sabotage it.

The Socialist Revolution

14. The global dynamic of the social struggle as it is manifested in the aftermath of the liberation operates in favour of creating a socialist opening for the revolution. The overwhelming majority of the peasants and workers, who live in conditions of extreme poverty, are struggling for the radical transformation of traditional colonial society and are applying all the measures which the government has adopted to this end. These measures have been speeded up by the abrupt disappearance of the true property-owning class of the country, the Europeans.

15. It is in the interaction of these objective conditions that we can find the origin of the decree annulling transactions (in the *biens-vacants*). This expressed the decision of the government to halt the growth of forces hostile to socialism by preventing them from appropriating the national patrimony which was regained during the war of national liberation thanks to the sacrifices of the peasants and workers.

16. Equally, it is in this interaction of objective conditions that we must look for the origin of the movement of the *comités de gestion*. This constituted a form of revolutionary continuity underlying the measures taken by the post-war political and military authorities. The movement, encouraged and institutionalized by the government, has led to the present system of *autogestion* – the principal characteristic, in Algeria, of the road to socialism.

17. *Autogestion* expresses the desire of the country's labouring strata to emerge on the political and economic scene and to make themselves its controlling force. Economically, *autogestion* has brought about the need to extend agrarian reform and nationalizations in agriculture and industry, and to reorganise internal and external trade and the banking system. Politically, it places the reciprocal relations of the state, party, unions and masses in a new light, which implies the constant development of the democratic character of all these institutions in their relations with the masses. Democratic socialism, which is indispensable, must make itself known and become concrete through the existence at the base of truly democratic organs for the management of the economy, truly popular organs for the democratic administration of the communes, truly democratic unions and an effective administration controlled by the masses.

18. The uninterrupted development of the popular national revolution into the socialist revolution is, and will go on being, manifested in *autogestion*. This poses all the economic and political problems resulting from the present transition from colonialism to the emergence of a state opening the way to socialism. In this process the role of the urban

La Charte d'Alger

workers, together with the agricultural workers of the self-managed sector, will become more and more decisive because the social bases of revolutionary power can only be the working masses allied to the poor peasants of the traditional sector and the revolutionary intellectual elements.

19. The nature of revolutionary power is to be the defender of the interests of the labouring strata which constitute its social bases. That is why we cannot avoid a confrontation with the privileged strata which contain, on the one hand, all those who own, in varying degrees, the means of production and, on the other, the bureaucratic bourgeoisie.

20. In respect of these privileged strata, the revolutionary power must adopt a political stance based on the distinction between private property that is exploitative and private property which is not exploitative.

21. The revolutionary power can allow no delay in the struggle against exploitative private property, whether it is in the countryside or the town. Any underestimation of the social base of the capitalist elements, who find allies outside the country, can only constitute a check in the affirmation of revolutionary politics. The working masses of town and country alike are equally anxious to overcome the difficulties born of the resistance and the sabotage carried out by anti-socialist forces. The duty of the party and the revolutionary power is to show the masses the danger of these forces and mobilize them against them.

22. In relation to the petit-bourgeois strata of the tertiary sector and the middle peasantry, the policy of the revolutionary power must be to neutralize them through a whole series of measures which, while containing the potential bourgeois development of these strata, does not, at first, threaten or worsen their situation. On the contrary, the duty of the party will be to explain to these strata that the policy of the revolutionary power will lead to the ending of their own exploitation by big commercial, banking and industrial capital; something which will make their own situation considerably better.

23. The socialist transformation of the countryside poses some particular problems. It must be limited to the consolidation and dynamism of the socialist agricultural sector, and to the voluntary acceptance of socialist management by the small proprietors. The non-exploitative small proprietor must be respected.

24. The struggle for the triumph of socialism does not develop harmoniously. Only the conscious action of the controlling social forces and the propagation of socialist ideas can make it possible to overcome the economic, social and political contradictions which are a result of the low level of the forces of production, the underdeveloped nature of the

social consciousness of the workers, the bureaucratic deformations of the state apparatus and the absence of any real roots to the unions or party. These objectives demand a constant struggle to tighten the links with the working masses and to uproot the reactionary attitudes forged in the conditions of exploitation of man by man. Parasitism, the search for illegal profits or social advantages, must be denounced and combated, their consequences frankly exposed to the masses.

25. The need to create social and political ideas rooted in our own values, fed with scientific principles and fore-armed against erroneous attitudes, indicates the importance of a new conception of culture.

26. Algerian culture will be national, revolutionary and scientific.

(a) Its role as a national culture will consist, primarily, in giving back to the Arab language – itself the very expression of the cultural values of our country – its dignity and efficacy as a civilizing language. To do this, it will apply itself to reconstitute, revalorise and make known the national heritage and its dual humanism – classic and modern – before reintroducing them into the intellectual and educational life of the people. Thus, it will fight the cultural cosmopolitanism and Western impregnation which have helped to inculcate a disdain for their own language and national values among many Algerians.

(b) As a revolutionary culture it will contribute to the task of freeing the people; a task which consists of liquidating the remnants of feudalism, anti-social myths and reactionary and conformist habits of thinking. It will be neither a caste culture, closed off to progress, nor a luxury. Being popular and militant, it will clarify the struggle of the masses in the political and social combats. Through its conception as a culture active in the service of society, it will help in the development of a revolutionary consciousness by ceaselessly reflecting the aspirations of the people, their realities and new victories. It will also reflect all the forms of its artistic traditions.

(c) As a scientific culture in its means and scope, Algerian culture must define itself in terms of its rational character, its technical equipment, the spirit of research which animates it, and its methodical and generalized diffusion to all levels of the society.

27. From this stems the need to renounce routinized conceptions which might block creative effort and paralyse teaching by aggravating the obscurantism inherited from colonial domination. This necessity is all the greater because the language has suffered such a setback as an instrument of modern scientific culture that it must be promoted, in its future roles, by the most vigorously concrete and perfected methods.

For the Development of a Socialist Way of Thinking

28. Far from depending merely on professions of socialist faith, socialism is the result, foremost, of the irreversible affirmation of socialist social, economic and political structures; that is to say, the exclusion of all forms of exploitation of man by man. Because, above all, men are what they are and not what they say they are.

29. But socialism thus inscribed in objective reality must at the same time have as an indicator and catalyst a clear socialist consciousness, widely distributed and continually radicalized. It is a fatal error to underestimate the political factor in the march of socialism.

30. In consequence, to ensure socialization and to deepen it we must keep watch to see that the elaboration and diffusion of our socialist ideas are developed in every possible way.

31. We must, above all, impregnate the life of the nation with the convictions which constitute the pillars of our socialist option and which revolve round the struggle against imperialism, capitalism and bureaucracy. By means of unceasing campaigns, of the appropriate *mots d'ordre*, we must refill the Algerian political stage with slogans that mark the stages of our revolution by making the people assimilate its gains and by helping them to become conscious of the dangers and obstacles to be overcome.

32. It is a necessary supplement to this that, at the level of all intellectual activity, the content of socialism should be popularized in such a way as to mould our mentality definitively. To this end, the importance of education, at every level, as an instrument of ideological training must be insisted on. This implies, notably, a revolutionary reorganization of the programmes left by colonialism and capitalism. Also, we must undertake a systematic programme of socialist education for the workers, for example, by a vast number of popular universities and this must be pursued throughout the country.

33. At the level of the political formation of the country, the greatest importance must be given to the profound and institutionalized study of the problems of socialism and its application in Algeria as the main means of allowing militants to continue the revolutionary struggle through which will emerge our socialist country.

Part II   Chapter 1   From Capitalism to Socialism

The Period of Transition

18. The period of transition is when the political organization of the society prepares for socialism, starting with the abolition of the ex-

ploitation of man by man, the establishment of the material and social bases for a rapid development of the forces of production, and the freeing of the workers' creative activity. None of these aspects must be given precedence over the others, since they are an indissoluble whole.

19. The suppression of economic exploitation, the abolition of colonial and neo-colonial relationships, the expropriation of dominant foreign capital, the agrarian revolution, the socialization of the means of production will all allow us to end economic anarchy and make it possible to plan effectively and harmoniously in the real interests of the community.

20. These general conditions imply the construction of a popular state which will express the will of the masses to build socialism and which will organize the defence of revolutionary achievements, at the same time as inspiring a dynamic policy in its relations with other countries and peoples.

21. The primary task of such a state is to preserve the existing socialist experience and to help overcome the inevitable difficulties, to intervene in the private sector to speed up the process of socialization, to make good the lack of direct [workers'] management, where it is not yet possible, without ever losing sight of the fact that this exceptional managerial role, which it has to assume, is only a temporary phase in the preparation for full self-management.

22. These political preconditions open the way for industrialization, but do not, in themselves, resolve the problem. In countries with a basically agrarian structure the peasants are demanding that their living standards should be better than they were. This demand, which is reflected in an increase in consumption, leads to a diminution of the social surplus. There is a contradiction here which must be clearly grasped.

23. Reducing the diminution of the social surplus by relying, in an unprincipled way, on foreign aid compromises independence itself. Organizing society by constraint to reduce the standard of living in an authoritarian manner leads to the development of a bureaucracy which is the complete negation of socialism.

24. Confusing the optimum level of accumulation with the maximum level can only lead to grave crises. An optimum level (which must be our aim) cannot come through the imposition of constraints on the workers. That would entail depolitization, a tendency to desert the villages, towns and factories, and a general spirit of social irresponsibility.

25. Even on an economic level the unnatural search for a maximum level [of accumulation] is unprofitable and *can have totally the opposite effect*. In effect, the level of productivity is dependent on the level of

La Charte d'Alger

consumption and an underfed worker is not an efficient worker. Moreover, the open or masked resistance of the workers would mean having to develop a coercive apparatus and a parasitic administration which would raise the level of unproductive consumption.

26. One of the factors limiting accumulation is under-employment, which means that an important percentage of the population consumes without producing. The entrance of this 'reserve army' into the cycle of economic production would certainly raise levels of consumption but it would be less than the increase in production. The result would be a possibly very important increase in accumulation.

27. Opening public works, putting the rural unemployed to work, is not, however, a panacea for industrialization but an economic means for giving the initial impulse. The solidarity, based on reciprocal interests, between nations at different levels of development but with common perspectives, should not be neglected.

28. The problem of the construction of the economic structures of socialism cannot be separated from the problem of the necessary technical cadres. There are not enough of these in countries that stagnated under foreign bondage. Thus they must be carefully nurtured at the same time as we develop a policy of rapid intellectual and professional training.

29. This problem of cadres cannot be isolated from the world context, particularly the attractions they may feel for jobs offered in the private sector abroad. Obviously, biasing wages in favour of cadres poses a problem not only for any policy of austerity but also for the principles of equality. But it is necessary to be aware of certain realities which, though transitory, are contradictory.

30. What we must avoid is allowing privileges based on technical ability to be transformed into political privilege; also, that the cadres, themselves a particular stratum, do not organize society on a technocratic model. Here also the real solution lies in *autogestion*.

31. The essential principle of the period of transition is that the means must be related to the ends. There is an intrinsic relationship between the instruments used and the results obtained. A new society cannot be developed using methods and structures that were part of the development of capitalism. The principle of creating controlling groups which organize the masses, who obey, is the basic principle of capitalist society.

32. The basic questions in the new society are these: Who controls and sanctions the obligation to work? Who establishes the norms? Who controls production? If the solution leads to a separation between the social group [*catégorie sociale*] charged with controlling the work of

Workers' Self-Management in Algeria

others and the producers, then socialism is compromised. Only the organized collectivity of the workers can assume this task. Only it can establish plans that are more than artificial schema only capable of realization on paper. Only it can give a collective solution to a collective problem. That is the meaning of *autogestion*.

33. The transitional programme is a necessary stage in realizing the material and human conditions of socialism. The poverty of the economy justifies the division of labour. It could never justify the persistence of exploitation in any form.

34. During this period it is impossible to create, immediately, a situation any better than the one the country inherited. It is illusory to believe that plenty comes at the wave of a wand. But the real difficulty does not lie there. It lies in justice and equality.

35. In such a period the salary and social advantages given to the ruling strata and the state apparatus are very important. It would be quite illegitimate if a privileged caste was installed, whether it was privileged in terms of its prestige or financial position. Also, extravagant expenditure* not only increases the difficulties of accumulation but forms a basis for discontent and a quite comprehensible opposition.

36. Knowledge of the perspectives of socialism is necessary, not just to achieve a rounded picture of the changes or to justify the effort needed to create them but, even more, because it serves as a touchstone to judge whether events are progressing or degenerating. Each one of the characteristics of future society must be prepared for during the present struggle.

37. *Autogestion* is the basic principle of this society. With it are reached the end of exploitation, and the understanding by each worker of the meaning of his actions because economic and political activities will become inseparable: it is the direct involvement of the producer in production, i.e. the complete opposite of wage labour. With it is realized the beginning of the reign of liberty.

* The original is *dépenses somptuaires* which is meaningless in the context.

APPENDIX III

ECONOMIC INDICES

THE problem of finding accurate statistics on anything relating to Algeria is enormous. Most of the figures published in the past by the government and its agencies have fluctuated wildly and provide no real basis for analysis. Comparisons with the period before independence are of limited use as, from 1958 onwards, the internal market was deformed by the presence of up to a million military and auxiliary personnel, while the war itself severely distorted all forms of economic activity.

The following tables are drawn from three main sources: *The Economist* Intelligence Unit reports; *La Zone Franc*; *Marchés Tropicaux*. Another, irregular but useful, source is *L'Annuaire de l'Afrique du Nord*.

TABLE 1. *Algerian government revenue and expenditure, 1962–8 (in millions of* DA)

	1962	1963	1964	1965	1966	1967	1968
current revenue	3,272	2,575	2,632	2,831	2,890	3,151	3,280
current expenditure	3,270	2,573	2,632	3,053	3,200	3,332	3,539
balance	+2	+2	—	−222	−310	−181	−259
investment receipts	—	2,245	2,198	967	1,450	1,294	1,590
investment expenditure	—	2,245	2,198	1,169	1,746	1,375	1,537
total revenue	—	4,820	4,830	3,798	4,190	4,156	4,530
total expenditure	—	4,818	4,830	4,222	4,946	4,707	5,076
balance	—	+2	—	−424	−756	−651	−546

TABLE 2. *Algerian government investment receipts and sources (in millions of* DA*)*

	Algerian	External	Total
1963	154	2,091	2,245
1964	500	1,698	2,198
1965	337	630	967
1966	900 (oil – 750)	550	1,450
1967	1,039 (oil – 750)	225	1,264
1968	1,340 (oil – 1,000)	250	1,590

TABLE 3. *Investment expenditure (in millions of* DA*)*

	1963	1964	1965	1966	1967	1968
agriculture	803	709	190	118	161	213
industry	342	553	273	626	399	515
infrastructure	459	360	183	303	243	338
education	218	200	249	129	215	195
housing/health	392	267	124	98	101	145
total (including other unclassified expenditure)	2,245	2,198	1,169	1,746	1,375	1,537

TABLE 4. *Algerian foreign trade figures, 1960–68 (in millions of* DA*)*

	1960	1962	1963	1964	1965	1966	1967	1968
exports	1,947	2,329	3,465	3,710	3,490	3,069	3,528	3,873
imports	6,298	2,424	3,900	3,740	3,680	3,153	3,154	3,428
balance	–4,351	–95	–435	–30	–190	–84	+374	+445

The figures for both 1960 and 1962 are exceptional. They do not include oil in the export figures. The severe drop in imports in 1962 is a result of the dislocation of the settler market and economic activity in general.

Economic Indices

The breakdown of the 1968 figures is as follows (per cent):

	imports	exports
food, drink, tobacco	16·5	16·3
fuel and lubricants	1·4	69·0
raw materials	6·0	5·4
semi-manufactured goods	23·6	5·1
finished products for agriculture	2·9	0·2
manufactured goods for industry	28·2	3·0
consumer goods	21·4	1·0

TABLE 5. *Agricultural production, 1962–8 (in thousands of tons)*

	1962–3	1963–4	1964–5	1965–6	1966–7	1967–8
wheat	1,495	1,580	1,121	1,323	627	1,266
barley	800	950	278	379	138	340
wine	1,228	1,258	1,048	1,043	682	1,100
olive oil	15	15	15	14	13	22
citrus fruit	366	464	415	402	401	400

TABLE 6. *Indices of industrial output, 1958–68*
(in thousands of tons, unless otherwise stated)

	1958	1963	1964	1965	1966	1967	1968
cement	842	602	730	739	657	731	866
superphosphates	101	52	88	79	74	74	114
steel	24·1	9·4	19·8	20·1	20·9	22·6	28·1
cigarettes/tobacco	10·0	0·5	0·5	6·2	8·4	7·8	8·0
*cotton yarn	(1960 – 0·9)	0·2	0·5	1·0	2·0	2·9	6·9
*shoes (thousands of pairs)	546	1,080	1,400	1,900	2,600	2,975	3,095

* Both shoes and cotton are relatively new industries and their rise can be partially attributed to the opening of new factories.

TABLE 7. *Mining output, 1961–8 (in thousands of tons)*

	1961	1963	1964	1965	1966	1967	1968
iron ore	2,868	1,976	2,746	3,147	1,764	2,467	3,085
lime phosphates	426	348	73	86	94	198	360
zinc	77	56	59	57	25	13	26
coal	78	38	46	45	45	15	—

TABLE 8. (a) *Oil production, 1961–8 (in thousands of tons)*

1961	1962	1963	1964	1965	1966*	1967	1968
17,800	20,487	23,637	26,223	26,022	33,253	38,376	42,500

* A new pipeline to the coast was opened in 1966.

(b) *Gas production (in millions of cubic metres)*

1961	1965	1968
231	1,838	2,556

REFERENCES

Chapter 1   Workers' Councils: A Historical Perspective
1. J. L. and B. Hammond, *The Rise of Modern Industry* (London, 1951).
2. Patrick Renshaw, *The Wobblies* (London, 1967).
3. See Malatesta, *Life and Ideas*, ed. Vernon Richards (London, 1965).
4. For documents and discussion on the split between Marx and Bakunin, see James Guillaume, *L'Internationale, documents et souvenirs, 1864–1878*, 4 vols. (Paris, 1905–10) for a Bakuninist account. For an orthodox Communist account see Y. M. Stekloff, *History of the First International* (London, 1928).
5. Lenin, *The Russian Revolution of 1905* (London, 1931), though the seeds of his ideas can be seen in *What Is To Be Done?* (London, n.d.).
6. Lenin, *The State and the Revolution* (Moscow, n.d.).
7. For an account of both of these incidents from an anarchist viewpoint, see Voline, *The Unknown Revolution* (London, 1955).
8. Alexandra Kollontai, *The Workers' Opposition* (London, 1963).
9. For a case study of the Italian experience, see J. M. Cammett, *Antonio Gramsci and the Origins of Italian Communism* (London, 1967).
10. H. R. Isaacs, *The Tragedy of the Chinese Revolution* (Oxford, 1961).
11. José Peirats, *La CNT en la Revolución Española*, 3 vols (Toulouse, 1953).
12. Andy Anderson, *Hungary 56* (London, 1964).
13. See Oscar Lange, *On the Economic Theory of Socialism* (London, 1964).
14. The most thorough account of the Polish councils is André Babeau, *Les Conseils Ouvriers en Pologne* (Paris, 1960). Some of the original documents, etc., can be read in 'La courte expérience des conseils ouvriers en Pologne', *La Documentation Française*, no. 2453, August 1958.
15. A description of the legislation can be read in 'The New Law on Workers' Controls', *Polish Perspectives*, no. 3, March 1959. For a depth study from a sociological position, see J. Kolaja, *A Polish Factory: A Case Study in Workers' Participation* (Lexington, 1960).

Workers' Self-Management in Algeria

16. The classic, if liberal, description of the class character of the party *élite* is developed by Milovan Djilas, *The New Class* (London, 1957).
17. See especially E. Kardelj, *'Dix ans de révolution populaire à la lumière de l'histoire'*, *Questions Actuelles du Socialisme*, nos. 5–6 July–September 1951, and Milovan Djilas, *On New Roads to Socialism* (Belgrade, 1950).
18. For a confirmation of this viewpoint, see Isaac Deutscher, *The Unfinished Revolution* (London, 1967), p. 31.
19. For a discussion on this, see B. Macfarlane, 'Jugoslavia's cross roads', *Socialist Register*, 1966.
20. E. Bernstein, *Evolutionary Socialism* (London, 1909), p. 119.
21. For a description of works' councils during the Weimar period, see C. W. Guilebaud, *The Works Councils* (Cambridge, 1928).
22. H. J. Spiro, *The Politics of German Codetermination* (Cambridge, Mass., 1958), p. 8.
23. F. W. Taylor, *Scientific Management* (New York, 1947).
24. Elton Mayo, *The Social Problems of an Industrial Civilization* (Boston, 1945).
25. Expositions of this type of view can be seen in C. Argyris, *Personality and Organisation* (New York, 1957), and J. A. C. Brown, *The Social Psychology of Industry* (London, 1964).
26. R. Blauner, *Alienation and Freedom: The Factory Worker and His Industry* (Chicago, 1964).

Chapter 2   A Colonial Prehistory

1. Quoted by R. Barbé, *'La question de la terre en Algérie'*, *Économie et Politique*, November 1955.
2. Marshal Bugeaud in a despatch from Ouled Ysser, May 1844.
3. Colonel Bouteilleux, *Campagnes d'Afrique* (Paris, 1842), p. 273.
4. Thus, writing in 1929, E. F. Gautier, *L'Algérie d'Aujourd'hui et Demain* (Paris, 1929), could say: *'Il n'y a pas en Algérie une seule grande ville indigène.'*
5. A good account of the period of the French conquest can be found in Mostefa Lacheraf, *L'Algérie: Nation et Société* (Paris, 1963).
6. Poujoulat, *Voyage en Algérie*, p. 301 (quoted in above, p. 52).
7. See F. Jeanson, *La Révolution Algérienne* (Milan, 1962), p. 29.
8. P. Hernandez, *'Ceux qui étaient les pieds-noirs'*, *La Nef, Cahiers* 12–13, October 1962–January 1963.
9. Taken from Tom Wengraf, 'The Algerian Revolution', *New Left Review*, no. 22, December 1963.
10. Cited in Barbé, *'Les classes sociales en Algérie'*, *Économie et Politique*, Part I, September 1959; Part II, October 1959.
11. In this context, see M. Launay, *Paysans Algériens* (Paris, 1963), p. 102 (in 1959 a hectare of vines brought a net profit of 2,500–3,000 NF).

References

12. Barbé, op. cit.
13. For a good history of nationalist politics up to the formation of the FLN, see André Nouschi, *La Naissance du Nationalisme Algérien: 1914–1954* (Paris, 1962).
14. For a description of the founding of the *Étoile Nord Africaine*, see Mohammed Lebajoui, *Vérités sur la Révolution Algérienne* (Paris, 1970).
15. Maurice Violette had been Governor-General of Algeria from 1925–7 and favoured assimilation. See Violette, *L'Algérie, Vivra-t-elle?* (Paris, 1931).
16. Quoted by M. Clark, *Algeria in Turmoil: A History of the Rebellion* (New York, 1959), p. 56.
17. For a detailed history of the period 1954–62, see Charles-Henri Favrod, *Le FLN et l'Algérie* (Paris, 1962); Jeanson, op. cit.; Jacques Duchemin, *Histoire du FLN* (Paris, 1962) and André Mandouze (ed.), *La Révolution Algérienne par les Textes: Documents du FLN* (Paris, 1961).
18. According to Rabah Bitat, the rebel army consisted of less than 900 in 1954; see interview in *L'Express*, 7 November 1963.
19. The Évian Agreements are dealt with in two analyses: Serge Moureaux, *Les Accords d'Évian et l'Avenir de la Révolution Algérienne* (Paris, 1962), which is sympathetic to the nationalist cause and contains the text of the agreements, and Maurice Allais, *L'Algérie d'Évian* (Paris, 1962), which is critical of France's treatment of the settlers.

Chapter 3   The Formation of the Comités de Gestion

1. See Jean Lartéguy, *Les Centurions* (Paris, 1960) for a fictionalized but accurate description of the attitudes of many of the professional army officers.
2. For accounts of this period and OAS activities, see Paul Marie de la Gorce, 'Histoire de l'OAS en Algérie', *La Nef, Cahiers* 12–13, October 1962–January 1963, pp. 139–92; Albert-Paul Lentin, *Le Dernier Quart d'Heure* (Paris, 1963); Morland, Barange and Martinez, *Histoire de l'Organisation de l'Armée Secrète* (Paris, 1964); Maurice Edelman, *The Fratricides* (London, 1963), a novel which gives a good feeling of the atmosphere.
3. See Brian Crozier, *The Morning After: A Study of Independence* (London, 1963), pp. 110–12.
4. FLN, *Projet de Programme pour la Réalisation de la Révolution Démocratique Populaire* (Algiers, n.d.), p. 19.
5. Tripoli Programme, p. 26.
6. ibid., p. 28.
7. Ben Bella claims that he avoided pressing this point at the conference for fear of creating a split; see Robert Merle, *Ben Bella* (Paris, 1965).

8. See Hervé Bourges, *L'Algérie à l'Épreuve du Pouvoir* (Paris, 1967); Laid Debzi, *Les Étapes de la Création du Nouvel État d'Algérie* (Brussels, 1965).
9. Authors taking this viewpoint are: Gérard Chaliand, *L'Algérie: est-elle Socialiste?* (Paris, 1964); Daniel Guérin, *L'Algérie qui se Cherche* (Paris, 1964); Mohammed Boudiaf, *Où Va l'Algérie* (Paris, 1964); François d'Arcy, Annie Kreiger and Alain Marill, *Essais sur l'Économie de l'Algérie Nouvelle* (Paris, 1965).
10. Two noteworthy right-wing accounts in this context are François Buy, *La République Algérienne, Démocratique et Populaire* (Paris, 1965) and Bachaga Boualem, *L'Algérie sous la France* (Paris, 1964).
11. Alain Marill, '*L'expérience algérienne d'autogestion industrielle*', in d'Arcy, Kreiger and Marill, op. cit., p. 118.
12. *L'Autogestion: Un Système et non une Expérience* (Algiers, 1967), published by a dissident group of FLN militants.
13. Mohammed Harbi, '*L'Algérie et ses réalités*', *Économie et Politique*, May 1965, p. 56.
14. See Buy, op. cit., and Boualem, op. cit.
15. Grigori Lazarev, '*Remarques sur l'autogestion agricole en Algérie*', *Institutions et Développement Agricole du Maghreb* (Paris, 1965).
16. *Ordonnance*, 24 August 1962, especially articles 8–12.
17. See Jean Zeigler, '*L'autogestion ouvrière en Algérie – problèmes et perspectives*', *La Revue Syndicale Suisse*, no. 12, December 1964.
18. Sabadell, '*L'autogestion en Algérie*', *Rouge et Noir*, no. 34, June 1966.
19. *Le Monde*, 23 October 1962.
20. Lazarev, op. cit.
21. See the UGTA declaration of 31 July 1962, quoted in *L'Annuaire de l'Afrique du Nord*, 1962, p. 711.
22. *L'Ouvrier Algérien*, February 1962 (n.s.), no. 32.
23. Zeigler, op. cit.
24. Lazarev, op. cit.
25. UGTA declaration of 31 July 1962.
26. PRS declaration of 20 August 1962, quoted in *L'Annuaire de l'Afrique du Nord*, 1962, p. 711.
27. Decree no. 62.02.
28. Decree no. 62.38.
29. Decree no. 62.03.
30. FLN, *Comprendre l'Autogestion* (Algiers, 1963), p. 12.
31. See Jean Poncet, '*Quelques problèmes de l'agriculture algérienne*', *Tiers Monde*, vol. 5, no. 18, April–June 1964 – this is a depth study of the Tiaret department. See also H. F., '*Les comités de gestion agricoles; leurs chances et leurs problèmes*', *Confluent*, nos. 32–3, June–July 1963, who emphasizes the differences between the permanent workers in the Mitidja and the shepherds and smallholders in the Kabylie.

References

Chapter 4   The Décrets de Mars

1. See C. Roulette, '*Situation de l'industrie algérienne*', *Économie et Politique*, May 1965, no. 130. However, the destruction of records by the OAS meant that several thousand small workshops disappeared from administrative sight.
2. See Arslam Humbaraci, *Algeria: The Revolution that Failed* (London, 1966).
3. Decree no. 63.88.
4. ibid., Article I.
5. Decree no. 63.95.
6. FLN, *Comprendre l'Autogestion* (Algiers, 1963), p. 39.
7. For a detailed study on the law relating to public appropriation in Algeria, see F. Borella, '*Le Droit public économique positif en Algérie*', *Revue Algérienne des Sciences Juridiques, Politiques et Économiques*, December 1966.
8. Decree no. 63.168.
9. Decree no. 63.388.
10. *Comprendre l'Autogestion*, pp. 40–41.
11. Decree no. 63.95.
12. *Voix de l'Algérie Socialiste*, broadcast 12 May 1963.
13. *Comprendre l'Autogestion*, p. 42.
14. Speech by Ben Bella, 15 May 1963.
15. ONAT was created by the *Exécutif Provisoire* from the *Section Tourisme* of the colonial *Office Algérien de l'Action Commerciale*. ONRA was created from the remnants of the colonial body – *Caisse d'Accession à la Propriété et à l'Exploitation Rurale* (CAPER).
16. Decree no. 63.100, Article II.
17. Decree no. 63. 95, Titre II.
18. *Comprendre l'Autogestion*, p. 25.
19. Decree no. 63.98.
20. Decree no. 64.176.
21. Borella, op. cit., p. 796.

Chapter 5   The Economy: The Heritage of Colonialism

1. This table and preceding figures on growth rates are taken from Samir Amin, *Le Maghreb: Colonisation, Décolonisation et Perspective de Développement*, UN (Dakar, 1965).
2. ibid.
3. FLN, *L'Émigration Algérienne: Problèmes et Perspectives* (Algiers, 1966), p. 103. This is a report of the *Séminaire National sur l'Émigration*, 8–13 August 1966.
4. Amin, op. cit., p. 79.
5. René Gendarme, *L'Économie de l'Algérie: Sous-développement et Politique de Croissance* (Paris, 1959), p. 275.
6. ibid., p. 373.

7. Amin, op. cit.
8. These figures are taken from V., '*Inventaire de l'économie algérienne en bref aperçu des tendances du secteur privé*', *Confluent*, nos. 32–3, June–July 1963.
9. Alain Marill, in François d'Arcy, Annie Kreiger and Alain Marill, *Essais sur l'Économie de l'Algérie Nouvelle* (Paris, 1965).
10. Jean Teillac, *Autogestion en Algérie* (Paris, 1965), pp. 35–6.
11. Ben Bella's closing speech to the *Congrès des Fellahs*, 25–7 October 1963, quoted in *Confluent*, no. 36, December 1963.
12. Quoted in *Politique Économique du Gouvernement, Exposé de Bachir Boumaza devant l'Assemblée Nationale le 30 Décembre 1963* (Algiers, 1964), p. 14.
13. André Tiano, 'Le contenu économique du socialisme algérien', *Revue Algérienne*, March 1964.
14. See *Algérie Presse Service* (APS), *Bulletin Économique*, nos. 73–4, August 1966.
15. Grigori Lazarev, '*Remarques sur l'autogestion agricole en Algérie*', *Institutions et Développement Agricole du Maghreb* (Paris, 1965). But H. Sethom, '*Les mutations des campagnes algériennes depuis l'indépendance*', *Revue Tunisienne des Sciences Sociales*, February 1965, gives a figure of 1,500–2,000 hectares.
16. The figure of forty-five per cent and the quotation comes from *Office des Nouvelles Algériennes* (ONA), no. 128, 31 December 1966, p. 14. ONA is a non-government organization publishing a paper mainly devoted to economic information.
17. See Barbé, '*Les classes sociales en Algérie*', *Économie et Politique*, Part I, September 1959.
18. *Enquête Industrielle 1957, Sous-direction des Statistiques* (Algiers, 1957).
19. *Enquête Semestrielle sur la situation de l'emploi au printemps 1966, Sous-direction des Statistiques* (Algiers, 1966).
20. ibid.
21. Tiano, op. cit., pp. 97–8.
22. See ONA, no. 128, 31 December 1966.
23. See FLN, *L'Émigration Algérienne*, op. cit.
24. ibid., p. 29.

Chapter 6   Class and Ideology in Algeria
1. See Frantz Fanon, *Les Damnés de la Terre* (Paris, 1961).
2. See *La Revue du Plan et des Études Économiques* (Algiers, 1964) and *La Revue Algérienne du Travail* (Algiers, 1964).
3. Gérard Chaliand, *L'Algérie: est-elle Socialiste?* (Paris, 1964), p. 83.
4. René Gendarme, *L'Économie de l'Algérie: Sous-développement et Politique de Croissance* (Paris, 1959), p. 53.
5. See especially J. H. Servier, '*Essai sur les bases de l'économie tradi-*

References

tionelle chez les berbérophones d'Algérie', Cahiers de l'Institut de Science Économique Appliquée, no. 106, October 1960. See also Anon., 'Les Paysans en Algérie et l'amorce de la rénovation rurale par les communes', Cahiers Nord-Africains, no. 103, July–August 1964.
6. G. Destanne de Bernis, 'Islam et développement économique', Cahiers de l'Institut de Science Économique Appliquée, no. 106, October 1960.
7. Pierre Bourdieu, The Algerians (New York, 1962), pp. 112–13.
8. See Max Weber, The Protestant Ethic and the Spirit of Capitalism (London, 1930).
9. For a detailed discussion on the general subject of Islam and capitalism, see Maxime Rodinson, Islam et Capitalisme (Paris, 1966).
10. These quotations and all the rest in this passage come from Karl Marx, Eighteenth Brumaire of Louis Bonaparte, in Marx and Engels, Selected Works, vol. 1 (Moscow, 1962), p. 334.
11. Bourdieu, op. cit., p. 94.
12. Samir Amin, Le Maghreb: Colonisation, Décolonisation et Perspective de Développement, UN (Dakar, 1965), Chapter I.
13. An exhaustive study of the problems of urbanization can be found in UNESCO, Social Implications of Industrialization and Urbanization in Africa South of the Sahara (Paris, 1956). A particular study of the Algerian situation is R. and C. Descloitres and J. C. Reverdy, 'Organisation urbaine et structures sociales en Algérie', Civilisations, vol. 12, no. 2, 1962.
14. See Pierre Bourdieu, A. Darbel et al., Travail et Travailleurs en Algérie (Paris, 1963), Chapter II.
15. The best of these are Pierre Bourdieu and A. Sayed, 'Paysans déracinés', Études Rurales, no. 12, January–March 1962, and Michel Cornation, Les Regroupements de la Décolonisation en Algérie (Paris, 1967).
16. Bourdieu, op. cit., p. 179.
17. R. Descloitres and J. C. Reverdy, 'Recherches sur les attitudes du sous-prolétariat algérien à l'égard de la société urbaine', Civilisations, vol. 13, nos. 1–2, 1963, p. 79.
18. Bourdieu, Darbel et al., op. cit.
19. ibid., pp. 320–46.
20. ibid.
21. ibid., p. 338.
22. Pierre Bourdieu, 'La hantise du chômage chez l'ouvrier algérien', Sociologie du Travail, October–December 1962.
23. Bourdieu, Darbel et al., op. cit., p. 270.
24. ibid., p. 284.
25. ibid., p. 367.
26. Roger le Tourneau, Le Développement d'une Classe Moyenne en Afrique du Nord, INCIDI, XXIX Session (London, 1955). Bourdieu in The Algerians estimates no business concern employed more than twenty workers. An interesting, if not very successful,

analysis of the class structure of pre-colonial Algeria is: René Galissot, *'L'Algérie précoloniale: classes sociales en système précapitaliste'*, *Cahiers du Centre d'Études et de Recherche Marxiste*, no. 60, 1968.

27. *Révolution Africaine*, 13 June 1964. André Michel, *'Les classes sociales en Algérie'*, *Cahiers Internationaux de Sociologie*, vol. 38, 1965, estimates that there were 50,000 active members of the middle class.
28. Chaliand, op. cit., p. 89.
29. Preparatory thesis 11, quoted in Michel, op. cit.
30. Preparatory thesis 12, quoted in Michel, op. cit.
31. Michel, op. cit.
32. *Révolution Africaine*, 24 October 1964.
33. See Milovan Djilas, *The New Class* (London, 1957).

Chapter 7   The Political Stage, 1963–8

1. *Rapport présenté par la direction de l'UGTA en Janvier 1963*, quoted in full by Gérard Chaliand, *L'Algérie: est-elle Socialiste?* (Paris, 1964), pp. 123–40.
2. Quoted in Werner Plum, *'Les problèmes du syndicalisme algérien'*, *Confluent*, nos. 32–3, June–July 1963.
3. Mohammed Boudiaf, *Où Va l'Algérie* (Paris, 1964), p. 167.
4. Sabadell, *'L'autogestion en Algérie'*, *Rouge et Noir*, no. 34, June 1966, p. 6.
5. Chaliand, op. cit., p. 66.
6. Speech in June 1963.
7. See Boudiaf, op. cit., for an account of his own arrest and that of Moussa Kebaili, Mohand Akli Benyounes and Ali Allouache.
8. See Hocine Ait Ahmed, *La Guerre et l'Après-guerre* (Paris, 1964).
9. Boudiaf, op. cit., p. 167.
10. Speech, 27 October 1963, quoted in *Confluent*, no. 36, December 1963.
11. Alain Marill, *'L'expérience algérienne d'autogestion industrielle'*, in François d'Arcy, Annie Kreiger and Alain Marill, *Essais sur l'Économie de l'Algérie Nouvelle* (Paris, 1965), p. 235: 'The basic foundation of *autogestion* was established on the material involvement of the worker in the success of the enterprise by means of a share in the profits.'
12. For an account of the conference, see Monique Laks, *Autogestion Ouvrière et Pouvoir Politique en Algérie 1962–5* (Paris, 1970), pp. 221–31.
13. See Boumaza's speech quoted on p. 123.
14. *Ministère de l'Orientation Nationale, Le Secteur Socialiste Industriel* (Algiers, 1964), p. 44.
15. On the eve of the congress the Association of the 'Ulemas denounced

References

the government for not realizing that 'the theoretical foundations of their action should be nourished, not by foreign doctrines, but from our Arab–Islamic roots'; see *Le Monde*, 18 April 1964.

16. Arslam Humbaraci, *Algeria: The Revolution that Failed* (London, 1966), p. 95.
17. The *Charte d'Alger* has not been translated into English. Some other extracts can be found in Henri Alleg, 'The revolutionary character of the Algiers Charter', *Political Affairs*, August 1965, vol. 44, no. 8. Two longer sections are in Appendix II.
18. FLN, *La Charte d'Alger* (Algiers, 1964), p. 63.
19. ibid., p. 59.
20. See quotes from the *avant-projet* in Chapter 6, p. 114.
21. *La Charte d'Alger*, p. 62.
22. ibid., p. 115.
23. ibid., p. 105.
24. ibid., p. 107.
25. ibid., p. 114.
26. ibid., p. 60.
27. The final text of the congress is quoted in FLN, *Thèses, Résolutions et Déclarations se Rapportant à l'Autogestion*, March 1967, p. 18.
28. See Juliette Minces, '*Autogestion et luttes de classe en Algérie*', *Temps Modernes*, June 1965. This is a good account of the workers' opposition.
29. Issued 16 April 1965.
30. *El Moudjahid*, 28 September 1965.
31. *Révolution Africaine*, 11 September 1965.
32. Speech by Boumédienne, 15 November 1965.
33. Speech by Boumédienne, 17 February 1966.
34. *L'Autogestion: Un Système et non une Expérience* (Algiers, 1967), p. 16.
35. Abdelaziz Zerdani, *Les Tâches de l'Édification Socialiste* (Algiers, 1967), p. 11.
36. Personal observation.
37. *L'Autogestion: Un Système . . .* , op. cit., p. 17.
38. Zerdani, op. cit., p. 10: 'The concept of *autogestion* can only be the result of a total vision of society and the change needed in it: not just a simple formula for economic management, like any other form of management.'
39. FLN, *Réorganisation de l'UGTA: Projet Analytique du Développement du Syndicalisme en Algérie* (Algiers, 1968), p. 7.
40. ibid., p. 27.

Chapter 8   *The Bureaucratic Emprise on the* Comités
1. Daniel Guérin, *L'Algérie qui se Cherche* (Paris, 1964).
2. Claude Estier, *Pour l'Algérie* (Paris, 1964), p. 33.

Workers' Self-Management in Algeria

3. Hamid Temmar, 'Le choix des organes de l'autogestion dans l'Algérie de l'ouest', Revue Algérienne des Sciences Juridiques, Politiques et Économiques, December 1964.
4. Quoted in Documents on Self-Management (Algiers, 1963), p. 45.
5. See Temmar, op. cit., and H. Sethom, 'Les mutations des campagnes algériennes depuis l'indépendance', Revue Tunisienne des Sciences Sociales, February 1965.
6. Sethom, op. cit.
7. Temmar, op. cit., p. 36.
8. Sabadell, Rouge et Noir, no. 37, March–April 1967, and Révolution et Travail, 19 November 1966.
9. Sous le Drapeau du Socialisme, May 1966.
10. Mohammed Harbi, 'L'Algérie et ses realités', Économie et Politique, May 1965, p. 56.
11. Révolution et Travail, 17 March 1966.
12. Alain Marill, 'L'expérience algérienne d'autogestion industrielle', in François d'Arcy, Annie Kreiger and Alain Marill, Essais sur l'Économie de l'Algérie Nouvelle (Paris, 1965), p. 198.
13. See Bulletin d'Autogestion, no. 2, May 1964.
14. See André Tiano, 'Le contenu économique du socialisme algérien', Revue Algérienne, March 1964, for a discussion on this.
15. Révolution et Travail, 17 March 1966.
16. For similar accusations against the administration, see Gérard Chaliand, L'Algérie: est-elle Socialiste? (Paris, 1964), and Mohammed Boudiaf, Où Va l'Algérie (Paris, 1964).
17. See Enquête Semestrielle 1966.
18. ibid.
19. Sabadell, Rouge et Noir, no. 37, p. 9.

Chapter 9 Workers and Managers

1. Révolution et Travail, no. 103, November 1965.
2. ibid., no. 99, October 1965.
3. Sabadell, Rouge et Noir, no. 37, March–April 1967.
4. See Juliette Minces, 'Self-administration in Algeria', International Socialist Journal, no. 22, August 1967.
5. Minces, 'Autogestion et luttes de classe en Algérie', Temps Modernes, June 1965, p. 2,210.
6. Hamid Temmar, 'Le choix des organes de l'autogestion dans l'Algérie de l'ouest', Revue Algérienne des Sciences Juridiques, Politiques et Économiques, December 1964.
7. Révolution et Travail, 15 October 1966.
8. François d'Arcy, Annie Kreiger and Alain Marill, Essais sur l'Économie de l'Algérie Nouvelle (Paris, 1965), p. 148. Jean Poncet, 'La rénovation rurale en Algérie', Économie et Politique, no. 130, May 1965, describes similar cases.

References

9. Grigori Lazarev, 'Remarques sur l'autogestion agricole en Algérie', *Institutions et Développement Agricole du Maghreb* (Paris, 1965), p. 167.
10. Pierre Bourdieu, 'La hantise du chômage chez l'ouvrier algérien', *Sociologie du Travail*, October–December 1962, p. 314.
11. Bachir Boumaza, speech, May 1963.
12. Jean Henri, 'Rétrospective sur l'économie algérienne en 1963', *Confluent*, no. 39, March 1964, p. 271.
13. Both quoted in *Révolution et Travail*, 17 September 1965.
14. Lazarev, op. cit., p. 27.
15. Kreiger, op. cit.
16. Gérard Chaliand, *L'Algérie: est-elle Socialiste?* (Paris, 1964).

Chapter 10 The Lessons of Algeria: Workers' Councils in Advanced Economies

1. Herbert Marcuse, *One-Dimensional Man* (London, 1964).
2. Henri Alleg, 'Algeria Seven Years After: Socialism or Capitalism?', *Marxism Today*, vol. 14, no. 3, March 1970, p. 8.
3. *El Moudjahid*, 30 December 1968.
4. See Joan Woodward, *Industrial Organization: Theory and Practice* (Oxford, 1965).
5. Serge Mallet, *La Nouvelle Classe Ouvrière* (Paris, 1963).
6. Marcuse, op. cit.
7. Karl Marx, *Economic and Philosophic Manuscripts of 1844* (London, 1970), p. 110.
8. See Charles R. Walker, *Toward the Automated Factory* (New Haven, 1957).
9. R. Blauner, *Alienation and Freedom: The Factory Worker and His Industry* (Chicago, 1964).
10. Private information from the researcher.
11. Marcuse, op. cit., p. 29.
12. ibid., p. 31.
13. John Goldthorpe, David Lockwood, Frank Bechoffer, Jennifer Platt, *The Affluent Worker in the Class Structure* (Cambridge, 1969).
14. André Gorz, *Stratégie Ouvrière et Néocapitalisme* (Paris, 1964), translation from *Towards Socialism*, ed. Perry Anderson and Robin Blackburn (London, 1965), p. 349.
15. Private information from the researcher.
16. See Goldthorpe, Lockwood et al., op. cit.
17. Marcuse, op. cit., p. 5.
18. ibid.
19. Gorz, op. cit., p. 349.
20. Guy Debord, *La Société du Spectacle* (Paris, 1967), para. 51, p. 36.

INDEX

Abbas, Ferhat, 32, 33, 34, 36, 41, 111, 120, 124, 131
Abdel Kader, Emir, 25, 26, 31, 53, 100, 178
Abdessalem, Belaid, 136, 138, 151
ACILOR, 88, 129
administrative cadres, 112–13, 163, 164, 166; superstructure, 65–70, 73–4, 142; *see also* bureaucracy
The Affluent Worker (Goldthorpe et al.), 196
Afro-Asian Conference, Algiers, 130
agriculture, 44; under French colonial rule, 28–31; formation of *comités de gestion* in, 44–56, 143–4; and *décrets de mars*, 58, 59, 60, 61–2; state supervision in, 67, 68; financing of *comités* in, 70, 71–2; and marketing, 72–3, 89; legacy of colonialism in, 75–81 *passim*, 92; modern v. traditional sectors of, 83–6; labour-intensive v. capital-intensive, 82–3; traditional value-system of peasants in, 96–101; and sub-proletariat, 101–5; opposition of land-owners to reform in, 111; decentralization by Boumédienne régime in, 137; machinery for, 151, 158; bureaucratic control of *comités* in, 151–61 *passim*, 164; and management relations, 164, 167–8, 169, 173, 174; investment in, 222; and production, 223

Ahlener Programme, 1947 (West Germany), 20
Ahmed, Kaid (alias Commandant Slimane), 43, 130, 136, 139, 140 and n., 141, 152
Ait Ahmed, Hocine, 37, 41n., 43 and n., 120–21, 124, 128, 131
Alger Républicain, 119
Algerian Communist Party (PCA), 34, 35, 50, 117, 124, 131, 184
Algerian independence (July 1962), 7, 23, 30, 39–44, 80, 87, 89, 92, 102, 104, 105, 111, 131, 167, 177, 179, 181, 183, 186
Algerian Revolution, nationalist politics and, 31–8; Tripoli Programme for, 42–3; *Charte d'Alger*'s approach to, 125–8; and 19 June *coup*, 130–34; analysis of, 177–92; nature of, 177–9; role of peasantry and sub-proletariat in, 179–81; and of working class, 182; contradictions in, 182–5; bureaucratic counter-revolution, 185–6; three stages of class struggle in, 186; global economic imperialism and, 187–9; class consciousness and, 190–91; *autogestion* as part of mythology of, 191–2
Algerian War (1954–62), 8, 22, 23, 36–8, 39, 41–2, 78, 79, 80, 85, 92, 101, 102, 167, 178–9, 183, 185
Algiers, 25, 27, 29, 43, 44, 133, 150, 164; French conquest of, 25, 26; OAS terrorism in, 40n.; workers' move into European

Index

Algiers *contd*
  areas of, 47; UGTA demonstration in, 49; *biens-vacants* in, 58; growth of Muslim population in, 102–3; before French conquest, 110; FLN Congress (1964) in, 123–8; and dissolution of UGTA centre, 141; *comités de gestion* in, 165, 169
L'Algérie à l'Épreuve du Pouvoir (Bourges), 41n.
Algérie française, 27, 39, 40
alienation, 21, 181, 193–200
ALLAL, 156–7
Alleg, Henri, 187
ALN, see *Armée de Libération Nationale*
ALUMAF, 89, 156–7
Amicale Générale des Travailleurs Algériens (Algerian workers in France), 50
Amin, Samir, 77–8
Amis du Manifeste de la Liberté (AML), 33
L'An V de la Révolution Algérienne (Fanon), 181
anarchism, anarcho-syndicalism, historical background to, 7–12
Annaba steel complex, 89, 134
ANP, see *Armée Nationale et Populaire*
el-Arab, Saout, 124
arabs, 25, 27n., 178, 180; see also Muslims
Armée de Libération Nationale (ALN, later ANP), 37, 41, 43, 48 and n., 118
Armée Nationale et Populaire (ANP, formerly ALN), 47, 48 and n., 50–51 and n., 53 and n., 124, 128, 131, 133, 139, 140, 153, 167
artisans, 68, 86, 87, 110
Arzew refinery, 90, 91; and gas liquefaction plant, 91
assemblée générale des travailleurs, 61–2, 63, 64, 71, 166–7

Association of the 'Ulemas, 32, 36, 41, 124, 132

Bakunin, Mikhail Alexandrovich, 9, 10
Bank of Algiers, 29
banking, nationalization of, 61, 88, 135
Banque Centrale d'Algérie (BCA), 72, 74, 155
Banque Nationale d'Algérie (BNA), 72, 135, 155
Barbé, Raymond, 86
Belkacem, Cherif, 130, 136, 140n.
Benallah, Hadj, 43n.
Ben Badis see *Entreprise Ben Badis*
Ben Bella, Ahmed, 7, 8, 45, 46, 112, 118, 135, 136, 152, 183; imprisonment by French of, 37, 42n.; political opposition to, 41–3, 49, 50, 111, 120–21, 124; as head of new government, 51, 111, 117; *comités de gestion* and, 55–6, 82, 90, 119, 122–3, 143–4, 158, 173; and *décrets de mars*, 57–67 *passim*; Khider and, 119–20; and piecemeal nationalizations, 121, 135; and profit-sharing, 122–3; workers' opposition to government of, 123; FLN Congress (1964) and, 124, 125, 128; armed internal resistance to, 128; and fall of (1965), 130–34, 161
Ben Bella (Merle), 42n.
Ben Khedda, Ben Youssef, 36, 41, 43, 124, 131
Ben Tobbal, Lakhdar, 41, 124
Ben Yahia, Mohammed, 136
Berbers, 25, 27n., 178, 180
Bergheaud, Edmond, 42n.
BERI (organ of industrial development), 138
Bernstein, E., 19
bidonvilles (shanty towns), 102, 104
biens-vacants (abandoned *colon*

Index

enterprises), 47–8, 51, 53n., 58, 59–61, 65, 68, 71, 72, 147, 151
Bitat, Rabah, 37, 43n., 128
Blanqui, Louis-Auguste, 11
Blauner, Robert, 194
Blida, 24, 50, 151
Blum, Léon, 32–3
Blum–Violette proposals, 32, 33, 34
BNA, see Banque Nationale d'Algérie
BNASS, see Bureau National d'Animation du Secteur Socialiste
Bolshevism, 10, 11, 12
Bonnot gang, 9
Boubidner, Salah, 139
Boudiaf, Mohammed, 37, 43, 50, 119, 120–21, 124, 131, 184
Boufarik, 50
Boumaza, Bachir, 66, 82–3, 92–3, 123, 129, 133, 136, 143, 172
Boumédienne, Col Houari, 41, 43, 44, 72, 90, 93, 111, 119, 125, 151, 152; Ben Bella and, 128, 131; 19 June 1965 *coup* and, 130; as leader of new régime, 133, 135, 136, 140; military rising against, 139
Boumédienne government, 19 June 1965 *coup* and establishment of, 130–34; ambivalent stand over *autogestion* of, 134–5; state capitalist ideology of, 135–6, 137; and frontal assault on *comités* of, 136–7; opposition to, 137–8; military rising against, 138; elimination of opposition by, 139–41; bureaucratic control of *comités* by, 142–61
Bourdieu, Pierre, 99, 100, 106, 108, 109, 190, 191
Bourges, Hervé, 41n., 134n.
bourgeoisie *see* bureaucracy; entrepreneurial bourgeoisie; middle class
Bourmont, General Louis de, 26

Bourouiba (UGTA leader), 49, 117
Boussouf, Abdelhafid, 41 and n., 124
Bouteflika, Abdelaziz, 130, 131, 136, 140n., 151
BP distribution network, 91
Bromberger, Serge, 41n.
Bugeaud, Marshal Thomas, 24
building (construction) industry, 29, 68, 79, 88, 137, 165
Bureau d'Études de Réalisation et d'Intervention Industrielles et Minières, 72
Bureau National d'Animation du Secteur Socialiste (BNASS), 67, 68
Bureau National pour la Protection et Gestion des Biens-Vacants, 58, 67
Bureau Politique, 43–4, 50, 117, 120, 128
bureaucracy, bureaucratic élite, 128, 135, 189; class struggle between workers and, 109–10, 122–3, 129, 130, 140, 184–6; emergence of, 114–15; supervision of *comités de gestion* of, 118–19; *Charte* warns of danger of, 126–7; support for 19 June *coup* by, 133; control of *comités* by, 142–61, 162; worker-management relations and, 163–76; revolutionary ideology of, 191

Caisse Algérienne de Développement, 72, 136
Caisses Régionales de Crédit (CRC), 72, 154–5
CAMEL (*Cie Algérienne du Méthane Liquide*), 91
capitalism, 55, 111, 154, 187; in nineteenth century, 8, 9; and Marxist approach to, 10, 11; workers under modern, 18–22, 179–80; Algerian colonial, 29,

Index

capitalism *contd*
75–6, 78, 170; Islam and, 99; analysis in *Charte* of, 125
Castro, Fidel, 7, 46, 51, 56
CCAA, *see Conseil Communal d'Animation d'Autogestion*
CCE, *see Comité de Coordination et d'Exécution*
CCRA, *see Centres Coopératifs de la Réforme Agraire*
cement production, 87, 223
centralism, *see* state capitalism, centralism
Centres Coopératifs de la Réforme Agraire (CCRA), 71, 72, 137, 154, 155
cereals, 76, 80, 223
CGT *see Confédération Générale du Travail*
Chaabani, Col Mohammed, armed revolt of, 128
Chaliand, Gérard, 96, 119
Challe, General, 37
Charte d'Alger, 8, 61, 114, 124–8, 137, 142, 164, 172, 176, 184, 185; extracts from, 211–20
chefs historiques, 37, 41, 43, 50, 117, 120
Cheliff, 50
chemical industry, 79, 88, 89, 135
Chena M'hand *comité de gestion*, 158
China, 1924–7 rising in, 12; People's Republic of, 8, 82, 188
Christian Democrats (German), 20
The Civil War in France (Marx and Engels), 11, 17
class, *see* social structure and ideology
class-consciousness, 109–10, 116, 171–6, 189–92, 193, 196
class struggle, 116, 140, 172, 195; development of, 109–10, 114–15, 124; 19 June *coup* and, 134; revolution and, 178, 180, 184; three stages of, 186

CNDR, *see Comité National de la Défense de la Révolution*
CNRA, *see Conseil National de la Révolution Algérienne*
CNT (*Confederación Nacional del Trabajo*, in Spain), 10
COBISCAL *comités de gestion*, 122, 146, 174
le code de l'indigénat (separate legal code for Muslims), 28
Codetermination Law, 1951 (West Germany), 20
COGEHORE, *see Comité de Gestion des Hôtels et Restaurants*
colons (*pieds-noirs*: European settlers in Algeria), 45, 55, 75, 89, 108, 111, 112, 114, 164; before independence, 25–31, 32–3, 35, 37, 38; OAS terrorism of, 39–40; flight from Algeria of, 40, 47, 52, 58, 76, 79, 80, 111; occupation of properties of, 44, 53, 55, 71, 72, 76, 121, 176, 182; Ben Bella on, 59–60
COMETAL (*Complexe Métallurgique d'Algérie*), 69
comités d'administration, 146, 148, 152
Comité de Coordination et d'Exécution (CCE: CNRA executive), 36, 41
comités d'entreprise, in France, 20; in Algeria, 145, 147, 149
comités de gestion (workers' management committees), revolutionary role of, 7, 8, 23, 39, 45–7, 50, 179–92 *passim*; spontaneous emergence of, 44–5; occupation of *biens-vacants* by, 47–8, 58–61, 76, 84; role of UGTA in creation of, 48–50, 117, 184; and army, 50–1; temporary decrees on (October–November 1962), 51–2, 58, 68; ideologies and motivations underlying, 52–6, 95; *décrets de mars* legal recogni-

240

Index

tion of, 57–61, 81–3; elective structure of *autogestion* and, 61–5, 166–7, 168; and superstructure, 65–70, 73–4; financing of, 70–72, 85–6, 129, 153–60; and marketing, 72–4, 85, 89, 157; agricultural, 79, 84–6; in industry, 88–90; and mining, 91; state bureaucratic control of, 92–3, 113–14, 118–19, 129, 134–9, 142–61, 179, 182; electoral manipulation within, 143–7, 163, 167, 170; incorporation into *sociétés nationales* of, 148–51; and denationalization, 151–3; economic controls over, 153–61, 162, 163; management relations within, 162–76; role of director in, 163–70; and workers, 170–76, 191
Comité de Gestion des Hôtels et Restaurants (COGEHORE), 152, 169
Comité National de Défense de la Révolution (CNDR), 128
Comité Révolutionnaire pour l'Unité et l'Action (CRUA), 36, 37, 140n.
comités de travailleurs, 136
commercial enterprises, under colonial rule, 29, 110; forced occupation of, 49; nationalization of, 53, 61; workers in, 54–5; *décrets de mars* on, 59, 60
commission d'autogestion, 50
Commission Nationale de Recrutement et Discipline, 63 and n.
communards (in nineteenth-century France), 11
communes (Algerian), 27, 69
Compagnie Française des Petroles, 90, 91
Complexe d'Ameublement et de Menuiserie de l'Algérois (CAMA), 69n.
Complexe Industriel du Bois (CIB), 69n.
Complexe Laitier de l'Algérois (COLAITAL), 69n.
Confédération Générale du Travail (CGT), 20, 34, 35, 49, 149; *see also* UGSA
Congrès des Fellahs (agricultural workers: October 1963), 122, 158
conseils d'administration, 69
Conseil Communal d'Animation d'Autogestion (CCAA), 63, 69–70
Conseil de la Révolution (1965), 130, 139
Conseil National de la Révolution Algérienne (CNRA), 36, 41, 179
Conseil Supérieur, 27–8
conseils des travailleurs, 62, 63, 64, 136, 146, 169
construction *see* building industry
Constantine, 27, 32, 102–3, 110
Constantine Plan (1959), 78
Constantinois, 25, 50
cooperatives, 52, 53, 54, 98, 101, 151–2
Coopérative Agricole d'Anciens Moudjahidins (ex-combatants), 153
Coopérative Frantz Fanon, 123, 145–6
Coopérative Laimeche Ali (Tizi Rached), 165
Coopérative Ouvrière Aissat Idir, 151–2
Coopératives de la Réforme Agraire (CORA), 72–3, 85, 157
COTEINTAL, 174
cotton yarn, 87, 223
CRUA *see Comité Révolutionnaire pour l'Unité et l'Action*
Cuba, 8, 82

Dar el Beida district, 145
décrets de mars (1963), 16, 52, 57–74, 81–2, 92, 113, 118, 119, 125, 128, 129, 130, 133, 137, 142–8 *passim*, 152, 154, 158, 160, 162, 163,

Index

décrets de mars contd
  164, 166, 170, 172, 173, 176, 184, 192; texts of, 201–9
Délégations Financières, 27–8, 29
denationalization, 135, 151–3; *see also* nationalization
Deutscher Gewerkschaftsbund, 20
directions collégiales (management committees), 46 and n.
director (of *comité de gestion*), role of, 61, 63, 64–5, 162, 163–70
Djermane, Rabah, 117
Domaine Amirouche, 173
Domaine Hassamène, 172
Domaine Megnouch Mustapha, 168
Domaine Sainte Louise, 144
Domaine Zair Houari, 153
Draa ben Khedda textile works, 89

The Economic and Philosophic Manuscripts (Marx), 194
economy, colonial, 28–31, 35, 40, 44, 75–81; dependence on France of, 75–6, 94, 153, 187; *autogestion* as solution to problems of, 81–3; agricultural sector of, 83–6; and industry, 86–90; hydrocarbons and mining sector of, 90–92; move to centralization of, 92–3; advantages of emigration to, 93–4; peasants' traditional attitudes to, 98; and working class, 106–7; *Charte*'s support for labour intensivity in, 128; bureaucratic control (in *comités*) of, 153–61, 163, 170; global neo-imperialistic domination of, 186–9; advance, technological, 192–6; indices on: revenue and expenditure, 221; investment, 222; foreign trade, 222–3; agricultural production, 223; industrial output, 223; mining output, 224; and oil production, 224; *see also* agriculture; industry

education, 28, 222
Eighteenth Brumaire of Louis Bonaparte (Marx), 99–100
electoral manipulation (in *comités de gestion*), 143–7, 163, 167, 170
electricity and gas, 61, 65, 79
Élus, see Fédération des Élus
emigration, 31–2, 35, 50, 93–4
Engels, Friedrich, 10, 11
entrepreneurial bourgeoisie, 40, 78, 110, 112, 114, 135, 142, 172, 189; *see also* middle class
Entreprise Ben Badis, 151
Entreprise de Filature et Tissage de Tlemcen, 147 and n.
entreprises mixtes, 88
Esso, 91
Estier, Claude, 144
Étoile Nord Africaine, 31–2, 33, 34
Éts. Veuve Côte, 147
Évian peace Agreements (1962), 38, 41, 42, 44
Exécutif Provisoire, 44, 47, 60
exports, 29, 75, 77, 79–80, 89, 90, 92, 94, 222
extended family, 52, 96, 182

FAI (*Federación Anarquista Ibérica*, Spain), 10
Fanon, Frantz, Fanonism, 99, 100, 180, 181, 185
La Fausse Industrie (Fourier), 8
Fédération des Cheminots (of UGTA), 149, 150
Fédération des Élus, 32–3, 111
Fédération Nationale des Travailleurs de la Terre (agricultural workers), 129
fellahs, see peasantry
FFS, *see Front des Forces Socialistes*
Fields, Factories and Workshops (Kropotkin), 9
fisheries, fishing, 29, 79, 68
FLN, *see Front de Libération Nationale*
Fonulpt-Esperaber, M., 34

242

Index

food and drink industries, 88, 150, 223
foreign aid, 80, 92
foreign trade, 186–9, 222–3
Fourier, Charles, 9
France, 71; Fourth Republic in, 7, 37; nineteenth-century communards in, 12; *comités de gestion* in, 20–21; emigrant Algerian workers in, 31–2, 35, 50; Blum-Violette project of, 32–3; Vichy government in, 33; de Gaulle returned to power (1958), 37–8; OAS terrorism and, 39–40; Algerian hydrocarbons and, 90, 91; nationalized industry in, 93, 136; Marx's view of peasants in, 100; emigration of landowners to, 111; trade between Algeria and, 187, 188; *see also* French colonial rule
Francis, Ahmed, 36, 120, 131
French army, colonial settlement policy and, 23–4; administrative control of Algeria by, 27 and n.; Algerian war and, 37–8; and abortive officers' *coup* (1961), 39; OAS attack on, 40n.; *regroupement* policy of, 103–4
French colonial rule in Algeria, 7; history of, 23–31; state administration under, 27–8, 35, 112, 113; nationalist opposition to, 31–6; and war of independence, 36–8; economic heritage of, 75–94; middle class under, 110–11; trained Muslim management under, 164; role of caïds under, 167; and workers, 171; Algerian revolution and, 177–8, 179, 181, 186; *see also* France
French Communist Party (PCF), 31–2, 34
Front des Forces Socialistes (FFS), 120, 125n., 128, 130, 131, 150
Front de Libération Nationale (FLN), 63n.; formation of, 36–7; OAS terrorism and, 39; splits within, 39, 41–4; *comités de gestion* and, 45–6, 47, 48, 51, 172; UGTA and, 49, 50, 117–18, 130, 140; peasantry and, 52–3; 'socialist' ideology of, 53, 55–6, 94; views on emigration of, 93–4; and on workers, 109; administrative cadres and, 112–13, 114; internal crisis over role and content of, 119–20; political opposition to, 120–21; adoption of *Charte* at first congress of, 123–8, 210–20; 19 June *coup* and, 131, 132, 133–4; opposition to Boumédienne régime in, 137–8; *comité* elections and, 145, 167; organization of, 163; role in Algerian revolution of, 177, 178–9, 181, 183, 184
fruit and vegetables, 77, 79, 80, 157, 223
Fundamental Works' Constitution Law, 1952 (Germany), 20

Galbraith, John Kenneth, 195
de Gaulle, Charles, 20, 33, 34 and n., 78; returned to power (1958), 37, 112; visit to Algeria of, 38n.; grants independence to Algeria, 37–8, 39
Gendarme, René, 78
Germany, 12, 19–20, 196; East, 12; West, 187
Gomulka, Wladyslaw, 14, 15
Gorz, André, 196, 198
Gouvernement Provisoire de la République Algérienne (GPRA), 37, 38, 41, 42, 43, 113, 124, 136, 139
government revenue and expenditure, 81, 85, 221
Grand Alger, 49; *see also* Algiers
Guérin, Daniel, 144

Hadj Ali, Bachir, 124, 131
Harbi, Mohammed, 46, 59, 67, 120, 124, 129, 154

Index

Harbi group (*pieds-rouges*), 128, 129, 133, 143, 172
Hassie Messaoud oil field, 90
Hassi R'Mel, natural gas production in, 90–91
Ho Chi Minh, 7
housing, 58, 59, 222
Huileries Modernes d'Alger (HMA), 137, 156
Humbaraci, Arslam, 58
Hungary, 10, 12, 16
hydrocarbons (oil and natural gas), 29, 61, 75, 76, 77, 79, 80, 88, 90–91, 92, 135, 224

ideology, *see* social structure and ideology
imports, 29, 75, 77, 80, 222
Indochina, 7, 37, 39
Industrial Workers of the World, 10
industry, industrialization, historical background to, 9–17 *passim*; under colonialism, 29, 30; *comités de gestion* in, 44, 45, 47–8, 51, 82–3, 143–4; nationalization in, 53; and workers, 54–5; *décrets de mars* and, 58, 59, 60, 61; and state supervision, 67–8; financing of *comités* in, 70, 72; and marketing, 72–3; legacy of colonialism for, 75, 76; employment reduction in, 80–81; and lack of investment capital for, 81; labour-intensive v. capital-intensive production in, 82–3, 88–9, 90, 93; before independence, 86–7; and after, 87–90, 92; bureaucratic control of *comités* in, 143–61; and management relations, 169–70; investment, 222; and output in, 223
insurance, nationalization of, 61, 88, 135
investment, investment capital, 78, 79, 81, 82, 85, 89, 91, 92, 136, 222

International, First, 9; Third, 35; Fourth, 59
iron ore, 91, 92, 165, 224
irrationality (among lower-paid workers), 106–8
Islam, 99, 124; *see also* Muslims

Kabylie revolt (1870–71), 28n., 31
Kabylie region, 25, 36, 43, 50, 53–4, 120, 165
Khaled, Emir, 31
Khan, Lamine, 136
Khider, Mohammed, 37, 43 and n., 117, 119–20, 128, 131, 140
Krieger, Annie, 168
Krim, Belkacem, 41, 43
Kronstadt mutiny, 10, 11, 12
Kropotkin, Peter, 9

land, *see* agriculture
Lange, Oscar, 13, 14
Lassel (UGTA leader), 49, 117
Lazarev, Grigori, 46, 168
League of Communists (Yugoslavia), 17
Lebajoui, Mohammed, 41n.
Lenin, V. I., 11, 15, 126
Lentin, Albert-Paul, 38n.
Lesieur (French company), 156
Lieberman, 13
lime phosphate production, 91, 92, 224
livestock, 29, 44 and n.
Lotfallah, Soliman, 51n., 59

Al-Madani, Tewfik, 36
Magasins Pilotes Socialistes, 73
Mahsas, Ali, 136
Mallet, Serge, 193, 195
Mandouze, André, 53
Manifeste des Élus Algériens, 33
manufacturing, 53, 86, 87, 88, 223
Mao Tse-tung, Maoism, 7, 46, 51, 121, 187

Index

maquis, maquisards, 36, 41, 43
Marcuse, Herbert, 180, 181, 195, 198
Marill, Alain, 45
marketing (in *autogestion*), 70, 72–3, 85, 89, 157; in *sociétés nationales*, 136
Marx, Karl, 9, 10, 11, 17, 100, 194, 196
Marxism, Marxism-Leninism, 8, 10, 17, 49, 99, 100, 121, 132, 139, 179; as basic philosophy of *Charte*, 124, 125, 128
Mayo, Elton, 21
Medeghri, Ahmed, 130, 136, 140n., 151
Mendjli, Commandant Ali, 43
Messali Hadj, Ben Ahmed, 32, 33, 34, 36
metallurgy, 79, 86, 89
Michelet (Kabylie), 120
middle class (bourgeoisie), 47, 56, 74, 78, 95, 135; before French conquest, 110; traditional, 110–11, 142, 185; new administrative, 111–15, 134, 140, 162, 164; class struggle and, 109–10, 116, 124, 185; 19 June 1965 *coup* and, 131–2, 135; *see also* bureaucracy; entrepreneurial bourgeoisie
migration (of sub-proletariat to urban areas), 101–3
Minces, Juliette, 166
mining, 29, 51, 58, 59, 61, 68, 75, 76, 79, 88, 91–2, 135, 144, 165, 224
Ministry of Agriculture, 68, 86, 137, 151
of the Economy, 68, 129
of Finance, 145
of Industry and Energy, 63n., 145, 156
of the Interior, 144
of Labour, 63n.
of Public Works, 68
of Tourism, 152

Mitbestimmung (West German works councils), 20, 196
Mitidja, *comités de gestion* in, 50, 145; Zbiri armed rising in, 139
Mobil, 91
Mohammedi, Said, 43n.
money, peasants' attitude to, 98
Morocco, 36, 37, 44
Morris, William, 9
MORY (transport company), 121
Mouvement pour le Triomphe des Libertés Démocratiques (MTLD), 34, 35, 36, 41
Mozabites, 99 and n.
Muslims, 39; hostility of *colons* to, 26; under colonial rule, 24, 26, 27–8, 30–31; growth of nationalist movements among, 31–6; and revolution, 36–8, 178; OAS terrorism against, 40 and n.; middle class, 47, 110, 112, 164; political groups of, 52; in agriculture, 54, 83–4; and in industry, 86; urban sub-proletariat, 102; and working-class sector of, 105–6; Paris police section of, 164
Mutual Aid: A Factor in Evolution (Kropotkin), 9
MVD (Soviet 'Ministry of Internal Affairs'), 16

Napoleon III, Emperor, 27
national liberation army *see Armée de Libération Nationale*; *Armée Nationale et Populaire*
nationalism, Algerian, 25, 31–8, 41–4, 133, 135, 179
nationalization, 21, 53, 60–61, 65, 81, 89, 90, 91, 92–3, 121, 132, 135–6, 139, 148–9, 150, 187; *see also* denationalization
natural gas, *see* hydrocarbons
Neuloh, Otto, 196
New Economic Laws, 1965 (Yugoslavia), 17–18
News from Nowhere (Morris), 9

Index

19 June 1965 *coup*, 147, 153; causes of, 130–32; leaders' aims in, 132–3; and opposition to, 133–4
Le Nouveau Monde Industriel et Sociétaire (Fourier), 8
La Nouvelle Classe Ouvrière (Mallet), 193

OAS, see Organisation de l'Armée Secrète
Obradovic, Josip, 194
Office National de Commercialisation (ONACO), 72–3, 157
Office National de la Pêche (ONP), 67
Office National de la Réforme Agraire (ONRA), 67, 68, 71–2, 74, 85, 86, 129, 145, 154, 155
Office National de Tourisme (ONAT), 67
Office National des Transports (ONT), 68, 145
oil, see hydrocarbons
olive oil, 77, 79, 156, 223
One-Dimensional Man (Marcuse), 195
Oran, 24, 27, 29, 40n., 49, 102–3, 110, 133, 165
Oranie, 25, 53n.
Organisation de l'Armée Secrète (OAS), 39–40, 47, 76
Organisation Politico-Administrative (OPA), 112
Organisation Spéciale (OS), 36
Orléansville, 50
Ottoman Empire, rule in Algeria of, 24–5, 110
Ou el-Hadj, Col Mohand, 120, 124, 139
Oujda group, 136, 139
L'Ouvrier Algérien, 49
Owen, Robert, 9

Pablo, see Raptis, Michaelis
Paris Commune, 10, 11

Parti Communiste Algérien see Algerian Communist Party
Parti du Peuple Algérien (PPA), 33, 34
Parti de la Révolution Socialiste (PRS), 50, 117, 119, 120, 125n., 128, 130, 131, 132, 151, 172, 184
party, the, *Charte d'Alger*'s views on, 127, 142
PCA, see Algerian Communist Party
PCF, see French Communist Party
peasantry, 46; army attitude towards, 50–51, 52; and government, 51–2; motivation for occupation of *colon* farms by, 52–4; landless, 61–2 and n.; social structure and traditional value-system of, 95, 96–101, 180; revolutionary role of, 118, 178–9, 180, 181–2, 185, 190; see also sub-proletariat
Pétain, Marshal Philippe, 33
pieds-noirs, see colons
pieds-rouges, see Harbi group
primes, see production bonuses
Poland, 12, 13–16
Popular Front (France), 32–3, 35
Poznan riots (Poland), 14, 15, 16
PPA, see Parti du Peuple Algérien
president (of *comité de gestion*), role of, 62–3, 64–5, 166, 168, 169
productivity (production) bonuses (*primes*), 70, 71, 158
profit-sharing, 70, 71, 122–3, 158–60, 173, 174, 192
Proudhon, Pierre Joseph, 11
PRS, see Parti de la Révolution Socialiste
public works, 79, 88

Rabat, 41
Ramdane, Abane, 41n., 121
Raptis, Michaelis (alias Pablo), 59
raw materials, 75, 81, 89, 94, 154, 157, 188, 223
Rebba, Slimane, 136

246

Index

Les Rebelles Algériens (Bromberger), 41n.
regroupement (French policy of), 37, 44, 62, 80, 102, 103–4
Renault car industry (France), 136
Révolution Africaine (FLN organ), 45 and n., 59, 110, 129
La Révolution Algérienne par les Textes (Mandouze), 53
Révolution et Travail (UGTA paper), 157
Rocher Noir (French administrative centre of), 44
Ruskin, John, 9
Russia, libertarian socialism in, 9, 10, 11–12; *see also* Soviet Union
Russian Revolution, of 1905, 11; of 1917, 10, 11, 15, 179, 210

Sahara, 25, 27n., 31; oil fields in, 90 and n., 91
SAP, *see Sociétés Agricoles de Prévoyance*
Sartre, Jean-Paul, 180
SATAC (transport company), 121
SATAS (transport company), 121
sections syndicales (union shop-floor committees), 148, 150
senatus consulte, 28
services, service industries, 29, 75, 77, 86, 88
Setif, Muslim riots in, 33, 34, 35
settlers, *see colons*
shoe manufacturing, 87, 223
Skikda, gas liquefaction plant at, 91; dissolution of UGTA centre at, 141
Slimane, Commandant, *see* Ahmed, Kaid
Smain, Hadj, 136
SNCFA, *see Société Nationale des Chemins de Fer Algériens*
S. N. Repal, 90
SNTA, *see Société Nationale des Tabacs et Allumettes*
SNTR, *see Société Nationale des Transports Routiers*

social democracy, West European, workers under, 18–22
Socialist Industrialist Sector Conference (June 1966), 138
social structure and ideology, 75, 95–115; of peasantry, 52–4, 96–101; of sub-proletariat, 101–5; of working class, 54–6, 105–10; of middle class, 110–15
Sociétés Agricoles de Prévoyance (SAP), 71, 154, 158, 164
Société Algérienne des Boissons, 150, 175n.
Société d'Entreprise de Routes en Algérie, 165
sociétés nationales, 66, 89, 136, 137, 138, 145, 148–51, 161, 187–8
Société Nationale des Chemins de Fer Algériens (SNCFA), 149
Société Nationale des Tabacs et Allumettes (SNTA), 148
Société Nationale des Transports Routiers (SNTR), 137, 145, 149
Soldiers' Councils, in Russia, 11–12; in Poland, 13; *see also* workers' councils
SONACO (textiles), 147n.
SONATIBA (construction), 137, 149
SONATRACH (hydrocarbons), 90, 91, 137, 138
SONITEX (textiles), 148
SOPEFAL (French company for hydrocarbons), 91
SOTRAPPA, 122
Soult, Marshal Nicolas (duc de Dalmatie), 23–4
Soummam valley, FLN meeting in, 36
Sous le Drapeau du Socialisme (PRS paper), 151
Soviet Union, 101; authoritarian socialism in, 7; Hungarian uprising and, 12; political and economic system of, 12–13; Poland and, 14, 15; Yugoslavia and, 16–17, 18; 'socialism in one

247

Index

Soviet Union *contd*
country' doctrine of, 35; state capitalism in, 49, 66; class characteristics in, 115; *Charte*'s rejection of socialism in, 125; NEP period of, 126; and imperialism, 187; trade between Algeria and, 188; *see also* Russia
Spain, 26; Civil War (1936–9) in, 10, 12
Spartakist rising (in Germany), 19
Stalin, Josef, Stalinism, 12, 15, 16, 187, 210
the state, *Charte d'Alger*'s view of, 126–7, 142
state administration *see* bureaucracy
The State and Revolution (Lenin), 126
state capitalism, centralism, historical perspective on, 7–18 *passim*; in Algeria, 49, 75, 83, 88, 89, 93, 95, 116, 118, 143; of Boumédienne régime, 135–7, 140, 177
state farms, 51, 53, 59, 101
state socialism, 114–15
Statute of 1947, 34
steel, 135, 223
strikes, 118, 134, 147, 149
sub-proletariat, 54, 84–5, 95, 101–5, 108, 176, 180–81, 182, 191
superphosphates, 87, 223

Taylor, Frederick W., 21
technology, 193–6
Temmar, Hamid, 144, 167
terre brulée (scorched earth), OAS policy of, 40
textiles, 79, 87, 89, 135
Thoreau, Henry David, 9
time, peasants' concept of, 97–8; and sub-proletariat's, 104
Tito, Josip Broz, Marshal, 16
Tizi-Ouzou (Kabylie), 43, 44
Tizi-Rached (Kabylie), 165
Tlemcen, 43, 50, 110

tobacco industry, 77, 87, 148, 223
transport, 29, 61, 65, 121, 135, 137, 145, 174; railway, 149–50; road, 68, 165
trade-union shop-floor committee *see sections syndicales*
traffiquants, 54
Transports Sidi M'Hamed (road haulage firm), 145
Tripoli, CNRA meeting at, 41 and n.
Tripoli Programme, 42–3, 49, 53, 55, 58, 81, 82, 179, 183
Trotsky, Leon, Trotskyism, 12, 126, 128, 184
Tunis, Tunisia, 36, 37, 41, 44

UDIBA, *see Union Départementale des Industries du Bois*
'Ulemas *see* Association of the 'Ulemas
Union Démocratique du Manifeste Algérien (UDMA), 34, 36, 41, 111, 120
Union Départementale des Industries du Bois (UDIBA), 156
Union Générale des Syndicats Algériens (UGSA), 35n.; *see also* Confédération Générale du Travail
Union Générale des Travailleurs Algériens (UGTA), 63n., 82, 135; formation of, 35; *comités de gestion* and, 47, 48–50, 51, 55, 69, 117, 122, 172; socialist ideology of, 55; nationalization and, 60; conflict between FLN and, 117–18, 120, 130, 133, 135; *union centrale* and *unions locales* of, 118 and n.; conditional support for 19 June coup by, 133; conflict between Boumédienne régime and, 137–8, 140–41; bureaucratic control of *comités* and, 145, 147, 148–9, 150–51, 155, 157, 159, 166, 168, 176; role in revolution of, 183, 184

248

Index

Union Nationale des Étudiants Algériens, 133
Union Nationale des Industries Métallurgiques et Électriques Socialistes, 69
Union Populaire Algérienne, 33
Union Regionale du Bois de l'Algérois, 69
United Nations, 37n.
United States, 105, 180, 187, 188, 194
urban population, 101-3, 104
Usine Gabet, 123

Veblen, Thorsten, 9
Verreries de l'Afrique du Nord (VAN), 88, 89, 129, 149
Vietnam, 7, 8; *see also* Indochina
Vichy government (France), 33
Violette, Maurice, 32
viticulture *see* wine production

willayas, 43 and n., 44, 51, 117, 124, 139
wine production, 29, 76-7, 80, 223
workers, working class, under modern capitalism, 18-22, 125; agricultural, 47, 54, 55, 84-5, 95, 97, 106; industrial, 54-5, 95, 106; seasonal, 61-2, 97; social structure and ideology of, 105-10, 115; class struggle between new middle class and, 109-10, 115, 116, 124; hostility to Ben Bella of, 130, 133-4; participation in *sociétés nationales* of, 136, 148; opposition to Boumédienne régime of, 137-8, 140; bureaucratic control of *comités* and, 142-61 *passim*; and *comités* hierarchy, 163-70; attitude to work of, 170-71, 173, 192; concept of *autogestion* and, 162, 170, 171-6; role in Algerian revolution of, 179-92 *passim*; in advanced technological economies, 192-200; *see also comités de gestion*; sub-proletariat
workers' councils, historical survey of, 7-18, 190; social democratic and capitalist containment of, 18-22; *see also comités de gestion*
workers' management committees *see comités de gestion*
World War, First, 10, 11, 21; Second, 12, 14, 16, 20, 33, 187
The Wretched of the Earth (Fanon), 180

Yahia, Ali, 139
Youcef, Katib, 139
Yugoslavia, workers in, 12, 13, 16-18, 21, 22, 45, 61, 67, 70, 101, 163, 194, 197

Zaccar iron-mining complex, 164-5
Zbiri, Col Tahar, armed rising of, 139
Zerdani, Abdelaziz, 137-8, 139
zinc, 91, 224